The
HIDDEN INNS
of
CENTRAL AND SOUTHERN SCOTLAND

Edited by
Barbara V

Published by:
Travel Publishing Ltd
7a Apollo House, Calleva Park
Aldermaston, Berks, RG7 8TN
ISBN 1-902-00761-1
© Travel Publishing Ltd

First Published: *2000*

Regional Titles in the Hidden Inns Series:

West Country	Southeast England
South of England	Central & Southern Scotland
Wales	

Regional Titles in the Hidden Places Series:

Cambridgeshire & Lincolnshire	Channel Islands
Cheshire	Chilterns
Cornwall	Derbyshire
Devon	Dorset, Hants & Isle of Wight
East Anglia	Essex
Gloucestershire & Wiltshire	Heart of England
Hereford, Worcs & Shropshire	Highlands & Islands
Kent	Lake District & Cumbria
Lancashire	Northeast Yorkshire
Northumberland & Durham	North Wales
Nottinghamshire	Potteries
Somerset	South Wales
Suffolk	Surrey
Sussex	Thames Valley
Warwickshire & W Midlands	Yorkshire

National Titles in the Hidden Places Series:

England	Ireland
Scotland	Wales

Printing by: Ashford Colour Press, Gosport
Maps by: © MAPS IN MINUTES ™ (2000)
Line Drawings: Rodney Peace
Editor: Barbara Vesey
Cover Design: Lines & Words, Aldermaston
Cover Photographs: The Auld Cross Keys, Denholm, Roxburghshire; Colintraive
Hotel, Colintraive, Argyll; The Stair Inn, Stair, Ayrshire

*F*OREWORD

The *Hidden Inns* series originates from the enthusiastic suggestions of readers of the popular *Hidden Places* guides. They want to be directed to traditional inns "off the beaten track" with atmosphere and character which are so much a part of our British heritage. But they also want information on the many places of interest and activities to be found in the vicinity of the inn.

The inns or pubs reviewed in the *Hidden Inns* may have been coaching inns but have invariably been a part of the history of the village or town in which they are located. All the inns included in this guide serve food and drink and many offer the visitor overnight accommodation. A full page is devoted to each inn which contains a line drawing of the inn, full name, address and telephone number, directions on how to get there, a full description of the inn and its facilities and a wide range of useful information such as opening hours, food served, accommodation provided, credit cards taken and details of entertainment. *Hidden Inns* guides however are not simply pub guides. They provide the reader with helpful information on the many places of interest to visit and activities to pursue in the area in which the inn is based. This ensures that your visit to the area will not only allow you to enjoy the atmosphere of the inn but also to take in the beautiful countryside which surrounds it.

The *Hidden Inns* guides have been expertly designed for ease of use. *The Hidden Inns of Central and Southern Scotland* is divided into 7 regionally based chapters, each of which is laid out in the same way. To identify your preferred geographical region refer to the contents page overleaf. To find a pub or inn simply use the index and locator map at the beginning of each chapter which refers you, via a page number reference, to a full page dedicated to the specific establishment. To find a place of interest again use the index and locator map found at the beginning of each chapter which will guide you to a descriptive summary of the area followed by details of each place of interest.

We do hope that you will get plenty of enjoyment from visiting the inns and places of interest contained in this guide. We are always interested in what our readers think of the inns or places covered (or not covered) in our guides so please do not hesitate to write to us. This is a vital way of helping us ensure that we maintain a high standard of entry and that we are providing the right sort of information for our readers. Finally if you are planning to visit any other corner of the British Isles we would like to refer you to the list of Hidden Inns and Hidden Places guides to be found at the rear of the book.

Travel Publishing

LOCATOR MAP

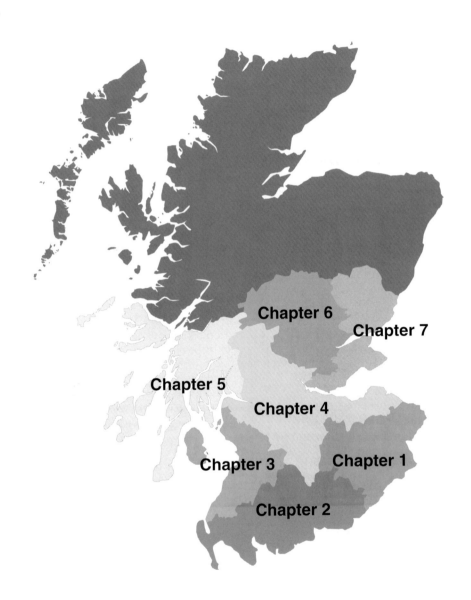

Chapter 6

Chapter 7

Chapter 5

Chapter 4

Chapter 3

Chapter 1

Chapter 2

CONTENTS

TITLE PAGE   i

FOREWORD   iii

LOCATOR MAP   iv

CONTENTS   v

GEOGRAPHICAL AREAS:

    Chapter 1: The Borders   1
    Chapter 2: Dumfries and Galloway   29
    Chapter 3: Ayrshire and the Isle of Arran   55
    Chapter 4: Central Scotland   77
    Chapter 5: Argyll and Bute   115
    Chapter 6: Perthshire and Kinross   147
    Chapter 7: Fife, Dundee and Angus   171

INDEXES AND LISTS:

    Alphabetic List of Pubs and Inns   197
    Special Interest Lists of Pubs and Inns:
        With accommodation   201
        Opening all day   203
        With childrens facilities   206
        Accepting credit cards   207
        With garden, patio or terrace   210
        With occasional or regular live entertainment   212
        With a separate restaurant or dining area   214
    Index of Towns, Villages and Places of Interest   217

ADDITIONAL INFORMATION

    Reader Reaction Forms   219
    Order Form   223

1 The Borders

PLACES OF INTEREST:

Ancrum 3
Ayton 3
Bowhill 4
Coldstream 5
Duns 5
Galashiels 6
Hawick 6
Innerleithen 7

Jedburgh 7
Kelso 8
Lauder 9
Melrose 9
Peebles 10
St Abb's 10
Selkirk 11

PUBS AND INNS:

The **Auld Cross Keys**, Denholm 12

The **Black Bull Hotel**, Duns 13

The **Castle Hotel**, Coldstream 14

Churches Hotel, Eyemouth 15

The **Commercial Inn**, Coldstream 16

The **Craw Inn**, Auchencrow,
  nr Reston 17

The **Crown Hotel**, Coldstream 18

Dryburgh Arms Hotel,
  Newtown St Boswells 19

The **Fox & Hounds**, Denholm 20

The **Liddesdale Hotel**, Newcastleton 21

Linton Hotel, West Linton 22

The **Pheasant Inn**, Jedburgh 23

The **Plough Hotel**, Leitholm 24

The **Royal Hotel**, Jedburgh 25

The **Ship Inn**, Melrose 26

Traquair Arms Hotel, Innerleithen 27

The Hidden Inns of Central and Southern Scotland

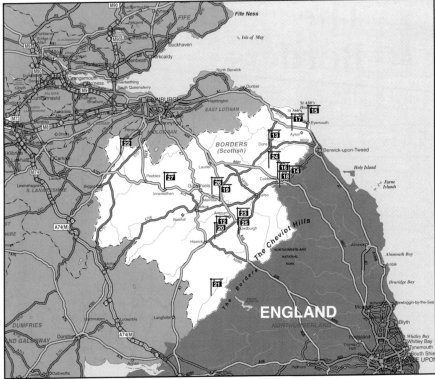

© MAPS IN MINUTES ™ (1999)

12	The Auld Cross Keys, Denholm	20	The Fox & Hounds, Denholm
13	The Black Bull Hotel, Duns	21	The Liddesdale Hotel, Newcastleton
14	The Castle Hotel, Coldstream	22	Linton Hotel, West Linton
15	Churches Hotel, Eyemouth	23	The Pheasant Inn, Jedburgh
16	The Commercial Inn, Coldstream	24	The Plough Hotel, Leitholm
17	The Craw Inn, Auchencrow, nr Reston	25	The Royal Hotel, Jedburgh
18	The Crown Hotel, Coldstream	26	The Ship Inn, Melrose
19	Dryburgh Arms Hotel, Newtown St Boswells	27	Traquair Arms Hotel, Innerleithen

Please note all cross references refer to page numbers

The Borders

For many centuries the setting for bloody warfare between the fiercely independent Scots and the "Sassenachs" (English) to the south, The Borders region is today pastoral and peaceful, dotted with neat little market towns. Its 1,800 square miles extend from the rocky Berwickshire coastline, with its picturesque fishing villages, through the gentle valley of the River Tweed to the rolling hills and moorland of the west.

In medieval times, four great Abbeys dominated the area: Jedburgh, Kelso, Melrose, and Dryburgh, all of them now in ruins but still magnificent. The heart of Robert the Bruce is buried at Melrose Abbey. Dryburgh Abbey was the last resting place of Sir Walter Scott, whose beloved home, Abbotsford House near Melrose, is still lived in by his descendants. Traquair House, a mile or so south of Innerleithen, boasts an even longer record. The oldest continuously inhabited dwelling in Scotland, it has been lived in by the Maxwell-Stuart family since 1491. Floors Castle at Kelso, the hereditary home of the Dukes of Roxburghe, is a mostly Victorian, mock-medieval extravaganza of turrets and castellations, while by contrast, Paxton House is a gem of 18th century classical restraint, a masterwork of the gifted Adam brothers. Perhaps the most august of all the great houses is Bowhill, the main Scottish residence of the Duke of Buccleuch, although multi-turreted Thirlestane Castle runs it a close second.

These historic houses are set in an inspiring landscape where grand vistas sweep across the majestic Eildon Hills or the crumpled masses of the Cheviots; where broad green valleys unfold and huge tracts of forest shelter a varied wildlife and unspoilt countryside which generously repays a leisurely exploration.

Wherever you travel in the Borders you will come across memories of the area's most famous son, Sir Walter Scott, who sang its praises in many of his poems.

PLACES OF INTEREST

ANCRUM

Prettily located beside Ale Water, a tributary of the River Teviot, Ancrum saw one of the last of the major Border conflicts, the **Battle of Ancrum Moor** in 1544. A much later and better-known battle is commemorated by the Waterloo Monument, some two miles northeast, erected in 1815 by the Marquis of Lothian and his tenants.

A mile or so east of Ancrum, **Monteviot House Gardens** on the banks of the River Teviot offers a variety of gardens, a water garden of islands linked by bridges, an arboretum, greenhouses and a plant stall. For a perfect family day out, combine Monteviot House with a visit to **Harestanes Countryside Visitor Centre** which is almost next door. There are beautiful woodland walks, an outdoor play area, lots of countryside activities throughout the season, a gift shop and a tea room.

AYTON

This small village on the River Eye, only a mile or so from the A1, is dominated by **Ayton Castle**, a fairyland fantasy of pepperpot turrets and crow-stepped gables. The castle was built in 1846 and is still a private residence, but is open to visitors on Sunday afternoons during the season.

From Ayton, five miles of country lanes lead southwards to **Paxton House**, "the most perfect example in Scotland of the style now known as neo-Palladianism". A melancholy tale is attached to this gracious house, designed by

4

the Edinburgh brothers John and James Adam in the 1750s. It was commissioned by Patrick Home, Lord Billie, a rich and personable young man who, while visiting Berlin on his Grand Tour of Europe, bedazzled the court of King Frederick the Great of Prussia. The king's only acknowledged child, Charlotte de Brandt, became besotted with the smooth-talking Scotsman. She absolutely rejected her father's long-held plans for a politically more useful dynastic connection with a plump and terminally boring Silesian prince. The king, surprisingly, finally agreed to her marriage with the wealthy, handsome but politically insignificant Scottish laird. Patrick gleefully returned to Scotland and spent lavishly on building a noble house at Paxton worthy of his intended royal bride. Charlotte never entered its stately portals or passed through its sublimely-decorated rooms, however. She died young before the house became habitable; her marriage not yet consecrated.

The sad story of Patrick and Charlotte was to be duplicated a few years later when Patrick became engaged to Jane Graham of Dugaldstone. Their marriage did indeed take place, in Naples in 1771, and the couple spent three years touring Europe. Once again, Patrick commissioned Robert Adam to design and build a new marital home, Wedderburn Castle. He returned to it alone: Jane stayed in Europe with a new lover. No wonder the striking portrait of Patrick Home by John Hoppner, on display in Paxton House, depicts an elderly man with a choleric complexion, a set jaw and a sour expression. It is part of a large collection which Patrick bequeathed to his nephew George, who was then 77 years old. Despite his age, George enthusiastically set about building what is still the largest private picture gallery of any country house in Scotland. A rich selection of other paintings on display here are on loan from the National Galleries of Scotland (for whom Paxton House is an outstation), and are changed frequently.

Paxton House is also notable for its outstanding collection of furniture by Chippendale, with more than 60 pieces ranging from the entire furnishing of the dining-room (not just tables and chairs but window-seats, wine-coolers and knife-boxes) to pier tables with marvellous marquetry inlays, desks and secretaries, and mahogany armchairs and sofas.

Outside, the 80 acres of gardens, parkland and woodland were laid out in the late 1770s in the style of "Capability" Brown and are set within a great loop of the River Tweed, which here marks the border between Scotland and England.

A few miles upstream from Paxton House, the ruins of **Norham Castle** stand on the south bank of the Tweed and are therefore in England, though the Castle is generally considered one of the Border attractions. Its great Norman Keep, which inspired several landscapes by J. M. W. Turner, is regarded as one of the finest examples in England. Built in the 1150s, Norham was the principal stronghold of the Prince-Bishops of Durham and witnessed many battles before Elizabeth I abandoned it in favour of the newly-fortified Berwick-upon-Tweed.

BOWHILL

The principal Scottish residence of the Duke of Buccleuch, Bowhill is a monumental building 437 feet long, most of it built in the first half of the 19th century. The 4th Duke's kinsman and neighbour, Sir Walter Scott, whose own home, Abbotsford, is just six miles away, was a frequent visitor to Bowhill and advised on the early stages of the massive new construction. The famous portrait by Henry Raeburn of the affable poet and novelist with his beloved dog "Camp" at his feet hangs in the Scott Room, which also contains Sir Walter's tartan and the original manuscript of *The Lay of the Last Minstrel*.

Bowhill boasts a superlative collection of other works of art - family portraits by Lely and Reynolds, landscapes by Claude Lorraine and Ruysdael, as well as sumptuous French furniture and priceless displays of Meissen and Sèvres china.

The house alone provides a full and rewarding day, but there's also the **Bowhill Country Park** where miles of footpaths and cycle trails criss-cross the estate. There's a very well-designed Adventure Playground, a Victorian Fire Engine Display, a Gift Shop, Courtyard Tea Room, and the thriving Bowhill Little Theatre housed in the former stables.

Apart from visits by educational groups which can be pre-arranged at any time, the house is only open to the public on afternoons during July; the Country Park on afternoons from April to September (daily during July, closed Fridays during the other months). Disabled visitors have free entry to the house and Little Theatre.

Two miles south of Bowhill, on the B7009, **Aikwood Tower** is the legendary home of Michael Scott the wizard, although nowadays occupied by the former Liberal leader (Lord) David Steel. It's a rather austere looking building, its forbidding appearance somewhat softened by the surrounding wooded slopes of the Ettrick Water Valley. In the former byres of the 16th century tower there's an exhibition celebrating the life and work of James Hogg, a self-taught poet and friend of Scott who enjoyed great fame in the late 1700s but whose verse requires sincere dedication from modern readers. The Tower also hosts temporary exhibitions of the work of local artists and sculptors, and there's an interesting garden devoted to medieval plants.

COLDSTREAM

This pleasant little town sits beside the Tweed and is linked to England by the graceful five-arched **Smeaton's Bridge**, built by John Smeaton in 1766 on the site of the original ford by which Edward I had invaded Scotland nearly five centuries earlier. Like Gretna Green, Coldstream was a favourite with eloping couples, who until 1856 could get married in the Toll House at the Scottish end of the bridge. Robert Burns crossed here on his first visit to England in May 1787, an event commemorated by a plaque on the bridge. Nearby, a huge obelisk erected in 1832 to a little-known MP soars above the town.

Coldstream's name is perhaps best known in connection with the Coldstream Guards. Officially designated the 2nd Regiment of Foot Guards of the British Army, the regiment was formed here in 1659 by General Monck with the intention of marching on London to help restore Charles II to the throne. The Guards' distinguished reputation is recorded at the Coldstream Museum in the attractive, pedestrianised Market Square.

To the northwest of the town, **The Hirsel** was the home of former Prime Minister Sir Alec Douglas-Home. His family still live here and the house is not open to the public, but visitors are free to wander through large parts of the 3,000-acre estate. On the western edge of the estate, former homestead outhouses have been converted into the **Homestead Museum &** **Centre for Arts & Crafts**, incorporating craft shops, a tea room and a museum which interprets the management of the estate, past and present.

About four miles southeast of Coldstream, near the village of Branxton, is **Flodden Field**, the site of Scotland's most disastrous battle against the English. On 9 September 1513, at least 10,000 men perished, among them the Scottish leader, James IV, and "not a family of note in all Scotland was left without cause to mourn that dreadful day." In 1910, a tall Celtic cross was erected on the hill overlooking the battlefield. It is inscribed simply "Flodden 1513. To the brave of both nations."

DUNS

The former county town of Berwickshire, this quiet little market town sits at the foot of **Duns Law** - 714 feet high and well worth the 20-minute walk to the summit for its grand views and to see the **Covenanters' Stone**, which marks the spot where Alexander Leslie gathered his troops for an expected battle with Charles I's army. In the event, Charles' troops thought better of it and retreated without a fight. Duns Castle, 14th century with early 19th century extensions, is not normally open to the public, but the surrounding **Duns Castle Nature Reserve** offers some pleasant trails for walkers through its 190 acres.

Duns was the birthplace of two well-known figures. The medieval theologian Duns Scotus was born here around 1265. Those who subscribed to his views were contemptuously called "Dunses", hence the word "dunce". A more contemporary figure is Jim Clark, who was twice world motor racing champion in the 1960s. His dazzling career, brutally cut short by a fatal crash on the track at Hockenheim in Germany in 1968, is recalled at the **Jim Clark Room** in Newtown Street.

Two miles east of Duns on the A6105, **Manderston House** is one of the finest examples of a lavish Edwardian house in Britain. Set in some 50 acres of gardens which are noted for their rhododendrons and azaleas, Manderston was built between 1871 and 1905 for the Miller family. who had made their fortune in herrings and hemp. No expense was spared. The architect John Kinross installed the exquisite plasterwork ceilings, an inlaid marble floor and an immensely costly staircase

6

modelled on one in the Petit Trianon at Versailles, its rails plated in silver.

GALASHIELS

Lying in the valley of the Gala Water, Galashiels has for centuries been an important centre for wool and cloth-making, so much so that in 1777 the town's textile manufacturers adopted the motto "We dye to live and live to die." The Scottish College of Textiles was established here in 1909; today, the **Lochcarron of Scotland Cashmere & Wool Centre** offers guided tours of tartan and tweed production from raw yarn to finished product. Within the Mill, Galashiels Museum records the development of the town.

Old Gala House, home of the Lairds of Gala for many generations, is now a Museum and Art Gallery, beautifully set in landscaped gardens. There are more flowers in Bank Street Gardens in the heart of the town, a pleasant spot to linger for a while breathing in the fragrance.

Every year in July, Galashiels hosts the Braw Lads Gathering - which, it is claimed, began as a celebration of the marriage of James IV and Margaret Tudor, sister of Henry VIII, in 1503. Whatever its roots, it provides the excuse for a week of ceremonies and events. A "braw lad" of another kind is commemorated by the dramatic statue of a Border Reiver which commands the east end of Bank Street.

Sadly no more is St Trinnean's School which once stood on the edge of the town. Visiting Galashiels in 1941, Ronald Searle met two of the girls from St Trinnean's; their accounts of the pupils' disorderly conduct furnished some memorably comic material for his St Trinian's novels.

Not to be missed by any devotee of Sir Walter Scott is a visit to his home for the last 20 years of his life, **Abbotsford**, a mile or so south of Galashiels. It is a masterpiece of the Scottish Baronial style of architecture, surrounded by trim gardens and looking out to the River Tweed. Inside, visitors pass through a grand barrel-ceilinged entrance hall to the galleried and book-lined study where each morning at 6 o'clock Scott would seat himself at the small writing desk made of salvage from wrecked ships of the Spanish Armada. His chair, his spectacles, the portrait of Rob Roy hanging on the wall - all remain just as he left them. In the superb library next door, with a richly moulded ceiling copied from Rosslyn Chapel, are housed the 9,000 books Scott collected during his lifetime, along with a fascinating assortment of Scottish memorabilia, including Rob Roy's purse and skene dhu (knife), and a lock of Bonnie Prince Charlie's hair. Perhaps the most poignant place in the house is the dining room. In September 1832, his health destroyed by overwork, Sir Walter's bed was placed here so that he could gaze out on his beloved River Tweed. On the 21st, his family was at his bedside, among them his son-in-law and biographer, John Lockhart: "It was a beautiful day - so warm that every window was open - and so perfectly still that the sound of all others the most delicious to his ear, the gentle ripple of the Tweed over its pebbles, was distinctly audible as we knelt around his bed, and his eldest son kissed his eyes and closed his eyes."

HAWICK

The largest of the Border burghs, like so many Border towns Hawick was regularly attacked by the English. There was a particularly violent onslaught in 1570 which left scarcely a building standing. A notable exception was **Drumlanrig's Tower** which, after extensive and sensitive restoration, opened in 1995 as a museum recording the town's turbulent history. The tower also houses Hawick's Tourist Information Centre.

In June, the "Common Riding" ceremony of riding the boundaries commemorates the gallant defence of the town against English raiders in 1514 by the youths of the town - only the youths, because virtually all Hawick's menfolk had been slain the year before in the frightful carnage of the Battle of Flodden. The "Common Riding" became something of a battle itself in 1996 when two local women asserted their right to join the previously all-male ride. They faced bitter opposition but their claim was eventually upheld by the Sheriff Court.

Hawick (pronounced Hoyk) is a thriving community, its prosperity based on the manufacture of quality knitwear, clothing and carpets. The town is the home of such names as Pringle of Scotland, Lyle and Scott, Peter Scott, and many other smaller firms producing knitwear in cashmere, lambswool and Shetland yarns.

On the edge of the town, the award-winning **Wilton Lodge Park** on the banks of the River

The Horse Monument, Hawick

the original 19th century machinery.

Innerleithen's premier attraction, though, is undoubtedly historic **Traquair House**, a mile or so to the south of the town. Traquair is the oldest house in Scotland to have been continuously inhabited by the same family, the first of the line being James Stuart, who took up residence in 1491. More than 500 years later, James' descendants, the Maxwell-Stuarts, still live here. The family were staunch Catholics and suffered grievously for their adherence to the Old Religion. A succession of priests lived in hiding in the claustrophobic Priest's Room, and during the Jacobite rebellions the Stuarts, now Earls of Traquair, compounded their problems by supporting Bonnie Prince Charlie. The 5th Earl was host to the Prince at Traquair in the autumn of 1745, and when his guest was leaving escorted him to the famous "Bear Gates" guarding the entrance. As the Prince passed through, the Earl vowed that "The gates of Traquair wad be opened nevermair till a Stuart king was crooned in London." They have remained firmly closed ever since.

The long and romantic history of the Stuarts of Traquair comes alive in every part of this fascinating house - in the exquisite 18th century Library, in the corkscrewing stone staircases and in family mementos like the list compiled by the 4th Earl's wife detailing the 17 children, including two sets of twins, with which she presented her husband over a period of 14 years.

Teviot offers a whole range of recreational facilities within its 107 acres - woodland and riverside walks, tennis, bowling and putting, as well as a walled garden with special floral displays. Riders can follow the 18-mile Hawick Circular Riding/Walking Route or tackle the famous Buccleuch Ride which wanders for some 56 miles through the Borders. There is a wonderful 100-acre riverside award-winning park only a mile's walk from Wiltonburn and, for the more energetic, a 200-acre hill to climb with wonderful panoramic views of the town and surrounding countryside.

INNERLEITHEN

The Rivers Tweed and Leithen meet in this charming little town which has a famous watering place known as St Ronan's Wells (free) whose sulphurous waters were once regularly sampled by Sir Walter Scott. In the High Street, Robert Smail's Printing Works (National Trust for Scotland) is popular with children who are allowed to try their hand at typesetting using

JEDBURGH

Approached along the lovely Jed Valley, Jedburgh's glory is the **Abbey**, magnificent even in its ruined state. Built in glowing red sandstone, the Abbey was founded in 1138 by David I but suffered grievously and often from English attacks during the interminable Border wars. The final blow came in 1523 when the Earl of Surrey ordered the Abbey to be burned. Some 40 years later Scotland's monarch came to the town, a visit commemorated at **Mary, Queen of Scots House**. The name is slightly misleading since Mary didn't own the house but stayed there as the guest of Sir Thomas Kerr. The exhibits include a death mask of the hapless Queen and a rare portrait of her third husband, the Earl of Bothwell. The Queen's host at Jedburgh, Sir Thomas Kerr, lived at **Ferniehurst Castle** just outside the town, still the family home of his descendant, Lord Lothian. The Castle and **Kerr Museum** are occasionally open to the public.

A winner of the country town prize in the "Beautiful Scotland in Bloom" competition,

Jedburgh Abbey

Jedburgh is a pleasant place to walk around, perhaps following the riverside walk or just lingering in the Abbey precincts.

KELSO

Sir Walter Scott considered Kelso "the most beautiful, if not the most romantic, village in the land". Sir Walter was very familiar with this dignified little town, set around the meeting of the rivers Tweed and Teviot. As a boy he attended the Old Grammar School which was actually based within the melancholy ruins of **Kelso Abbey**. Founded in 1128 by King David it became the richest and most powerful monastery in southern Scotland. Successive English invasions culminated in the Earl of Hertford's merciless attack in 1545 when all the monks

were murdered and the Abbey set on fire. The fine Norman and Gothic detail of the remaining transepts and façade give some idea of the glorious building that once stood here.

From Kelso's elegant and spacious **Market Square**, believed to be the largest in Scotland, Bridge Street leads to John Rennie's fine five-arched bridge over the Tweed. It was built in 1803 and Rennie was clearly pleased with his work since, some eight years later, he used virtually the same design for his Waterloo Bridge in London.

There are grand views from the bridge of **Junction Pool**, the famous salmon fishing beat where the waters of the Tweed and Teviot mingle. If you want to try your angling skills here you must book years ahead and pay somewhere around £5,000 per rod per week.

A short walk along Roxburgh Street to another alley leads to the delightful Cobby Riverside Walk. A short stroll will bring you to the breathtaking extravagance of **Floors Castle**, hereditary home of the Dukes of Roxburghe. Originally a rather austere early-Georgian building, the mansion was transformed in the 1830s by the Edinburgh architect William Playfair into a dramatic masterpiece of the Scottish Baronial style, its roofscape fretted with a panorama of stone pinnacles and turrets crowned by lead-capped domes. This palatial transformation was undertaken by the 6th Duke, who had succeeded to the title at the age of seven. His father's succession had occurred under rather unusual circumstances. When the 4th Duke died childless, the inheritance was disputed between several claimants. After a seven-year legal battle the House of Lords decided that Sir James Innes held the superior right to the title of 5th Duke. Sir James was then 76 years old and childless, prompting fears that on his death the succession would again be contested. Rising nobly to the challenge, the new Duke married the youthful Harriet Charlewood and became a father for the first time in his 81st year.

The 6th Duke was a discriminating collector of works of art. The magnificent State Rooms of the Castle display many fine paintings, among them portraits by Gainsborough, Reynolds, Allan Ramsay and Henry Raeburn, a collection that has since been supplemented by modern masters such as Matisse, Bonnard and Augustus John. Other attractions at Floors Castle include the extensive parklands and grounds, a picnic area overlooking the Tweed, a garden centre, gift shop and licensed restaurant.

LAUDER

The main town in Lauderdale, the Royal Burgh of Lauder nevertheless has a population of little more than a thousand people. Surrounded on three sides by the gentle Lammermuir Hills, the town has preserved its medieval plan with a single main street widening into a Market Place dominated by the quaint old Tolbooth. **Lauder's Parish Church** of 1673 is decidedly unusual, built in the form of a Greek cross with the pulpit in the centre under the octagonal bell tower. The original box pews are still in place.

A short walk from the centre of this picturesque conservation village brings you to the imposing pile of **Thirlestane Castle**. The castle was built in the 1670s for John Maitland, 1st (and only) Duke of Lauderdale. A close confidant of Charles II and a member of the notorious Cabal, the Duke's power was such that he was regarded as the uncrowned King of Scotland. In those days political power meant rich pickings by way of bribes, and the Duke spared no expense on the building, decorating and furnishing of his opulent castle. The famous English plasterer George Dunsterfield was commissioned to create the marvellous ceilings, most notably in the Red Drawing Room where garlands of leaves and flowers cascade from the ceiling. The Castle's other attractions include a wonderful collection of historic toys which children are actually *encouraged* to play with, a

Border Country Life exhibition, and a superb park where the Scottish Championship Horse Trials are held in late August.

MELROSE

Melrose is an enchanting little town, set beside the River Tweed at the foot of the three peaks of the Eildon Hills. Behind the town square, the noble ruins of **Melrose Abbey** stand in shattered glory. Founded in 1136 by David I, the original building was repeatedly attacked by the English and the present structure dates mostly from the late 1300s. Modelled on the abbeys of northern England, the building reflects the splendidly intricate Gothic style of that age. (Look for the curious gargoyle of a pig playing the bagpipes).

For centuries, tradition asserted that the heart of Robert the Bruce was buried near the Abbey's high altar. In 1996 the legend was proved true when a casket was uncovered containing a withered heart. Two years later the casket was ceremonially re-buried and a commemorative stone tablet erected.

Next door to the Abbey, the inviting **Priorwood Garden** (National Trust for Scotland) specialises in growing plants suitable for dried flower arranging. The walled garden encloses an apple orchard walk and a picnic area, and there's a shop selling the dried flowers. Also within the Abbey precincts is the 16th century Commendator's House, formerly the "Estate Office" for the Abbey's extensive properties,

Thirlestane Castle

10

now housing a collection of ecclesiastical artefacts. In the town itself the Trimontium Exhibition gives an insight into the Roman occupation of the area, while Teddy Melrose is Scotland's first teddy bear museum with displays recording the full history of the British teddy bear.

About four miles east of Melrose, on the B6356, **Scott's View** looks across the River Tweed to the Eildon Hills and was one of the great novelist's favourite viewpoints. When the hearse taking him to his final resting place at Dryburgh Abbey reached this point, it's said that the horses stopped of their own accord.

Dryburgh Abbey itself (Historic Scotland) lies a couple of miles to the south, beautifully set within a curve of the River Tweed. Scott and members of his family are buried in St Mary's Aisle; close by is the grave of Field Marshal Earl Haig, Britain's disastrous Commander-in-Chief during World War I. Originally founded during the 12th century, like its sister Abbeys in

Dryburgh Abbey

the Borders Dryburgh was repeatedly attacked by the English and little of the Abbey Church remains. But the cloister buildings are remarkably well preserved and the lovely surroundings create a sense of deep peace.

PEEBLES

The Royal Burgh of Peebles enjoys a superb position surrounded by hills and with the River Tweed running through its centre. Spacious parklands extend along the river banks and the town itself has a genteel, almost demure charm, its houses presenting a pleasing medley of architectural styles.

Natives of the town are known locally as "gutterbluids" and they have included William

and Robert Chambers, creators of the famous encyclopaedia. In 1859 the brothers presented the town with the Chambers Institute, which today houses **The Tweeddale Museum & Picture Gallery**.

Peebles folk also have their own word for a visitor or incomer to the town - "stooryfit" (dusty-footed). Among stooryfits who made Peebles their home were Robert Louis Stevenson, novelist, soldier and politician John Buchan and his sister, the novelist O. Douglas, and the celebrated explorer of Africa, Mungo Park.

A mile to the west of Peebles, **Neidpath Castle** stands dramatically on a steep bluff overlooking the River Tweed. Its 14th century walls are more than 10 feet thick, but when Cromwell's artillery relentlessly pounded them with cannon, the castle's owner, the Earl of Tweeddale, was forced to surrender. The castle later passed to the Douglas family, Dukes of Queensberry. In 1795 the 2nd Duke found himself strapped for cash; he ordered the felling of every marketable tree on the estate. This spectacular act of environmental vandalism resulted in the Duke becoming the target of a wrathful sonnet by William Wordsworth which begins with the words "Degenerate Douglas ..."

ST ABB'S

St Abbs is one of the most picturesque fishing villages on Scotland's east coast, one of the few safe havens along this rocky stretch of coast. Jagged cliffs, some of the highest in Britain, rise 300 feet above the shore and fishermen's cottages are shoe-horned in wherever they can fit.

For the active there are many lovely walks in the vicinity, opportunities for both sea and river fishing, and boat trips from the harbour. Or you may prefer to just relax in the tea garden, observing the cormorants and the fishermen mending their nets, while keeping an eye open for a sighting of the occasional seal.

The village is named after St Ebba, a 7th century princess of Northumbria who was shipwrecked here. She managed to reach shore and founded a nunnery in gratitude for her escape. Just to the north of the village, **St Abb's Head** is a spectacular promontory, now a National Trust for Scotland Marine Reserve. A lighthouse was built here in 1862 but, because of the height of the cliffs on which it stands, no tower was necessary and keepers actually walk *downhill* to reach the light.

Three miles to the west of St Abb's Head is one of Scotland's most extraordinary castles. **Fast Castle** is perched precariously on a stack of rock, barely accessible by the steep cliff footpath and best viewed from above. Sir Walter Scott used the castle as his model for Wolf's Crag in his novel *The Bride of Lammermuir*.

SELKIRK

The twin valleys of Ettrick and Yarrow contain some of the most glorious scenery in the Borders. High on the hillside, the Ancient and Royal Burgh of Selkirk enjoys superb views across Ettrick Water. Sir Walter Scott had close connections with the town, serving as Sheriff of Selkirkshire from 1799 until 1832. There's a striking statue of him in front of the Courthouse where he presided so often and where visitors can see a video recounting the story of Scott's associations with the area and its people.

Another statue in the High Street commemorates Mungo Park, the famous explorer and anti-slavery activist who was born in Selkirkshire in 1777. Two finely-worked bas-reliefs depict his adventures along the River Niger which ended in his death by drowning in 1805.

11

Selkirk's oldest building, **Halliwell's House**, is now home to the town's Museum and the Robson Gallery (both free), the latter a venue for touring art exhibitions. The museum's most prized possession is the "Flodden Flag". Eighty men of Selkirk marched off to fight in the calamitous Battle of Flodden; only one of them returned. He stumbled into the Market Square bearing a captured English flag. Unable to express his grief, the soldier simply waved the flag towards the ground. His gesture is symbolically re-enacted each year in June during the Common Riding, one of the oldest of the Border Festivals, dating back to the year of Flodden Field, 1513. As many as 400 riders take part in the ceremony.

The town's other visitor attractions include **Selkirk Glass** where you can watch glassmakers at work and purchase the high quality products, factory shops selling the local tweed, and the unusual **Robert Clapperton Daylight Photographic Studio**, an original daylight studio from 1867. There's a small family-owned museum with many photographic artefacts, and a negative archive from which visitors can order prints.

12 The Auld Cross Keys

Denholm,
Roxburghshire TD9 8NU
Tel: 01450 870355
Fax: 01450 870778

Directions:

Denholm is on the A698 Hawick to Kelso road, about 5 miles northeast of Hawick. The Auld Cross Keys Inn is set beside the village green

Denholm village grew up alongside the important bridge over the River Teviot. Close by, overlooking the village green, you'll find the **Auld Cross Keys Inn** which enjoys an exceptional reputation in the area for good food, excellent ales and topflight entertainment. The premises were built in 1800 as a bakehouse, later becoming a coaching inn. Today, the Auld Cross Keys is well-known for its real ales (which have earned it a place in the CAMRA Good Beer Guide), and for its cuisine (which is praised in the Good Pub Food Guide). The comprehensive menu ranges from dishes such as Creamy Mushroom Crepes to Denholm Beef Sausages which won the "Best Beef Sausages in Scotland" award in 1996. The inn serves a traditional carvery between12.30 and 18.00 each Sunday.(Do note that the kitchen is closed on Mondays).

The Auld Cross Keys stocks a good range of ales, amongst them the local Broughton real ale and an ever-changing guest ale. Peter and Heather Ferguson, who have owned and run the inn since 1987, also provide their customers with an outstanding programme of quality folk music, presenting regular performances every other Thursday. Artistes who make their way to this country inn include nationally-known performers as well as local folk-singers. The inn is also a popular venue for weddings, private parties, conferences and other functions at which guests can enjoy the same high standards of food, drink and service that have earned the Auld Cross Keys its enviable reputation.

Opening Hours: Mon: 17.00-23.00; Tue-Wed: 11.00-14.30; 17.00-23.00; Thu: 11.00-14.30; 17.00-24.00; Fri: 11.00-14.30; 17.00-01.00; Sat: 11.00-24.00; Sun: 12.30-23.00

Food: Tue-Sat: 12.00-14.00; 18.00-20.30; Sun: Carvery 12.30-18.00

Credit Cards: All major cards except Diners

Facilities: Parking

Entertainment: Pool; darts; satellite TV; quiz nights; live entertainment every other Thursday

Local Places of Interest/Activities: Golf, 2 miles; Waterloo Monument, 9 miles; Teviot Water Gardens, 12 miles; Bowhill, 15 miles

The Black Bull Hotel 13

Blackbull Street, Duns,
Berwickshire TD11 3AA
Tel: 01361 883379

Directions:

Duns is 12 miles northwest of Coldstream on the A6112. Blackbull Street is just off the main square

The former county town of Berwickshire, this quiet little market town sits at the foot of Duns Law - 714ft high and well worth the 20-minute walk to the summit for its grand views. Duns Castle, 14th century with early 19th century extensions, is not normally open to the public but the surrounding Duns Castle Nature Reserve offers some pleasant trails for walkers through its 190 acres. Duns town was the birthplace of two well-known figures. The medieval theologian Duns Scotus was born here around 1265. Those who subscribed to his views were contemptuously called "Dunses", hence the word "dunce". A more contemporary figure is Jim Clark who was twice world motor racing champion in the 1960s. His dazzling career, brutally cut short by a fatal crash on the track at Hockenheim in 1968, is recalled at the Jim Clark Room in Newtown Street.

Just across the road from the Jim Clark Room, the **Black Bull Hotel** stands at the heart of the town. This appealing old hostelry was built in the late 1700s as a coaching inn and the former stables still stand alongside. The Black Bull is owned and run by Margaret Sturrock who offers her customers a warm welcome, a comprehensive menu of main meals and snacks, and a good selection of beers and ales, including the locally-brewed Bellhaven Ales. Food is served every day, all day and you can enjoy it either in the atmospheric bar, the separate restaurant or, in good weather, on the lovely secluded patio overlooking the garden. And if you are looking for somewhere to stay in the area, the hotel has 3 pleasant and comfortable letting rooms: a single and a twin with shared facilities, and a single en suite.

Opening Hours: 11.00-23.00, Summer; 12.00-23.00, Winter

Food: Available all day until 21.00

Credit Cards: Access, Mastercharge, Visa

Accommodation: 3 rooms, (1 single en suite; 1 single & 1 twin with shared facilities)

Facilities: Beer garden; parking

Entertainment: Pool table; Occasional live entertainment

Local Places of Interest/Activities: Jim Clark Room, nearby; Duns Castle Country Park, 1.5 miles; golf, 1.5 miles; Manderston House, 2 miles

14   The Castle Hotel

11 High Street,
Coldstream,
Berwickshire TD12 4AP
Tel/Fax: 01890 882830

Directions:

Coldstream is on the A697 Edinburgh to Newcastle road, about 48 miles southeast of Edinburgh. The Castle Hotel is located on the main road

Coldstream's name is perhaps best known in connection with the Coldstream Guards. Officially designated the 2nd Regiment of Foot Guards of the British Army, the regiment was formed here in 1659 by General Monck with the intention of marching on London to help restore Charles II to the throne. The Guards' distinguished reputation in subsequent years is recorded at the Coldstream Museum in the pedestrianised Market Square. To the northwest of the town, The Hirsel was the home of former Prime Minister Sir Alec Douglas-Home. His family still live there and the house is not open to the public but visitors are free to wander through large parts of the 3000-acre estate. Former homesteads here have been converted into the Homestead Museum & Centre for Arts and Crafts.

Back in the town centre, **The Castle Hotel** has been dispensing hospitality and providing comfortable accommodation for more than 150 years. The interior, with its vintage tables, looks very inviting and the owners, Derek and Linda Nimmo, who arrived here in October 1999, have been steadily upgrading the hotel's amenities. Children are welcome and so too are Old Age Pensioners who will find special price meals and drinks available. There's a good choice of bar meals or you can dine à la carte. If you are planning to stay in this pleasant little town, The Castle can offer you a choice of 7 rooms, all of them en suite, and equipped with TV and hospitality trays.

Opening Hours: Mon-Thu: 11.00-24.00; Fri-Sun: 11.00-01.00

Food: Available 12.00-14.30 & 18.00-21.00

Credit Cards: All major cards except Amex & Diners

Accommodation: 7 rooms, all en suite

Facilities: Beer garden; parking nearby

Entertainment: Live music monthly

Local Places of Interest/Activities: Coldstream Guards Museum, nearby; The Hirsel Museum & Country Craft Centre, 1 mile; Flodden Field, 4 miles; Floors Castle and Kelso Abbey, 9 miles

Churches Hotel 15

Albert Road, Eyemouth,
Berwickshire TD14 5DB
Tel: 01890 750401
Fax: 01890 750747

Directions:

From the A1 about 7 miles north of Berwick, turn right on the A1107 to Eyemouth (2 miles)

Still an active little fishing port, Eyemouth has long since abandoned its other main source of income in times past, smuggling. Contraband goods were furtively conveyed to Gunsgreen House on the far side of the harbour and thence by way of underground tunnels to eager purchasers in the town itself. The elegant 1750s house, designed by James Adam, has now retrieved its respectable status by becoming fully restored to its former glory. Eyemouth Museum's most striking exhibit is a contemporary tapestry depicting the traumatic disaster of 1881 when 189 fishermen from this small town perished in one of the worst North Sea storms on record. More upbeat celebrations of the town's maritime history take place in July with the Herring Queen Festival, and August with the RNLI.

Enjoying views across the harbour, **Churches Hotel** was originally built in 1790 as a manse but has been completely refurbished and brought up to the standard of a 4-star hotel. The interior is exquisitely decorated and furnished, with paintings and antique pieces, beautiful wooden floors and concealed lighting all adding to the appeal. The cuisine at Churches is in keeping with these stylish surroundings. Locally caught fish, naturally, are a speciality of the house and the menu, which changes regularly, also offers plenty of other choices. The gardens are another major attraction, beautifully laid out and with those splendid views of the harbour - an ideal setting for afternoon tea. Churches is a place to linger and there are 6 guest bedrooms, all individually styled and decorated to the same high standards as the rest of the hotel.

Opening Hours: Hotel open all day

Food: Available all day until 21.00

Credit Cards: Access, Mastercharge, Visa & Switch

Accommodation: 6 rooms

Facilities: Extensive gardens, conference facilities

Local Places of Interest/Activities:
Eyemouth Museum nearby; St Abb's Head, 4 miles; Paxton House, 12 miles

Internet/Website:
www.churcheshotel.co.uk

16   The Commercial Inn

32 High Street,
Coldstream
TD12 4AS
Tel: 01890 882135

Directions:

Coldstream is on the A697 Edinburgh to Newcastle road, about 48 miles southeast of Edinburgh. The Commercial Inn is located on the main road

This pleasant little town sits beside the River Tweed and is linked to England by the graceful 5-arched Smeaton's Bridge built by John Smeaton in 1766 on the site of the original ford by which Edward I had invaded Scotland nearly 500 years earlier. Like Gretna Green, Coldstream was a favourite with eloping couples who until 1856 could get married in the Toll House at the Scottish end of the bridge. Robert Burns crossed here on his first visit to England in May 1787, an event commemorated by a plaque on the bridge. Nearby, a huge obelisk erected in 1832 to a little-known MP soars above the town.

    Situated in the heart of the town, **The Commercial Inn** is a substantial mid-Victorian building with a lovely stone frontage. The interior is much more spacious than the outside leads you to expect and features an unusual two-level Function Room. The inn is owned and run by Stephen Wilson and his mother, a family team which has made many improvements to the old inn in recent years. A special attraction here is that food is served throughout the day, right up until 8.30pm. The menus are varied, there are regular daily specials and children's portions are available.

Opening Hours: Sun-Thu: 11.00-24.00; Fri-Sat: 11.00-01.00

Food: Available all day until 20.30

Credit Cards: Cash only

Facilities: Function room; parking nearby

Entertainment: Pool table; quiz nights

Local Places of Interest/Activities:
Coldstream Guards Museum, nearby; The Hirsel Museum & Country Craft Centre, 1 mile; Flodden Field, 4 miles; Floors Castle and Kelso Abbey, 9 miles

The Craw Inn

17

Auchencrow,
Reston,
Berwickshire
TD14 5LS
Tel: 01890 761253

Directions:

From the A1, about 12 miles north of Berwick-upon-Tweed, turn left on the B6438 to Reston and Auchencrow (3 miles)

Only a few minutes from the A1, the village of Auchencrow stands in peaceful countryside with the Lammermuir Hills rising to the west. It's an unspoilt village and one of its most attractive buildings is **The Craw Inn**, Built in the early 18th century and now a listed building. It has been completely refurbished, but the old charm still survives. The Inn has 3 guest bedrooms, all with private modern facilities.

The Inn has a good reputation for its food, with the emphasis on traditional Scottish fare. The extensive menu includes fresh local fish and shellfish, game in season,and excellent steaks.There are delicious home-cured hams and wonderful local cheeses. Fine wines and real ales on tap compliment the food. Dining is available in the bar, or in the more formal atmosphere of the restaurant. A warm welcome awaits you at the Craw Inn.

Opening Hours: 11.00-24.00, daily

Food: Available 12.00-14.00; 18.00-21.00

Credit Cards: Access, Mastercharge, Visa & Switch

Accommodation: 3 rooms

Facilities: Beer garden; parking

Entertainment: Occasional live music evenings - jazz and folk

Local Places of Interest/Activities:
Eyemouth Museum, 7 miles; Manderston House, 7 miles; Duns Castle Nature Reserve, 9 miles; Jim Clark Room, Duns, 9 miles; Paxton House, 10 miles

Internet/Website:
e-mail: thecraw.inn@virginnet.co.uk
website: www.virgin.net/

18   The Crown Hotel

Market Square,
Coldstream,
Berwickshire TD12 4BG
Tel: 01890 882558

Directions:

Coldstream is on the A697 Edinburgh to Newcastle road, about 48 miles southeast of Edinburgh. The Crown Hotel is located in the Market Square

This small Border town is famous for the 2nd Regiment of Foot Guards, founded here in 1659 by General Monck. Another famous name associated with the town is Sir Alec Douglas-Home, Prime Minister in the early 1960s, whose family still live at The Hirsel to the north-east of the town. The unusual name of the house derives from an old Scottish word meaning the amount of land which could be tended by a single shepherd. The Hirsel is not open to the public but the extensive grounds are. A few miles east of Coldstream lies the site of the most disastrous battle in Scottish history, Flodden Field. Here, in 1513, ten thousand Scotsmen, including their king James IV, perished at the hands of the English.

Located in the heart of this historic town, **The Crown Hotel** is an early Victorian building where landlady Dorothy Hetherington has established a reputation for serving good food and fine ales. Wholesome and appetising traditional Scottish fayre is the order of the day, with prices that represent real value for money. Food is available every lunchtime and evening, and the menu is supplemented by daily specials. There's a pool table and anglers can purchase permits here for trout fishing in the nearby River Tweed. The hotel has a warm, family atmosphere which makes it a very pleasant place to stay. There are 5 guest bedrooms, 2 of them en suite and all equipped with TV and tea/coffee-making facilities.

Opening Hours: Mon-Fri: 11.00-24.00; Sat-Sun: 11.00-23.30

Food: Available every lunchtime & evening

Credit Cards: Access, Mastercharge & Visa

Accommodation: 5 rooms, 2 en suite

Facilities: Pool table; fishing permits available

Local Places of Interest/Activities: Coldstream Guards Museum, nearby; The Hirsel Museum & Country Craft Centre, 1 mile; Flodden Field, 4 miles; Floors Castle and Kelso Abbey, 9 miles

Dryburgh Arms Hotel 19

Melbourne Place,
Newtown St Boswells
Border TD6 0PA
Tel: 01835 822704

Directions:
Newtown St Boswells is off the A68, about 11 miles north of Jedburgh

Newtown St Boswells stands close to the River Tweed and there are some lovely riverside walks alongside the famous waterway. Also within easy walking distance is Dryburgh Abbey, beautifully set within a curve of the river. Sir Walter Scott and members of his family are buried in St Mary's Aisle and close by is the grave of Field Marshal Earl Haig, Britain's disastrous Commander-in-Chief during World War I. About a mile from the Abbey is, Scott's View looks across the Tweed to the Eildon Hills and was one of the great novelist's favourite viewpoints. When the hearse taking him to his final resting place at Dryburgh Abbey reached this point, it's said that the horses stopped of their own accord.

Back in Newtown St Boswells, the **Dryburgh Arms Hotel** is a striking building in glowing pinkish stone. Built in late Victorian times it has all the spaciousness and quality features of that era. The owner, Fred Bell, is a welcoming host, and if you happen to be a keen golfer you will find a kindred spirit! The hotel serves excellent value for money food, with a wide choice that ranges from bar snacks to 4 course meals. In good weather, you can enjoy your refreshments in the peaceful beer garden where there's also a children's play area. The Dryburgh Arms makes a very good base for exploring this historic area with its wealth of old buildings and its many associations with Walter Scott. The hotel has 3 guest bedrooms, all of them en suite and provided with TV and tea/coffee-making facilities.

Opening Hours: 11.00-24.00, daily

Food: 12.00-14.30 every day

Credit Cards: Cash only

Accommodation: 3 rooms, all en suite

Facilities: Beer garden; games room

Entertainment: Occasional live entertainment

Local Places of Interest/Activities: St Cuthbert's Way passes through the town; Dryburgh Abbey, 1.5 miles; Wallace Monument, 2 miles; Eildon Hills, 2.5 miles; Scott's View, 3 miles; Melrose Abbey, 5 miles; Abbotsford, 8 miles

20 The Fox & Hounds

Main Street,
Denholm,
Roxburghshire
TD9 8NU
Tel: 01450 870247

Directions:

Denholm is on the A698 Hawick to Kelso road, about 5 miles northeast of Hawick. The Fox and Hounds is on the main street

This small village set beside the River Teviot was the birthplace of both John Leyden, the 18th century poet and friend of Sir Walter Scott, and Sir James Murray, editor of the monumental Oxford English Dictionary. Leyden is commemorated by an obelisk to his memory and by a plaque on the thatched cottage where he was born. Murray's monument is his ground-breaking dictionary of which millions of copies have been sold. Across the river and about 2 miles to the east, atop Minto Crags, stand the ruins of the curiously named Fatlips Castle, built in the late 1500s for the Lockhart family.

Located in the heart of the village **The Fox & Hounds** is an attractive building of grey stone, offset by hanging baskets and tubs of flowers. It dates back to 1741 when it was built as a coaching inn and today it continues a long tradition of hospitality. Landlady Christine Purvis offers her customers a good choice of wholesome and appetising food which is available throughout the day until 8pm. Outside, there's a peaceful beer garden and children's play area, and Christine also organises occasional folk music evenings. If you are planning to stay in this pleasant part of the Borders, The Fox & Hounds has 3 guest rooms, available all year round.

Opening Hours: Mon-Thu: 11.00-15.00; 17.00-23.00; Fri-Sat: 11.00-01.00; Sun: 11.30-23.00

Food: 12.30-14.30, 17.30-20.00 every day

Credit Cards: Access, Mastercharge, Visa & Switch

Accommodation: 3 rooms

Facilities: Beer garden; children's play area; parking

Entertainment: Occasional folk music evenings

Local Places of Interest/Activities: Golf, 2 miles; Waterloo Monument, 9 miles; Teviot Water Gardens, 12 miles; Bowhill, 15 miles

Internet/Website: vijstew@quista.net

The Liddesdale Hotel   21

Douglas Square,
Newcastleton,
Roxburghshire TD9 0QD
Tel: 013873 75255
Fax: 013873 75569

Directions:
From the A7, about 14 miles north of Carlisle, take the B6357 towards Newcastleton (10 miles)

Located in the heart of beautiful Liddesdale, on the edge of the vast Border Forest Park, Newcastleton is a classic estate village, built by the 3rd Duke of Buccleuch as a 'new town' in 1793. A handsome bridge spans Liddel Water and. the gridiron pattern of the streets links three attractive squares. In one of these stands **The Liddesdale Hotel**, owned and run by Denis Kackeen who hails from south of the border. He's very proud of the food served and swears that his chef is the best in the whole of the Border Country! There's a choice of à la carte or table d'hôte menus as well as bar meals. All the dishes are prepared from fresh local produce with local trout and pheasant among the appetising choices on offer. The hotel has 5 guest rooms, all of them en suite, attractively furnished and meticulously clean, and provided with TV and tea/coffee-making facilities. Be aware that if you are planning a visit to Newcastleton in July you should book well ahead since that is when the hugely popular Newcastleton Folk Music Festival takes place.

The area around Newcastleton is marvellous walking and touring country and it can also boast one of the few great fortresses in the Borders. Hermitage Castle, a few miles to the north, dates back to the 14th century. It's a grim place associated with some gruesome legends and with the true story of Mary, Queen of Scots who fleetingly visited the castle one day in 1566 to tend her wounded lover, Bothwell.

Opening Hours: Sun-Thu: 11.00-23.00; Fri-Sat: 11.00-01.00

Food: Available 12.00-14.00 & 18.00-21.00 daily

Credit Cards: Access, Mastercharge, Visa & Switch

Accommodation: 5 rooms, all en suite

Facilities: Function Room; parking

Entertainment: Music by local people, visitors welcome to join in

Local Places of Interest/Activities: Golf nearby; Border Forest Park, 2 miles; Hermitage Castle, 6 miles

22   Linton Hotel

Main Street,
West Linton,
Peeblesshire
EH46 7EA
Tel: 01968 660228

Directions:
West Linton is on the
A702 about 18 miles
south of Edinburgh.

West Linton is a picturesque medieval village lying on the southern edge of the Pentland Hills, a favoured area for walkers. At the heart of the village is the **Linton Hotel**, a sturdy building of grey local stone which is very much the centre of village life. The inn is owned and run by Jim and Helen Clark, a friendly and welcoming couple with a great deal of experience in the hospitality business. The public bar here seems to be always thronged with locals - a good place for visitors to experience the genuine Scottish atmosphere. To the rear of the bar is the Drovers Log Cabin, a western themed restaurant with a decor recreating the log cabin dwellings of America's Wild West. The cuisine also has the true flavour of the west with steaks, venison, port, chicken and fish dishes all chargrilled. The Linton Hotel is a lively place with, in addition to the large screen TV, regular music evenings with live entertainment.

Opening Hours: Mon-Thu: 11.00-24.00; Fri-Sat: 11.00-01.00; Sun: 12.00-24.00

Food: Available all day

Credit Cards: All major cards except Amex & Diners

Facilities: Beer garden; Western Themed restaurant

Entertainment: Regular live entertainment; large screen TV

Local Places of Interest/Activities: Walking in nearby Pentland Hills; Hillend Country Park, 13 miles; Neidpath Castle, 14 miles; City of Edinburgh, 18 miles

The Pheasant Inn   23

61 High Street,
Jedburgh,
Roxburghshire
TD8 6CQ
Tel: 01835 862708

Directions:
The Pheasant Inn is located in the centre of the town

Approached along the lovely Jed Valley, Jedburgh's glory is the Abbey, magnificent even in its ruined state. Built in glowing red sandstone, the Abbey was founded in 1138 by David I but suffered grievously and often from English attacks during the interminable Border wars. The final blow came in 1523 when the Earl of Surrey ordered it to be burned. Some 40 years later, Scotland's monarch visited Jedburgh, an honour commemorated at Mary, Queen of Scots House. The name is slightly misleading since Mary didn't own the house but stayed there as a guest. Amongst the fascinating exhibits is a death mask of the hapless Queen.

A short walk from the Abbey, **The Pheasant Inn** is an inviting hostelry in the traditional Scottish style. It was originally built in 1904 as the Liberal Club and didn't become a pub until 1987. Roy Spowart bought the inn two years later and has been running it ever since. It's a lively place, with all the usual pub games available and live music at weekends. There's a function room upstairs which can cater for up to 60 people and food is served every lunchtime and evening in the spacious bar area. Customers have the choice of either a full à la carte menu or an appetising range of bar snacks. Children have their own menu, as do vegetarians. A genial and attentive host, Roy maintains the best traditions of Scottish hospitality.

Opening Hours: Mon-Thu: 11.00-23.00; Fri-Sat: 11.00-01.00; Sun: 12.30-23.00

Food: Available daily 12.00-14.30; 18.00-21.00

Credit Cards: Access, Amex, Mastercharge, Visa & Switch

Facilities: Function room; parking nearby

Entertainment: Darts; dominoes; live music at weekends

Local Places of Interest/Activities: Jedburgh Abbey; Mary, Queen of Scots House, both nearby; Waterloo Monument, 7 miles; Teviot Water Gardens, 8 miles

Internet/Website: e-mail: royspowart@hotmail.com

24 The Plough Hotel

Main Street,
Leitholm,
Berwickshire
TD12 4JN
Tel/Fax: 01890 840252

Directions:

From Coldstream, take the A697 towards Edinburgh. About 3 miles along this road, turn right on the B6461 to Leitholm (2 miles)

About 5 miles northwest of Coldstream, the picturesque village of Leitholm is well worth seeking out in order to visit **The Plough Hotel**. It's an attractive building with whitewashed walls, windows with black surrounds set off by hanging baskets and tubs of flowers. It was built in 1843 as an inn and although it has been expanded and modernised over the years it retains all the charm of a traditional Scottish hostelry. Traditional is the right word also for the appetising food on offer which draws on the country's renowned wealth of quality local produce. Complement your meal with one of the real ales on tap. Customers can eat in the beautifully furnished restaurant, the spacious public bar or, in good weather, in the delightful garden at the rear of the inn.

Joan Pitman is the owner of The Plough, a lady who works astonishing hours, (she is both chef and bar manager), but thrives on it as she loves meeting people. Children are welcome here and if you are planning to stay in the area, The Plough has 3 guest bedrooms, one a family room, two of them doubles, and all of them en suite and equipped with TV and tea/coffee-making facilities.

Opening Hours: Summer: 12.00-24.00 daily; Winter: Mon-Fri: 17.00-24.00, Sat-Sun: 12.00-24.00

Food: Available daily 12.00-14.00, (Sun 14.30); 18.00-21.00

Credit Cards: Cash or cheque with card

Accommodation: 3 rooms (1 family, 2 double, all en suite)

Facilities: Beer garden with fish pond & barbecue area; separate restaurant; parking

Entertainment: Darts; live music

Local Places of Interest/Activities: The Hirsel, & Coldstream Guards Museum, Coldstream, 4 miles; Kelso Abbey & Floors Castle, 8 miles; Norham Castle, 7 miles; Manderston House, 10 miles

Internet/Website:
e-mail: jp@plough19.fsnet.co.uk

The Royal Hotel 25

Canongate, Jedburgh TD8 6AN
Tel: 01835 863152 Fax: 01835 862019
Directions:
The Royal Hotel is just off the main street, along-
side the Abbey

A winner of the country town prize in the
"Beautiful Scotland in Bloom" competition,
Jedburgh is a pleasant place to walk around,
perhaps following the riverside path or stroll-
ing in the lovely Abbey precincts. Founded
by King David I around 1138, the Abbey was
often attacked by the English and as often
rebuilt. Built of glowing red sandstone, the
ruins are notable for St Catherine's Wheel,
(a rose window on the west front), and intricate carvings on the west door. Another place
of interest is the Jedburgh Jail Museum. Built
as a Georgian prison in 1820 on the site of
Jedburgh Castle, the Museum provides an insight into the town's 19th century social history.

Dating back to 1777, **The Royal Hotel**
began life as a coaching inn called The Har-
row Inn. It was rebuilt and extended in 1865 and two years was renamed following
the visit of Queen Victoria's children Prince Leopold and Prince Beatrice. Today, The
Royal is a warm and comfortable family-run hotel with modern facilities offering hearty
home cooked meals, a cosy residents' lounge and a lively public bar. A full and varied
menu is served throughout the year with bar lunches also available during the season.
Seafood is a speciality but you'll also find prime Sirloin steak, vegetarian options and
a children's menu. (There's also a children's play area beside the hotel). With 10 en
suite rooms, including family rooms, the hotel can accommodate up to 24 guests.
There are special packages for golfers and walkers, and in addition, The Royal caters
for weddings, private parties, business meetings and conferences for up to 100 people.

Opening Hours: Sun-Thu: 11.00-24.00;
Fri-Sat: 11.00-01.00

Food: Available all day

Credit Cards: Access, Mastercharge, Visa

Accommodation: 10 rooms, all en suite

Facilities: Function room; parking

Entertainment: Karaoke nights; live music
discos with DJ

Local Places of Interest/Activities:
Jedburgh Abbey; Mary, Queen of Scots
House; Jedburgh Jail Museum, all nearby;
Waterloo Monument, 7 miles; Teviot
Water Gardens, 8 miles

26 The Ship Inn

East Port, Melrose,
Roxburghshire
TD6 9RA
Tel: 01896 822190
Fax: 01896 820061

Directions:

Melrose is on the A6091, about 5 miles southeast of Galashiels. The Ship Inn is in the centre of the town very close to the local youth hostel.

Melrose is an enchanting little town, set beside the River Tweed at the foot of

the three peaks of the Eildon Hills. Behind the town square, the noble ruins of Melrose Abbey stand in shattered glory. For centuries, tradition asserted that the heart of Robert the Bruce was buried near the Abbey's high altar. In 1996 the legend was proved true when a casket was uncovered containing a withered heart. Two years later, the casket was ceremonially reburied and a commemorative stone tablet erected. Adjoining the Abbey grounds is Priorwood Garden which specialises in growing plants suitable for dried flower arranging. Sheltered by a high wall, its orchard has an interesting "Apples through the Ages Walk".

A short stroll from the garden, in the town's main square, is **The Ship Inn** - the only pub in Melrose - which dates back to the early 1800s. The name was the idea of the original owners, a great seafaring family who made their fortunes in Jamaica. Vivien McDonald has owned and run this charming old hostelry since 1996 - and she also does the cooking. The lunchtime specials offer appetising and wholesome dishes at value for money prices and are available every day. During the summer season, Vivien also serves evening meals. When the weather is favourable you can enjoy your refreshments in the quiet beer garden at the rear of the inn. The Ship has a childrens certificate and pool table, and Vivien also organises a variety of entertainment - quiz nights, karaoke nights and evenings featuring music of the 60s and 70s.

Opening Hours: Mon-Thu, 11.00-23.00; Fri-Sat, 11.00-01.00; Sun 12.00-23.00

Food: Available lunchtimes, daily; evening meals in summer only

Credit Cards: Cash only

Facilities: Beer garden; games room; parking nearby

Entertainment: Quiz Nights; karaoke nights; 60s & 70s nights

Local Places of Interest/Activities: Melrose Rugby Sevens every April; Melrose Abbey and Priorwood Garden (NTS) nearby; Southern Upland Way, 1 mile; Abbotsford, 4 miles; Dryburgh Abbey, 7 miles, Golfing, Fishing, Horse Riding.

Traquair Arms Hotel | 27

Innerleithen,
Peeblesshire EH44 6PD
Tel: 01896 830229
Fax: 01896 830260

Directions:

From Peebles, take the A72 towards Galashiels. Innerleithen is on this road, about 7 miles east of Peebles.

The Rivers Tweed and Leithen meet in this charming little town which has a famous watering place known as St Ronan's Well whose sulphurous waters were once regularly sampled by Sir Walter Scott. In the High Street, Robert Smail's Printing Works is popular with children since they are allowed to try their hand at typesetting using the original 19th century machinery. Innerleithen's premier attraction though is undoubtedly Traquair House, about a mile south of the town. Traquair is the oldest house in Scotland to have been continuously inhabited by the same family, the first of the line being James Stuart who took up residence in 1491. More than 500 years later, James' descendants, the Maxwell-Stuarts, still live there.

Located close to the River Tweed which meanders through the town, the **Traquair Arms Hotel** promises its visitors the chance to "slow down a little - and relax a lot". This friendly family run establishment was built in 1875 as a luxury hotel and the present owners, Gig and Dianne Johnston, maintain those high standards. All food is prepared fresh on the premises by the hotel's chefs who take great pride in offering an imaginative selection of menus created using only the finest Scottish produce. They are often asked for their recipes. Guests can relax in front of the blazing log fires in both the lounge and the well-stocked bar which serves a number of locally brewed ales and also has an excellent wine lost. The hotel has 10 warm and comfortable guest bedrooms, all with en suite bathrooms, direct dial telephones and tea/coffee making facilities. You may be tempted not to leave the hotel at all but it would be a pity not to explore the surrounding countryside of soft rolling hills and deep valleys peppered with natural woodland.

Opening Hours: Hotel open all day

Food: Available from 11.00-21.00, daily

Credit Cards: Access, Amex, Mastercharge, Visa & Switch

Accommodation: 10 rooms, all en suite

Facilities: Ample parking

Local Places of Interest/Activities:
Fishing on hotels beat on Tweed, 3 miles; Golf, horse riding, nearby; Robert Smail's Printing Works (NTS), St Ronan's Well, town centre; Traquair House, 1 mile; Kailzie Gardens, 4 miles

Internet/Website:
e-mail: traquair.arms@scottishborders.com

The Hidden Inns of Central and Southern Scotland

2 Dumfries and Galloway

PLACES OF INTEREST:

Caerlaverock 31
Castle Douglas 31
Colvend 32
Crossmichael 32
Dalbeattie 32
Dumfries 32
Ecclefechan 34
Glenluce 34
Gretna Green 34
Kirkcudbright 34

Lockerbie 35
Moffat 35
New Abbey 35
New Galloway 36
Newton Stewart 36
Port Logan Bay 37
Stoneykirk 37
Stranraer 37
Wanlockhead 37
Whithorn 37

PUBS AND INNS:

Aberdour Hotel, Dumfries 38

Black Bull Hotel, Moffat 39

The Carrutherstown Hotel,
  Carrutherstown 40

The Courtyard, Eaglesfield,
  by Lockerbie 41

Craigdarroch Arms Hotel, Moniaive 42

Cressfield Country House Hotel,
  Ecclefechan 43

The Cross Keys Hotel, Canonbie 44

Dinwoodie Lodge Hotel, Johnstonebridge,
  by Lockerbie 45

The Farmers Inn, Clarencefield 46

The George Hotel, Stranraer 47

The George Hotel, Thornhill 48

The Lochann Inn, Lochans 49

Nithsdale Hotel, Sanquhar 50

The Station House Hotel, Annan 51

The Thistle Inn, Crossmichael 52

The Waterfront, Portpatrick 53

The Hidden Inns of Central and Southern Scotland

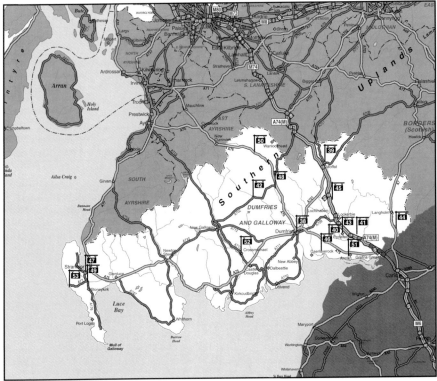

© MAPS IN MINUTES ™ (1999)

38 **Aberdour Hotel**, Dumfries	**46** **The Farmers Inn**, Clarencefield
39 **Black Bull Hotel**, Moffat	**47** **The George Hotel**, Stranraer
40 **The Carrutherstown Hotel**, Carrutherstown	**48** **The George Hotel**, Thornhill
	49 **The Lochann Inn**, Lochans
41 **The Courtyard**, Eaglesfield, by Lockerbie	**50** **Nithsdale Hotel**, Sanquhar
	51 **The Station House Hotel**, Annan
42 **Craigdarroch Arms Hotel**, Moniaive	**52** **The Thistle Inn**, Crossmichael
43 **Cressfield Country House Hotel**, Ecclefechan	**53** **The Waterfront**, Portpatrick
44 **The Cross Keys Hotel**, Canonbie	
45 **Dinwoodie Lodge Hotel**, Johnstonebridge, by Lockerbie	

Please note all cross references refer to page numbers

Dumfries and Galloway

Turn west off the M74 at Gretna Green and discover what the local Tourist Board calls "Scotland's best-kept secret". It's true that most visitors press on northwards and miss one of the most beautiful and unspoiled areas of the country.

Over 200 miles of superb coastline offer an infinite variety of beaches, bays and inlets. Inland stretch the vast expanses of the Galloway Forest Park where a patient observer may well spot a peregrine falcon or golden eagle, and just within the Dumfries and Galloway border is the highest village in Scotland, Wanlockhead, 1,500 feet above sea level.

The towns of Dumfries and Moffat are as appealing as any in Scotland and the region boasts more than its fair share of historic buildings, most notably romantic Sweetheart Abbey and the mighty medieval fortress of Caerlaverock Castle.

The area also has strong literary connections. Thomas Carlyle was born at Ecclefechan and the even more illustrious Robert Burns spent the last eight years of his life in and around Dumfries.

PLACES OF INTEREST

CAERLAVEROCK

Caerlaverock Castle (Historic Scotland) meets everyone's idea of a medieval fortress with its moat and mighty gatehouse flanked by blank-walled towers. In fact, Caerlaverock's ground plan is atypical of castles of the period since the design is triangular. Edward I made a ferocious attack on the castle in 1300 and held it for 11 years. The king's balladeer, Walter of Exeter, considered that "You will never see a more finely situated castle." Parts of the original structure of 1270 have survived but most of the present building dates from the 15th century, with Renaissance additions by the 1st Earl of Nithsdale in 1634. Six years later the castle surrendered to the Covenanters after a 13-week siege. They did their best to make Caerlaverock militarily useless and the castle has not been inhabited since. Attractions include a model siege engine, children's adventure park, a nature trail and, during July and August, the archaeological dig is open to visitors.

About three miles to the west of the castle, the 1,350 acres of the **Caerlaverock Wildfowl and Wetlands Trust** attract thousands of barnacle geese and other birds which can be seen from well-located hides and observation towers. In summer, nature trails meander through flower meadows alive with wildlife and you may even catch sight of a rare natterjack toad. There are free Wildlife Safaris starting at 2 p.m. each day during the summer months.

Continuing westwards to the village of **Ruthwell**, pick up the keys to the church (free) for a view of the magnificent **Ruthwell Cross**. Eighteen feet high, this internationally famous stone cross dates to around AD 680, its marvellously preserved surface decorated with intricate carvings illustrating episodes from the Gospel stories. Around its edge runs a poem written in both runic symbols and Northumbrian dialect.

CASTLE DOUGLAS

In the late 18th century when it was still possible for the rich to purchase whole villages, Sir William Douglas spent £14,000 on a cluster of settlements around Carlingwark Loch and proceeded to create his very own town, Castle Douglas. Sir William had made his fortune in what was murkily described as "the American trade", a term that covered anything from slave trading to straightforward piracy, but his new town was founded on the highest principles.

The result was a triumph of town planning. The three main streets running parallel and joined by five intersecting roads gave an orderly pattern to the town, and some fine Georgian

32

buildings enhanced its appearance. Today Castle Douglas remains one of the most pleasing towns in the country and in addition enjoys a reputation for being home to some of the best food shops, especially butchers, in Scotland.

A mile southwest of Castle Douglas, **Threave Garden & Estate** (National Trust for Scotland) is decidedly a garden for all seasons. It's best known for a spectacular springtime display of some 200 varieties of daffodil, but there are also lots of colourful summer displays and striking autumn tints in trees and the heather garden. The garden is also home to the National Trust for Scotland's School of Horticulture.

A visit to **Threave Castle** is something of an experience. It begins with a delightful 10-minute walk to the River Dee where the massive tower stands on an island. Visitors ring a brass bell and the castle custodian rows over to ferry them to the island. A forbidding build-

Threave Castle

ing, the castle was built in the late 1300s by Archibald the Grim, one of the notorious "Black Douglases". The family earned its nickname by exhibiting a blood-thirstiness that was appalling even by the standards of that barbarous age. The stories of the clan's reign of terror throughout the area fit well with the brooding, gloomy fortress.

COLVEND

Beautifully set beside the White Loch, Colvend formed part of what the Victorians called "The

Scottish Riviera", the lovely stretch of the Solway Coast between Southerness and Rascarrel blessed with fine beaches and ravishing scenery.

It was near Colvend in 1793 that Robert Burns, as an Excise Officer, led an armed attack on a French smuggling ship that had run aground near Gillis Craig and was waiting for the next tide. Whatever credit Burns received from his employers was soon dissipated: they took grave exception when Burns went to the auction of the smugglers' confiscated property and bought their guns with the intention of despatching them to France to assist the revolutionaries.

CROSSMICHAEL

Located on the shore of Loch Ken (actually a man-made reservoir), this sizable village is well worth seeking out, lying roughly halfway between the superb sandy beaches at Southerness and the unspoilt acres of the **Galloway Forest Park**.

DALBEATTIE

Lying in the wooded valley of Urr Water, Dalbeattie is built almost entirely of the local granite, a shining grey stone which has been shipped all over the world and used in building London's Embankment, the Bank of England and Manchester Town Hall. A mile or so outside the town, Old Buittle Tower is a 16th century **Lairds Tower House** with displays of arms and armour plus mounted displays of Border Reivers. The Tower is only open on occasional weekends or by appointment.

About four miles south of Dalbeattie, a signposted lane off the A711 leads to the **Orchardton Tower** (Historic Scotland, free), a late 15th-century tower house in an idyllic setting. It is built in cylindrical style, a design unique in Scotland although common in Ireland.

DUMFRIES

It was in this pleasant little town set beside the River Nith that Robbie Burns wrote some of his most famous songs, including *Auld Lang Syne* and *Ye Banks and Braes o' Bonnie Doon*. The poet had arrived in the town in 1791 to take up the improbable post of Excise Officer in charge of tobacco duties. To begin with Burns lodged in a house in Bank Street, at that time a noisome alley leading down to the river, which he nick-named "Stinking Vennel". He then moved to a more salubrious dwelling in Mill Street on the edge of town. The road has been re-named Burns Street and **Burns' House** (free) is now a museum containing his manuscripts and other memorabilia.

It was here that Burns died of rheumatic heart disease in 1796 at the age of 37. He was buried in a simple grave in the churchyard of nearby St Michael's Church, a Georgian building only a few years older than himself. Twenty years later his body was exhumed and re-interred in a splendid, columned mausoleum which also shelters a finely-executed statue of Scotland's national bard communing with the Muse of Poetry.

Another statue was erected to Burns' memory in the Market Square (also re-named **Burns' Statue Square**). This statue is a sentimental Victorian presentation of the roisterer and libertine as a clean-cut young fellow, clutching a posy of flowers in one hand and with a faithful canine curled around his feet.

A more authentic image of the partying poet is conjured up at the Globe Inn in the High Street, a down-to-earth hostelry established in 1610 and one of Burns' most favoured drinking dens, or "howffs" as they were called then. His preferred armchair is still in place but, before settling down in it, be warned that anyone who does so can be called upon to buy a round of drinks for everyone present.

The most comprehensive record of Burns' five-year residence in the town can be found at the **Robert Burns Centre** (free), located on the west bank of the River Nith and housed in an old water mill.

Another mill, an 18th century windmill perched on the hill above the Robert Burns Centre, is devoted to the many other years when the celebrated poet wasn't living here. **The Dumfries Museum** (free) contains an interesting series of exhibits recording the town's long history and, on its top floor, there's a camera obscura of the 1830s which provides fascinating panoramic views over the town.

Four bridges span the River Nith at Dumfries. The most appealing of them is **Devorgilla Bridge**, originally built by the 13th century Princess Devorgilla of Galloway whose poignant story of deep love and grievous loss is recounted later in this book under the entry for New Abbey. Now open only to pedestrians, this six-arched bridge was in medieval times the main thoroughfare for anyone travelling to or from the remote communities of southwest Scotland.

Dumfries boasts many handsome Georgian buildings. One of the most interesting is **Midsteeple** which dominates the High Street and was erected in 1707 as town hall, courthouse and prison. Sadly you can't go inside but on the outside you can see two curious features. On its southern wall is incised a line 37 inches long, an "ell" - the centuries old standard for measuring lengths of cloth. A table of distances from Dumfries rather surprisingly includes the small town of Huntingdon in Cambridgeshire. During the 18th century, Huntingdon was the cattle mart where Scottish drovers sold their stock. Huntingdon traders then herded the beasts down the Great North Road to the lucrative meat markets of London. Why the Scottish cattlemen didn't travel the extra 40 miles or so themselves remains a mystery - perhaps they didn't want to prolong their stay in England any longer than necessary!

Midsteeple, Dumfries

34 One of the most satisfying drives in the region is the 80-mile circular route from Dumfries, leaving southwards by the A710. It takes in Sweetheart Abbey, Arbigland Gardens and the Colvend Coast with its superb sandy beaches, then curves northwards to the gleaming grey granite town of Dalbeattie. Southwards again along the A711, past the Orchardton Tower to the East Stewartry Coast and on to the "irreproachable" little harbour town of Kirkcudbright. Heading northwards takes the visitor past Threave Garden and Threave Castle to Castle Douglas and back to Dumfries.

ECCLEFECHAN

This trim little hamlet was the birthplace in 1795 of Thomas Carlyle, a towering figure in the literary life of 19th century Britain. Carlyle's strict Calvinist upbringing imbued his prolific writings with a stern moralism, which together with his intellectual rigour and often pedantic prose do not endear him to modern readers. He was born in **The Arched House**, now Carlyle's Birthplace (National Trust for Scotland), which has been furnished to reflect domestic life in his time and has an interesting collection of portraits and personal memorabilia.

GLENLUCE

On the western edge of The Machars of Galloway, near Glenluce village, the ruins of **Glenluce Abbey**, founded in 1192 by Roland, Earl of Galloway, occupy a site of great natural beauty. The Abbey's 15th century Chapter House is surprisingly intact and its ribbed vault ceiling creates such astonishingly clear acoustics that opera singers often practise here. Look out for the carvings of the "green men", always depicted with foliage sprouting from their faces. These pagan symbols of fertility were often incorporated into the fabric of medieval Christian churches - but always on the outer walls, as a sign that they had been cast out by Mother Church.

During the late 1200s, the Abbey was the home of Michael Scot, a wizard and alchemist who was widely credited with enticing the plague that was decimating the population of Galloway into a secret vault here and imprisoning it. Scot's fame was such that he features as one of the damned in Dante's *Inferno*.

In the village itself, the **Glenluce Motor Museum** houses a splendid collection of vintage and classic cars, motor cycles, motoring memorabilia and even a vintage garage.

GRETNA GREEN

Scottish matrimonial law in the 18th century merely required a declaration by the couple in front of any two witnesses for their marriage to be legal. This relaxed attitude attracted many English runaway couples, and since Gretna Green was the first village across the Scottish borders, and the blacksmith's shop the closest dwelling to the stage-coach stop, it was here that most "solemnised" their marriages. Scottish law was changed in 1856, requiring that at least one of the partners had resided in Scotland for three weeks before the marriage.

At the Blacksmith's Shop you can enter the original Marriage Room where weddings still take place today, follow the Gretna Green Story in an interesting exhibition, visit the Coach Museum, buy a range of souvenirs in the gift shop, and refresh yourself in the Conservatory Bar or the restaurant. There's also a sculpture park, arts centre and animal park.

KIRKCUDBRIGHT

"An irreproachable Scottish town ... one of the most picturesque and fascinating Lowland towns I have seen." So enthused the travel writer H. V. Morton after visiting this enchanting little town (pronounced "Kir-coo-brit") set beside the River Dee. Morton was especially impressed by the ruins of **MacLellans Castle**, which towers over the tiny harbour. Built between 1569 and 1582, it was designed not for defensive purposes but as a private house for Sir Thomas MacLellan. Its Great Hall is particularly striking and there's a curious feature in the enormous lintel over the fireplace. A spyhole has been cut into the lintel and there's a small room behind it, a primitive but no doubt effective variant of today's bugging devices.

Just across the road, **Broughton House** is a handsome Georgian building which in the late 19th century was the home of the artist Edward Hornel, a major figure in the group calling themselves The Glasgow Boys. Some of their Impressionist-style work is on display here, including several of Hornel's paintings of Japan, a country he found mesmerising - so much so that he designed and built a lovely Japanese garden in the grounds of Broughton House.

At the corner of the L-shaped High Street stands the 16th-17th century Tolbooth, now an Art Centre featuring more of The Glasgow Boys' paintings, and with studios on the upper floor occupied by contemporary artists and craftworkers.

Just along the road from Baytree House is the Selkirk Arms Hotel, an essential port of call for any devotee of Robert Burns. The poet stayed at the hotel in 1794 and it was here that he penned his much-quoted 'Selkirk Grace':

'Some hae meat and canna eat,
And some wad eat that want it,
But we hae meat and we can eat,
And sae the Lord be thanket.'

In Kirkcudbright's St Mary's Sreet, the Stewartry Museum is well worth a visit for its huge collection of exhibits reflecting the life and times of the Solway Coast.

LOCKERBIE

For generations the Lamb Fair held at Lockerbie in August was Annandale's premier festival and as many as 70,000 animals were gathered in this small town. Its successor is the **Dumfries and Lockerbie Agricultural Show** which is also held in August but nowadays in Dumfries. But Lockerbie also hosts its own events. In June there's the Lockerbie Gala and Riding of the Marches; a Book Festival in September, followed by the Lockerbie Hot Jazz Festival in October.

The town is tranquil enough today, but in the 16th and 17th centuries it was often riven by the bitter disputes between the Maxwells from Nithsdale and the Johnstones and Jardines from Annandale. The animosity culminated in a full-scale battle on nearby Dryfe Sands in 1593 when the Maxwells were decisively routed and 700 of them killed.

Tragedy of another order struck Lockerbie on Wednesday, December 21st, 1988 when Pan Am Flight 101 exploded in mid-air. Its fuselage crashed into the town, killing 11 residents. A Remembrance Garden on the edge of the town has been planted in memory of all the innocent victims of this catastrophe.

MOFFAT

Boasting one of the broadest High Streets in Scotland, Moffat is also one of the most pleasing small towns in the country. It stands beside the River Annan, surrounded by Lowland hills, at the heart of a thriving sheep-farming

district. The town's dependence on sheep is symbolised by the striking **Colvin Fountain** at the top of the High Street. It is surmounted by a bronze sculpture of a sturdy ram, although unfortunately it was accidentally cast without any ears.

35

Moffat has been attracting visitors ever since Rachel Whiteford, the minister's daughter, discovered Moffat Well in 1633 and its history as a spa town began. A steady stream of distinguished visitors sampled the "magic waters", among them Robert Burns and James Boswell, who came in 1766 "to wash off a few scurvy spots which the warmer climate of Europe had brought out on my skin".

In 1878 the grandiose Moffat Hydropathic was built. At its peak, the 300-bedroomed hotel was welcoming some 25,000 guests each year. Sadly the Hydro was totally destroyed by fire in 1921 and Moffat's status as a spa town never recovered.

The local Tourist Information Centre has details of some excellent walks in and around the town, whether you just want a gentle riverside stroll or a brisk climb to the top of **Gallow Hill** where there are wonderful views over Annandale.

NEW ABBEY

The story of **Sweetheart Abbey** and Lady Devorgilla has been told many times but remains as touching as ever. In 1230, Devorgilla, daughter of Alan, last of the Kings of Galloway, married John Balliol, a marriage that by all accounts was supremely happy. There were a few setbacks, however. John Balliol managed to offend the powerful Prince-Bishop of Durham and as part of his penance was required to finance a hostel for students at Oxford, a modest establishment that his widow was later to expand into Balliol College.

John died in 1268 and Devorgilla, grief-stricken, had his heart embalmed and for the 21 years of her widowhood carried it with her in a casket of silver and ivory. She was now one of the richest women in Europe, owning most of Galloway along with estates in England and Normandy. She spent lavishly on founding several religious houses in memory of her husband, among them *Dulce Cor*, Sweet Heart, at New Abbey. It was here, in 1289, that she was buried beneath the High Altar together with her husband's heart. Sweetheart Abbey today is one

36

of the finest sights in the country, a romantic ruin of rose-red stone that seems to glow in the setting sun.

New Abbey has been described as "the most perfect unspoiled village in Galloway". Take time to walk to the lovely bridge built in 1715 and then up through the avenue of Scots pines planted between 1775 and 1780 to enjoy the classically romantic view over the beck to Sweetheart Abbey.

Sweetheart Abbey

Nearby is a restored 18th century **Corn Mill**, fully operational and with regular demonstrations during the summer months. Just outside the village, the **Museum of Costume** at Shambellie House provides an absorbing record of our sartorial fads, fancies and extravagances over the centuries.

About six miles south of New Abbey, follow the signs to **Arbigland Gardens** - especially if you are American. These famous semi-tropical gardens set around a secluded bay were originally laid out in the 1730s by a gardener named John Paul. One of his sons, also named John, was a lively youth who became a sailor at the age of 11 and later spent five years on an Ameri-

can slave ship. In Tobago he managed to get himself charged with murder; to avoid arrest he changed his name to John Paul Jones, the name by which he is honoured in the United States as the "Father of the US Navy". The tiny white-washed cottage where he was born in 1747 is now the **John Paul Jones Birthplace Museum**, restored to its mid-18th century appearance and housing some fascinating exhibits connected with the Admiral's life. Outside stand two flagpoles, one flying the Stars and Stripes, the other carrying Scotland's St Andrew's Cross. The latter, incidentally, is identical to the Empress Catherine of Russia's flag under which the restless John Paul Jones sailed as Admiral of her Black Sea Fleet during the Russo-Turkish war of 1788-89.

NEW GALLOWAY

With a population of just over 300, New Galloway holds the undisputed title of "Smallest Royal Burgh in Scotland". Little more than a single street of neat and attractive stone cottages, the village lies on the River Ken, noted for its fine angling. There's also a church which is well worth visiting for its unusual tombstones, an intriguing collection of curious carvings and strange epitaphs. A mile or so south of New Galloway the river flows into scenic Loch Ken, noted for its excellent bird-watching opportunities, coarse fishing and watersport facilities.

NEWTON STEWART

Running southwest from New Galloway to Newton Stewart, the 19-mile Queen's Way Tourist Route along the A712 passes through the rugged beauty of the Galloway Forest Park and provides some interesting locations along the way. First, six miles from New Galloway, there's **Bruce's Stone**, a massive boulder which marks the spot where Robert the Bruce defeated the English in 1307. Nearby is the **Clatteringshaws Forest Wildlife Centre**, an informative indoor display of forest wildlife, and a couple of miles further the **Galloway Deer Range**, where visitors can walk among red deer, handle them and take photographs close up. Near Newton Stewart, the **Kirroughtree Visitor Centre** offers a state-of-the-art children's play area, waymarked trails, cycle routes and a forest drive.

South and west of Newton Stewart stretches the area known as the **Rhins and Machars of**

Galloway, a peaceful peninsula of gentle farmland and broad landscapes culminating in the craggy coastline forming Scotland's most southerly point. (Burrow Head's latitude is actually several miles south of Durham in England). Peaceful though it is now, the region did not escape unscathed from the horrors of the Covenanter years. At **Wigtown**, a stone obelisk near the tidal sands of Wigtown Bay commemorates the Wigtown Martyrs, Margaret Machauchlan, aged 63, and Margaret Wilson, 18. In 1685, they were convicted of attending meetings of their sect, tied to stakes in the estuary and left to drown in the rising tide.

Port Logan Bay

Port Logan Bay is one of the most scenic locations on the west coast of the Rhinns of Galloway. Visitors can enjoy a wonderful view of the sweeping bight and the crescent-shaped beach with scarcely a human habitation (or, for much of the time, even a human being) in sight. staying in this idyllic spot,. This beguiling corner of west Galloway is often overlooked by visitors: do yourself a favour and don't make the same mistake!

Stoneykirk

South of Stoneykirk the A716 passes close by two outstanding gardens. **Ardwell Gardens** near Ardwell village has splendid displays of daffodils, rock plants, rhododendrons and flowering shrubs in a woodland setting overlooking Luce Bay. South of Ardwell, a minor road leads to **Logan Botanic Garden**, a specialist garden of the Royal Botanic Garden, Edinburgh. Logan is truly a plantsman's paradise, famous for tree ferns, cabbage palms, and many rare, unusual and interesting plants from the southern hemisphere.

Stranraer

This honest-to-goodness working port is well known to travellers by ferry to Belfast or Larne in Northern Ireland. While you're waiting for your boat, you could explore the **Castle of St John**, a late medieval tower which was later pressed into use as a Victorian prison, or drop into the **Stranraer Museum** in the Old Town Hall which has displays on Wigtownshire farming, folklife and archaeology.

Back in the 1950s, the citizens of Stranraer had a brilliant idea. Each would contribute a plant to help create a colourful public open space to be known as the **Friendship Gardens**. Almost half a century later, the Gardens are a splendid sight in summer, a living monument to the town's community spirit.

Wanlockhead

You would naturally expect the highest village in Scotland to be somewhere in the Highlands. In fact, it's here at Wanlockhead in Dumfries & Galloway. The village stands 1,500 feet above sea level. Small though the village is there's plenty here to keep you occupied. The Southern Uplands Way passes right through Wanlockhead, and the Scottish Lead Mining Museum tells the story of an industry that goes back to at least Roman times. Guided tours of Loch Nell Mine take place every half-hour and provide a chilling insight into the conditions under which the lead miners worked. As well as lead, there's also gold in "them thar hills" and the British, European and World Gold Panning Championships are all held in the village. Why not bring a pan along and try your luck?

At the nearby hamlet of **Leadhills** is the **Allan Ramsay Library**, founded in 1741 by lead miners employed by the Scots Mining Company. It is believed to be the first subscription library established in Britain and many of the books which have survived are rare outside private collections. The Library is usually open on weekend afternoons between May and September.

Whithorn

For centuries this little town attracted pilgrims from all around the country, with James IV making regular visits. They came to visit the church founded by St Ninian in 397, the first Christian place of worship north of Hadrian's Wall. During the 12th century a priory was built to meet the needs of the pilgrims. No trace remains of St Ninian's church but there are some remains of the Priory which can be explored with the help of a free guide service. In the nearby museum, **Cradle of Christianity in Scotland** (Historic Scotland), there's an impressive collection of ancient carved stones, amongst them the 7th century St Peter's Stone and 5th century Latinus Stone, possibly the oldest in Scotland.

38 Aberdour Hotel

16/20 Newall Terrace,
Dumfries DG1 1LW
Tel: 01387 252060
Fax: 01387 262323

Directions:

Dumfries is off the A75, 24 miles northwest of Gretna Green. The Aberdour Hotel is near the town centre

A large and imposing building of glowing red sandstone, the **Aberdour Hotel** began life in Victorian times as a girls' school. It's now a family run hotel established by John and Mary McLatchie in the late 1980s and their son Ian and daughter Tricia have only recently taken over. From the moment you arrive at the Aberdour you'll find a very warm and relaxed atmosphere, with the spacious rooms, their tall windows and the tasteful decoration all reflecting the high standards of a more leisured age.

The McLatchies take great care with the cuisine they offer, with all the dishes freshly prepared and based on prime local produce such as the superb Galloway beef. The hotel has 12 guest bedrooms, 9 of which are en suite and all of which have television and tea/coffee-making facilities. The hotel stands only a short walk from the centre of this charming small town set beside the River Nith and famous for its strong connections with Robert Burns who arrived here in 1791. He wrote some of his most celebrated songs here, amongst them Auld Lang Syne, and is commemorated by a statue in the market square and at the Robert Burns Centre. The house he lived in from 1791 until his death in 1796 is also open to the public.

Opening Hours: Hotel open all day

Food: Mon-Thu: 12.00-14.00 & 18.00-20.00; Fri-Sun: 12.00-14.00 & 18.00-21.00

Credit Cards: All major cards except Diners

Accommodation: 12 rooms, 9 en suite

Facilities: Function room; parking

Entertainment: Quiz nights

Local Places of Interest/Activities: Burns House, Robert Burns Centre, Dumfries Museum, all in Dumfries; Sweetheart Abbey, 6 miles; Caerlaverock Castle, 8 miles; Caerlaverock Wildfowl & Wetlands Trust, 10 miles

Internet/Website:

website: www.aberdour-hotel.co.uk

Black Bull Hotel & Railway Bar | 39

Churchgate,
Moffat DG10 9EG
Tel: 01683 220206
Fax: 01683 220483

Directions:

From Exit 15 of the
M74 take the A701 to
Moffat (1.5 miles)

Robert Burns knew a good "howff" when he found one and the **Black Bull Hotel** at Moffat was a favourite haunt for the celebrated poet and his friends. It was while he was drinking here that he wrote the famous "epigram to a scrimpit nature". More than 200 years later, the Black Bull is as popular as ever. In 1999, it was declared "Pub of the Year" and amongst its many awards is one for the quality of the real ales on offer. Food is available daily with value for money lunches and suppers served in the cosy lounge, in the Burns Room, or in the separate olde worlde restaurant. Children are very welcome and have their own special menu.

An attractive amenity here is the Railway Bar, situated across the courtyard. It contains some fascinating old railway relics and memorabilia, especially those from the old Caledonian Railway. A popular meeting place for locals young and old, the bar has all the traditional pub games as well as a more contemporary innovation, a quiz machine. Interestingly, the building dates back to the 1680s when it was the stables built for Graham of Claverhouse and his dragoons. They had been sent by the English king, James II, to suppress the religious rebels in the south west Borders. Moffat itself is a charming little town and if you are planning to stay in the area, the Black Bull has 7 guest bedrooms, all en suite and with colour TV, radio, direct dial telephone and hospitality tray. By the time you read this, a further 5 rooms should be available.

Opening Hours: Sun-Thu: 11.00-23.00; Fri-Sat: 11.00-24.00

Food: Available daily 11.00-14.30 & 18.00-21.00

Credit Cards: Access, Mastercard, Visa, Switch

Accommodation: Currently 7 rooms, all en suite; 5 more on stream

Facilities: Restaurant; lounge bar; public bar; parking

Entertainment: Pool table; darts; dominoes; quiz machine; quiz nights

Local Places of Interest/Activities: Moffat Museum nearby; Southern Upland Way, 1.5 miles; Lowther Hills, 2 miles; Grey Mare's Tail waterfall (NTS), 11 miles;

Internet/Website:
www.blackbullmoffat.co.uk
e-mail: jh@blackbull.co.uk

40 The Carrutherstown Hotel

Carrutherstown,
Dumfries DG1 4LD
Tel: 01387 840268
Fax: 01387 840302

Directions:

Carrutherstown is about
8 miles SE of Dumfries,
off the A75

Approached by an at-
tractive conservatory-
style entrance, **The
Carrutherstown Hotel**
is a friendly and wel-
coming hostelry owned

and run Brendan and Ann Magee, both of whom hail from Co. Down in Northern
Ireland. Since arriving here in 1997 they have completely transformed what was a
small 1950s cottage into a smart, completely refurbished pub. There's a lovely lounge
bar, a comfortable public bar and a brand new restaurant which has a fine reputation
for its steaks. These specialities of the house are prepared from prime cuts of Galloway
beef, cooked precisely as you prefer them and served with top quality fresh vegetables.
Real ale lovers will be pleased to find their favourite tipple and there's an extensive
choice of the leading brands of other beverages.

In good weather, you can enjoy your meal in the beer garden or at the picnic tables
set out at the front of the inn. Inside, there's a games room and the Magees lay on
regular quiz nights and live entertainment. The Carrutherstown is disabled friendly,
with a level entrance and also disabled toilets. And if you are looking for a good place
to stay in this attractive corner of the county, the hotel has 6 attractive guest bedrooms, all of them en suite and equipped with television, trouser press and hospitality
tray.

Opening Hours: Mon-Fri: 12.00-14.30,
17.30-23.00; Sat-Sun: 12.00-23.00

Food: Available daily 12.00-14.30 & 18.00-
21.00

Credit Cards: Access, Mastercard, Visa &
Switch

Accommodation: 6 rooms, all en suite

Facilities: Beer garden; parking

Entertainment: Games room; quiz nights;

live music

Local Places of Interest/Activities:
Ruthwell Cross, 3 miles; Burns' House,
Robert Burns Centre, Dumfries Museum,
all at Dumfries, 8 miles; Caerlaverock
Castle, Caerlaverock Wildfowl & Wetlands
Trust, both 8 miles; Thomas Carlyle's
Birthplace, Ecclefechan, 8 miles; Gretna
Green, 14 miles

The Courtyard 41

*Eaglesfield by
Lockerbie,
Dumfriesshire
DG11 3PQ
Tel: 01461 500215*

Directions:

From Exit 20 of the A74(M), Carlisle to Glasgow road, take the B722 into Eaglesfield (1 mile)

Comfortable and attractive accommodation; quality food based on fresh local produce - **The Courtyard** scores high on both counts. The restaurant is housed in a former draper's shop built in 1913 to the high standards of that time. Very well designed, it was converted in 1985 and decorated with an emphasis on providing an intimate setting ideal for special occasions. The cuisine is traditional Scottish with a French influence and the cuisine makes good use of fresh local produce, including many organically grown ingredients. The restaurant is fully licensed and offers a full range of wines, beers and spirits. The owner, Mike Mason, has been a restaurant manager for many years and certainly knows how to cosset his customers. No wonder he prides himself on his repeat business.

Accommodation at The Courtyard comprises 3 attractively converted single storey buildings, all of them provided with every modern convenience. One is suitable for a family, the other two can accommodate 2 people each. One of them has been equipped so that it is suitable for disabled guests. Conveniently close to the A74(M), Eaglesfield makes a good base for exploring Dumfries & Galloway and the Border Country. A popular destination, and only 4 miles away, is Thomas Carlyle's Birthplace at Ecclefechan. Born in 1795, Carlyle became a towering figure in the literary life of 19th century Britain and his birthplace contains an interesting collection of portraits and personal memorabilia.

Opening Hours: 12.00-14.00; 19.00-21.00, daily

Food: Traditional Scottish with French influence

Credit Cards: Access, Mastercharge, Visa

Accommodation: 3 chalets, (1 family, 2 double); one with disabled facilities

Facilities: Ample parking

Local Places of Interest/Activities: Thomas Carlyle's Birthplace, Ecclefechan, 4 miles; the Merkland Cross, 4 miles; Gretna Green, 9 miles

42   Craigdarroch Arms Hotel

High Street,
Moniaive,
Dumfries & Galloway
DG3 4HN
Tel: 01848 200205
Fax: 01848 200738
Mobile: 0771 4648573

Directions:

From the A76 about 15 miles north of Dumfries, turn left on to the A702. Moniaive is about 9 miles along this road.

The conservation village of Moniaive enjoys a lovely setting at the confluence of the Dalwhat, Craigdarroch and Castlefairn Waters. The meeting of these waters creates the Cairn Pool, the beginning of the River Cairn which is noted for its salmon and trout. Moniaive has many connections with James Renwick, one of the last of the rebellious Covenanters, and with Annie Laurie (of the famous song) who was born at nearby Maxwelton House. The village is a picturesque place and one where visitors are made to feel welcome and join in the local activities, whether on the bowling green or at the snooker tables in the village hall.

At the centre of this lively village, and at the heart of the community, is the **Craigdarroch Arms Hotel**, a welcoming hostelry which has been in existence for more than a hundred years. It's a warm, family run hotel with Deryck Watson is charge of the kitchen and his wife Mavis looking after the front of house. There's a traditional Scottish bar with log fires where the locals enjoy a 'blether', a lounge bar for a more relaxing atmosphere, and also a dining room used for formal dining and special functions. The hotel's 7 bedrooms are all en suite and equipped with colour television, central heating and tea/coffee-making facilities.

Situated in Upper Nithsdale, Moniaive lies at the heart of an unspoilt corner of Scotland which offers a wealth of outdoor activities, charming villages and grand castles together with a lovely countryside of rolling banks and braes that provided inspiration for the great Robert Burns.

Opening Hours: Hotel open all day

Food: Bar meals and à la carte available every lunchtime & evening

Credit Cards: Access, Visa

Accommodation: 7 rooms, all en suite

Facilities: Function room; parking

Local Places of Interest/Activities: Fishing, golf and walking nearby; Maxwelton House, 4 miles; Drumlanrig Castle, 12 miles

Cressfield Country House Hotel | 43

Ecclefechan,
Dumfriesshire
DG11 3DR
Tel: 01576 300281
Fax: 01576 300838

Directions:

From Junction 19 of the A74(M), follow the signs for Ecclefechan (0.3 miles)

Ecclefechan is best known as the birthplace of Thomas Carlyle and **Cressfield Country House Hotel** has a close connection with that grand old man of Victorian letters. The house was built as a private residence in 1873 for a member of Carlyle's family and the great sage no doubt visited the house before his death in 1881. Cressfield was sold in 1905 and then had several owners, including a cousin of Winston Churchill who is believed to have been a frequent visitor. An impressive building of rose red sandstone, Cressfield is now a quality hotel, owned and run by Nigel Jackson. Many original features have survived in the spacious public rooms, (notably an exquisitely carved fireplace in the lounge bar), and much of the furniture and decoration is in keeping with the house's Victorian origins. The food at Cressfield is outstanding, with full use being made of the finest of Scottish meat, fish and game in season. Meals are served in the elegant dining room with its imposing Adam fireplace and there's a select wine list to complement your meal. The hotel's 10 guest bedrooms are all en suite, attractively furnished, cosy and welcoming, and equipped with colour television and hospitality tray. With Gretna Green just a few miles down the motorway, Cressfield is ideally located for wedding parties and other special occasions. The hotel's superb function room has an enviable reputation for its ability to cater for up to 200 people.

Opening Hours: Hotel open all day

Food: Available daily 12.00-14.00 & 18.00-21.00

Credit Cards: Cash only

Accommodation: 10 rooms, all en suite

Facilities: Restaurant; function suite; adjacent caravan park; ample parking

Entertainment: Quiz night, Friday; live music weekly

Local Places of Interest/Activities: Thomas Carlyle's Birthplace, nearby; shooting, fishing on the River Annan, both nearby; Lochmaben Castle, Repentance Tower, 4 miles; golf, 6 miles; Gretna Green, 10 miles; Dumfries, 15 miles

Internet/Website: website: www.cressfield@btclick

44 The Cross Keys Hotel

Canonbie,
Dumfriesshire DG14 0SY
Tel: 013873 71382 /71205
Fax: 013873 71878

Directions:

From the A7 about 14 miles north of Carlisle, turn right on the B6357 to Canonbie (0.5 miles). The Cross Keys Hotel lies in the centre of the village on the right hand side

One of the oldest coaching inns in Scotland, **The Cross Keys Hotel** is a 17th century building standing in the heart of this picturesque village nestling in the valley of the Border Esk. The river is noted for its trout and salmon, and weekly fishing tickets are available from the inn's owners, Michael and Barbara Kitching, who can also provide information about how to fish the famous Willow Pool and Cauldron Beat. Canonbie itself is an attractive village adjoining the Duke of Buccleuch's estate. The houses, built in traditional stone, straggle along the banks of the Esk and there's also a fine church which was designed by William Atkinson, the architect of Sir Walter Scott's home, Abbotsford.

The Cross Keys has two bars: one is a cosy lounge with a log fire, the other is the public bar where visitors can soak up the local atmosphere. Bar lunches and evening meals are served daily in both bars, and the menu offers an extensive and varied choice based on seasonal fresh produce. The inn is also known far and wide for its Carvery which is served on Friday and Saturday evenings and also on Sunday lunchtimes. The intimate dining room is available for small private functions and guests requiring vegetarian meals can be catered for with a variety of interesting dishes. Canonbie is an ideal location from which to explore the lovely Borders area and the Cross Keys has 10 comfortably furnished guest rooms, all centrally heated with TV and tea/coffee making facilities. Residents also have the use of a small comfortable lounge with colour television.

Opening Hours: Hotel open all day

Food: Bar lunches & evening meals available every day

Credit Cards: All major cards accepted except Amex and Diners

Accommodation: 9 en suite bedrooms

Facilities: Ample parking

Entertainment: Large screen TV, darts, dominoes and pool table in public bar. Quiz nights Nov - Mar.

Local Places of Interest/Activities: Fishing and walking in Esk Valley nearby; Riding Stables, 0.5 miles; several golf courses within a 20-mile radius; Gretna Green, 9 miles; Carlisle, 14 miles

Dinwoodie Lodge Hotel 45

Johnstonebridge,
by Lockerbie,
DG11 2SL
Tel/Fax: 01576
470289

Directions:

From Exit 16 of the A74(M), take the B7076 south towards Lockerbie. Dinwoodie Lodge Hotel is about 1.5 miles along this road, off to the left

Located in the heart of Annandale, the **Dinwoodie Lodge Hotel** provides an excellent base for exploring Dumfries and Galloway. The hotel was built in the early 1800s as a very substantial hunting lodge. It's an impressive stone structure and in recent years an elegant conservatory has been added to the frontage. Stephen and Wendy Crawford took over here early in 2000 and this young, enthusiastic couple have already made significant improvements and have plans for further extension. The interior is quite delightful with lots of old features and attractive furnishings and decor. A big attraction at Dinwoodie Lodge is the food, traditional Scottish fare based on the very best of local produce and served in the conservatory restaurant. Guests have the use of an inviting and comfortable residents' lounge and there's also a well-stocked bar. At present, the hotel has 6 guest bedrooms, all of them en suite and equipped with television and tea/coffee-making facilities. The hotel is disabled-friendly and children will certainly enjoy the outdoor play area. Walkers will find some lovely woodland walks in Auchenroddan Forest, about a mile away, and a short drive will bring golfers to the course at Lockerbie. And if you are camping or travelling with a caravan, the hotel has a pleasant site within its grounds.

Opening Hours: Hotel open all day

Food: Food available Mon-Fri: 12.00-14.00 & 18.00-21.00; Sat-Sun: all day

Credit Cards: Access, Mastercard, Visa & Switch

Accommodation: 6 rooms, all en suite

Facilities: Disabled facilities; children's playground; caravan & camp site; parking

Entertainment: Occasional discos & live music

Local Places of Interest/Activities:
Walking in Auchenroddan Forest, 1 mile; golf, 6 miles; Lochmaben Castle, 7 miles; Rammerscales House, Hightae, 8 miles; Burns House, Robert Burns Centre, Dumfries, 13 miles

46   The Farmers Inn

Main Street,
Clarencefield,
Dumfries DG1 4NF
Tel: 01387 870675

Directions:
From the M6, take the A75 towards Stranraer. Take the second turn off for Annan, then first right. Follow the signs for Comlongon Castle until you get to Clarencefield

Situated in the peaceful village of Clarencefield, **The Farmers Inn** has had a varied history. Robert Burns visited in 1796 when he was taking the waters at nearby Brow Well. At that time it was a coaching inn and also housed the post office. Curiously, since 1995 the Farmers has again been serving as the village post office with a counter tucked away in one of the bars. Back in the 1890s the pub was closed following a sad incident when a labourer on the Earl of Mansfield's vast Dumfries Estates over-imbibed and drowned in a ditch on his way home. It re-opened as the Temperance Castle Hotel but understandably lacked the appeal of its predecessor and closed after a few years. It wasn't until 1983 that the Farmers Inn was once again serving ale - and real ale at that. The inn has been included in Camra's Good Beer Guide since 1991 and over the last ten years has served at least 300 different brews. The Farmers also offers a good selection of traditional meals as well as a variety of vegetarian dishes. Locally regarded as being of excellent value, the meals are all freshly prepared under the personal supervision of the owners, Colin and Jacquie Pearson. As in days gone by, the Farmers still provides a resting place for the weary traveller. The motel style bedrooms are in a self-contained annex, each room with its own 'front door'. The modern rooms are all en suite, well equipped and at ground floor level. One has a specially adapted bathroom for guests with mobility difficulties

Opening Hours: Daily: 11.00-24.00

Food: Available every lunchtime & evening

Credit Cards: None

Accommodation: 3 chalets, 1 with disabled facilities

Facilities: parking

Entertainment: Games room with pool, darts, jukebox and TV. Monthly quiz nights; Occasional barbeques

Local Places of Interest/Activities: Ruthwell Cross, 1 mile; Powfoot Golf Course, 4 miles; Caerlaverock Castle, 8 miles; Caerlaverock Wildfowl & Wetlands Trust, 10 miles

Internet/Website:
e-mail: mail@farmersinn.co.uk

The George Hotel   47

George Street,
Stranraer,
Galloway DG9 7RJ
Tel: 01776 702487
Fax: 01776 702488

Directions:

Stranraer is on the A77 (from Ayr) & A75 (from Dumfries). The George Hotel is on the main street (the A75)

Located in the heart of this market town and port, **The George Hotel** is an impressive 3-storeyed building dating back to the 1750s. It was then a coaching inn and in a sense it still is since the owners, brother and sister team of Susan Krejova and Phillip Miller, have geared the business to serve modern day coach travellers. The Miller family has owned the hotel since 1982 and their aim has always been to offer true value for money. To this end they have good English style cooking, with roasts and stews, and it is all under the watchful eye of Susan. Meals are based on fresh local produce with many of the vegetables and herbs coming from the hotel's own gardens.

The George consists of 28 bedrooms which, because of the age of the hotel, are all different, with some very quiet rooms and some bigger than others but all are en suite. Each bedroom is equipped with a kettle, television, ironing board and iron, as well as a trouser press. A baby-listening service is available. The hotel has a games room where guests can play pool, darts and 10-pin bowling and residents also have the use of the lounge bar and an entertainments room. Most evenings there is some form of entertainment, varying from live music to quizzes and bingo. Guests can hire a bicycle at the hotel, golf clubs or fishing equipment and one of the finest beaches in the country is at the nearby village of Sandhead where the seawater is some of the warmest in Britain. And if you're staying at the George on a Wednesday you can visit the Stranraer market which is held just 100 yards from the hotel.

Opening Hours: 12.00-23.00, daily

Food: English style cooking

Credit Cards: All major cards except Diners

Accommodation: 28 rooms, all en suite

Entertainment: Games room with mini 10-pin bowls, skittles & snooker; live music 3 nights a week; regular quizzes and bingo sessions

Local Places of Interest/Activities: Castle Kennedy gardens, 5 miles; Glenluce Abbey, 10 miles; Logan subtropical gardens, 15 miles

48 The George Hotel

*103/106 Drumlanrig
Street, Thornhill,
Dumfriesshire
DG3 5LU*
**Tel: 01848 330326
Fax: 01848 331713**

Directions:

Thornhill is on the
A76, 14 miles north of
Dumfries

A former coaching
inn, **The George Ho-
tel** stands on the old stage coach route from Dumfries to Cumnock and Kilmarnock,
now the A76. The road winds through scenic Nithsdale with the Forest of Ae and the
Lowther Hills rising to the west. The George is a small, friendly, family-run hostelry
offering excellent food and accommodation in charming surroundings. The original
coaching inn is now the Public Bar, down to earth, informal and lively, whilst the
dining room is small and elegant with an intimate atmosphere. There's also a Lounge
Bar, comfortably and tastefully furnished. Your hosts, the Nisbet family, offer their
customers an extensive bar meal menu, available 7 days a week to residents and non-
residents alike. An à la carte menu is also available but prior notice is requested, and
packed lunches can also be arranged. The 10 guest bedrooms are all en suite and as
well as Sky TV and a hospitality tray, you'll also find a useful hairdryer.

As Peter Nisbet says, "in this area, walking is a must" but there are also excellent
facilities for golf, shooting, riding, squash and, of course, fishing. If the water is not
suitable for salmon fishing, guests have the use of George Loch, a few miles from the
hotel, for trout fishing. Historic buildings within easy reach include the Duke of
Buccleuch's magnificent mansion, Drumlanrig Castle, and Ellisland Farm where Robert
Burns proved that whatever his talents in other directions, he was certainly not a
natural farmer!

Opening Hours: 11.00-24.00 every day

Food: Available 11.30-14.00 & 17.00-21.00
every day

Credit Cards: All major cards except Amex
& Diners

Accommodation: 10 rooms, all en suite

Facilities: Restaurant; function room;
parking

Entertainment: Occasional live music &
buffet dances

Local Places of Interest/Activities: Golf, 1
mile; Morton Castle, 3 miles; Drumlanrig
Castle, 4 miles; Forest of Ae, 5 miles;
Durisdeer Church, 6 miles; Ellisland Farm,
10 miles

The Lochann Inn 49

Main Street,
Lochans,
nr Stranraer,
Dumfriesshire
DG9 9AW
Tel/Fax:
01776 820252

Directions:

From Stranraer take the A77 south towards Portpatrick. Lochans is about 4 miles along this road

Lochans lies in the heart of the Rhinns of Galloway, a hammer-shaped peninsula that forms the most southwesterly tip of Scotland. This is hilly territory, dotted with small farming villages and with a fine stretch of sandy beach a few miles to the south of Lochans. From the busy little port of Stranraer there are regular ferries to Northern Ireland and is also notable for its Friendship Gardens. Back in the 1950s, the townspeople had a brilliant idea. Each would contribute a plant to help create a colourful public open space. Half a century later, the gardens are a splendid sight in summer, a living monument to the town's community spirit.

The tiny village of Lochans makes an excellent base for exploring the Rhinns and **The Lochann Inn** offers comfortable bed and breakfast accommodation together with all the amenities of a modern hostelry. The 3 guest rooms are all en suite and equipped with television and tea/coffee-making facilities. The inn opened in 1978 and it is still immaculate, a welcoming place with all the charm of a small Scottish hotel. The Lochann serves value-for-money food throughout the day, offering a menu with a good variety of dishes. Afternoon teas are also available. Your hosts are Eileen Mills and Peter Watson, both of whom take great pains to make sure their customers are well-looked after.

Opening Hours: Sun-Thu: 11.00-23.00; Fri-Sat: 11.00-01.00

Food: Available every lunchtime & evening

Credit Cards: Cash only

Accommodation: 3 family rooms, all en suite

Facilities: Small patio garden; parking

Entertainment: Games room with pool, darts & dominoes

Local Places of Interest/Activities: Castle of St John, Stranraer, 4 miles; Castle Kennedy gardens, 6 miles; Glenluce Abbey, 8 miles

50   Nithsdale Hotel

1 High Street,
Sanquhar,
Dumfriesshire
DG4 6DJ
Tel: 01659 50506
Fax: 01659 50081

Directions:

12 miles east of Cumnock on the A76

The Nithsdale Hotel looks very spruce and inviting with its ochre-coloured walls, hanging baskets and dormer windows on the second floor. Mine host is Owen Argue, an Irishman by birth who moved here in 1996 and has spent a great deal of time, effort and cash in refurbishing and upgrading the hotel. The Nithsdale has a long history which stretches back to the late 1700s when it is believed to have been used as a granary. It is now a warm and welcoming hostelry with a reputation for serving the best bar food for miles around. The menu offers an excellent choice of wholesome food at sensible prices and, best of all, it's available every day from noon until 8pm. For anyone wanting to explore Robert Burns Country, Sanquhar is an ideal base - within easy reach of both the Ayrshire and the Dumfries locations associated with the great poet. The Nithsdale Hotel has 7 guest bedrooms, 4 of them en suite, and all provided with TV, hospitality tray and hair dryers. Sanquhar itself is a pleasant little town on the River Nith which boasts the distinction of being a Royal Burgh and also of having the oldest working Post Office in Britain. It's housed in a building of 1712 where you'll also find the tourist information office. Also well worth a visit is the Tolbooth, or Town Hall, built in 1735 and now serving as the town's Museum.

Opening Hours: Sun-Thu; 12.00-24.00, Fri-Sat; 12.00 -01.00

Food: Available 12.00-20.00, every day

Credit Cards: Access, Delta, Visa

Accommodation: 7 rooms, (4 of them en suite)

Facilities: Ballroom/function room; parking nearby

Entertainment: Games room; live entertainment

Local Places of Interest/Activities: Sanquhar Church, Tolbooth Museum, Southern Upland Way, all nearby; golf, 1 mile; Drumlanrig Castle, 8 miles; Museum of Lead Mining, Wanlockhead, 10 miles

The Station House Hotel | 51

Annan,
Dumfriesshire
DG12 6AS
Tel/Fax: 01461 206999

Directions:

Annan is off the A75 Dumfries to Gretna Green road. In the High Street look for signs to the Station

This pleasant little town stands beside the River Annan, looking across the Solway Firth to the mountains of the Lake District. An ancient burgh, Annan was founded by the family of King Robert the Bruce and the Bruce coat of arms is used by the town. Once an important shipbuilding and trading centre, Annan now offers the visitor strolls around the attractive riverside park, lovely walks around nearby Hoddom Castle, and a golf course enjoying panoramic views over the Solway.

The town still has its railway link to Glasgow but the little branch line that ran cross-country to Kirtlebridge closed long ago. Small though it was, this line had a substantial station building in the typical red sandstone of the area. It is this interesting building that Jacqueline Lamberton has converted into a charming restaurant and hotel. Part of the spacious platform is now a Beer Garden with lots of plants and colourful sunshades. Inside, The Carriage Restaurant, decorated with a 1920s railway theme, serves excellent traditional Scottish fare, with a popular Carvery on Sundays. Bar snacks are also available. At the time of writing, Jacqueline is creating 3 attractive guest rooms, all en suite and one of them furnished as a bridal suite. Weddings are a special interest of Jacqueline's. She has co-ordinated every aspect of wedding arrangements for many couples from all around the world. With Gretna Green just up the road, Annan seems a very appropriate base for her co-ordinating activities!

Opening Hours: Sun-Thu: 11.00-14.30; 18.00-23.00; Fri-Sat: 11.00-14.30-24.00

Food: Bar meals and separate restaurant

Credit Cards: Not accepted

Accommodation: 3 rooms, all en suite, including 1 bridal suite

Facilities: Beer Garden; parking

Entertainment: Disco, Fridays; occasional live music; seasonal barbecues

Local Places of Interest/Activities: Thomas Carlyle's Birthplace, Ecclefechan, 6 miles; Gretna Green, 8 miles

52   The Thistle Inn

Main Street,
Crossmichael,
Dumfriesshire
DG7 3AU
Tel: 01556 670203

Directions:

From the A75 near Castle Douglas take the A713 north towards St John's Town. Crossmichael is about 5 miles along this road

Crossmichael village lies roughly halfway between the superb sandy beaches at Southerness and the unspoilt acres of the Galloway Forest Park. It's also close to Threave Gardens which are best known for their spectacular springtime display of some 200 varieties of daffodil, but there are also lots of colour summer displays and striking autumn tints in trees and the heather gardens. Also nearby is Threave Castle, a brooding, gloomy fortress built in the late 1300s by Archibald the Grim, one of the notorious 'Black Douglases'. It stands on an island and visitors are instructed to ring a brass bell to summon the castle custodian. He will row over to ferry them to the island.

Crossmichael village is located on the shore of Loch Ken (actually a man-made reservoir) and it's well worth seeking out to visit **The Thistle Inn**. There was a time in the 1950s when the Lady of the Manor had the inn's licence revoked and the village was dry for several years. Happily, those days are past and mine host Jim McLelland can offer visitors a good selection of well-kept ales and a staggering choice of more than 150 different whiskies. Jim has owned and run the inn for a quarter of a century and has a well-earned reputation for providing quality food. There's a separate dining area but you can eat throughout the inn. The menu is supplemented by daily specials and children are very welcome.

Opening Hours: Easter-early October
11.00-24.00

Food: Good wholesome food available every day

Credit Cards: Cash or cheque with card

Facilities: Off-road parking

Entertainment: Darts; dominoes; pub games; occasional live music

Local Places of Interest/Activities: Marina nearby; Threave Castle (NTS), 5 miles; Threave Gardens (NTS), 7 miles; Galloway Forest Park, 10 miles

The Waterfront | 53

North Crescent,
Portpatrick,
Wigtownshire
DG9 8SX
Tel: 01776 810800
Fax: 01776 810850

Directions:

From Stranraer take the A77 direct to Portpatrick (8 miles)

Portpatrick is a little gem of a place, cradled at the foot of cliffs and clustered around the harbour which was once a major embarkation point for travellers to Northern Ireland. The harbour also once sheltered a busy fishing fleet and locals recall that you could walk from one side to the other on the decks of the trawlers as they unloaded their catch of herrings. Those days are long gone - as are the days when the old church performed the same service for couples from Ireland as Gretna Green did for the English. Today Portpatrick is a popular holiday resort. Part of its appeal is due to the Gulf Stream which creates a mild climate in which sub-tropical plants and trees flourish.

Overlooking the charming harbour, **The Waterfront** is a stylish new hotel, opened in the summer of 1999, which is furnished to a very high specification and staffed by a small team dedicated to making visitors feel very special. Bar meals are available in the chic, intimate bar and can also be enjoyed on the terrace where you can watch the busy harbourside scene. For more formal dining, there's an elegant restaurant which serves an exciting and innovative selections of dishes, including vegetarian options, complemented by carefully chosen house and speciality wines. Fish dishes, naturally, are a speciality of the house. The hotel has eight beautifully appointed bedrooms, all en suite and many with a sea view. The rooms are individually designed and furnished and have been awarded a well-deserved 3 star rating.

Opening Hours: Hotel open all day

Food: Available from 10.00-21.30

Credit Cards: All major cards except Diners

Accommodation: 8 Double/Twin bedrooms en suite

Facilities: Harbourside terrace, On and off road Parking

Local Places of Interest/Activities: Golf & coastal walk nearby; Sandhead beach, 12 miles; Castle Kennedy Gardens, 14 miles; Logan Botanic Garden, 18 miles; Mull of Galloway; South Upland Way; Walking, Golf, Bowling Green, Tennis, Fishing, Pony Trekking, Sea Angling

Internet/Website:
e-mail: waterfronthotel@aol.com

The Hidden Inns of Central and Southern Scotland

3 Ayrshire and the Isle of Arran

PLACES OF INTEREST:

Alloway 57
Ayr 58
Ballantrae 58
Brodick 58
Dalmellington 59
Fairlie 59
Galston 59
Irvine 59
Kilmarnock 59

Kirkoswald 60
Lamlash 60
Largs 60
Mauchline 60
Maybole 61
Patna 62
Saltcoats 62
Tarbolton 62
Troon 62

PUBS AND INNS:

Allandale House, Brodick 63
The Annfield House Hotel, Irvine 64
The Bank, Prestwick 65
The Boswell Arms, Auchinleck 66
Catacol Bay Hotel, Catacol 67
Clachan Bar, Largs 68
The Coylton Arms, Low Coylton 69
The Crown Hotel, Tarbolton 70

The Harbour Bar, Troon 71
The Lochside House Hotel, New Cumnock 72
Scoretulloch House, Darvel 73
The Ship Inn, Irvine 74
The Stair Inn, Stair, nr Mauchline 75
The Wheatsheaf Inn, Symington 76

The Hidden Inns of Central and Southern Scotland

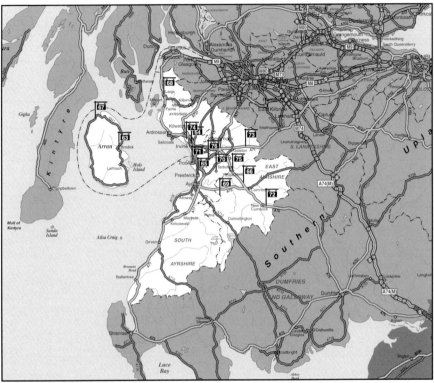

© MAPS IN MINUTES ™ (1999)

63	Allandale House, Brodick	**71**	The Harbour Bar, Troon
64	The Annfield House Hotel, Irvine	**72**	The Lochside House Hotel, New Cumnock
65	The Bank, Prestwick	**73**	Scoretulloch House, Darvel
66	The Boswell Arms, Auchinleck	**74**	The Ship Inn, Irvine
67	Catacol Bay Hotel, Catacol	**75**	The Stair Inn, Stair, nr Mauchline
68	Clachan Bar, Largs	**76**	The Wheatsheaf Inn, Symington
69	The Coylton Arms, Low Coylton		
70	The Crown Hotel, Tarbolton		

Please note all cross references refer to page numbers

Ayrshire & Isle of Arran

Within Ayrshire's 1,200 square miles there's a marked contrast between north and south. In the north there's a taste of the untamed Highlands, while the south is more reminiscent of the Borders, with rolling pasture lands and country villages. The long sandy shores and popular resort of Largs in North Ayrshire, the rural nature of East Ayrshire with its wide open spaces, and the broad beaches, seaside towns and verdant hills of South Ayrshire all add to the variety.

This is, of course, Robert Burns' homeland and wherever you go you'll almost certainly find that Scotland's national bard has been there before you and usually left behind a good anecdote to prove it. Pride of place in any Burns itinerary must go to the Burns Cottage & Museum, at Alloway near Ayr, where the poet was born. Homes of a statelier kind can be visited at Kelburn Castle, home of the Earls of Glasgow, and Culzean Castle, Ayrshire's top tourist attraction.

On the Isle of Arran, Brodick Castle has a history stretching back some 700 years, as does that of Crossraguel Abbey whose substantial ruins stand beside the A77 in the south of the county. And if you want a change of scenery from the mainland, there are regular ferries to the isles of Arran and Great Cumbrae.

With some justification, the Isle of Arran is often referred to as "Scotland in Miniature". Twenty miles long and 10 miles wide, the island unfolds dramatically from the Highland scenery of the north, capped by **Goat Fell** (2,866 feet), to the typically Lowland landscape of farmlands and rolling moors in the south. The island has suffered a turbulent history, having been over-run by the Dalriada Scots who invaded from northern Ireland, then by the Vikings - whose links with Arran are still celebrated - and finally by the Scottish Crown. Robert the Bruce stayed here in 1307 before leaving for the mainland to continue his struggle for Scottish independence, a mission he would finally achieve seven years later at the Battle of Bannockburn.

The island is almost entirely owned by the Duke of Hamilton and the National Trust of Scotland. Together they have successfully resisted any inappropriate development, ensuring that Arran is almost completely unspoilt. In addition, the island offers visitors a comprehensive range of recreational possibilities, from a choice of seven golf courses, to fishing, water-sports, pony-trekking, walking and climbing, as well as medieval castles and a wealth of prehistoric and Iron Age sites.

PLACES OF INTEREST

ALLOWAY

Today it is part of the Ayr suburbs, but Alloway was just a small village when Robert Burns was born here on January 25th, 1759. The long, low thatched cottage built by his father still stands and is now the **Burns Cottage and Museum** housing a wealth of Burns memorabilia including his original manuscript for *Auld Lang Syne*. To the south of the village, the lovely 13th century **Brig O'Doon** still spans the River Doon, a bridge familiar to all Burns' lovers from his poem *Tam O'Shanter*. Also featured in the poem is nearby **Kirk Alloway**, now a roofless but romantic ruin. Burns' father, William Burnes (sic), is buried in the graveyard here.

A few minutes' walk from the kirk, the **Burns Monument and Gardens** commemorate the poet with an impressive Grecian-style monument set in attractive gardens. From here a short stroll brings you to **The Tam O'Shanter Experience**, a 1990s visitor centre where you can watch a film about the life of Scotland's na-

58

tional bard and another telling the story of *Tam O'Shanter*, browse in the extensive gift shop, or sample the fare on offer in the "Taste of Burns Country" restaurant.

AYR

For centuries Ayr rivalled Glasgow as a major seaport. When its importance as a trading centre declined, the town's fine beaches provided a new lease of life - as a popular Victorian resort. A whole new town of wide streets, boulevards, imposing public offices such as the **County Buildings**, and an esplanade sprang up, making this part of Ayr stand in marked contrast to the narrow lanes and alleys of the Old Town - "Auld Ayr" as Robert Burns put it, "wham ne'er a toun surpasses for honest men and bonnie lasses".

The most notable survivor of medieval buildings in Ayr is the **Auld Brig**, a sturdy 15th century construction made famous by Burns in his poem *Twa Brigs*. Elsewhere, the poet described the bridge as *"a poor narrow footpath of a street where two wheel-barrows tremble when they meet"*. Auld Brig was restored in 1910 and is now only open to pedestrians.

A few yards from the bridge, the **Auld Kirk** was built by Cromwell after he incorporated the original town church into a massive fort he constructed here. (The fort has long since disappeared). Burns was baptised in the Auld Kirk; a plan of the graveyard in the lych gate indicates the resting-places of some of his friends. Also on the wall of the lych gate is an early 19th century "mort-safe", a heavy iron grille placed over newly-dug graves to discourage body snatchers.

The town honours two of Scotland's heroes with statues. Close to the Auld Kirk is **Wallace's Tower**, 113 feet high and built in 1828 on the site of a medieval tower in which, according to legend, William Wallace was imprisoned and from which he made a daring escape. About 400 yards to the south, Burns himself gazes thoughtfully over Burns Statue Square.

BALLANTRAE

Robert Louis Stevenson visited this attractive little holiday resort in 1876 to see the ruins of Ardstinchar Castle. Several years later he borrowed its name for his classic novel *The Master of Ballantrae*. The town has a busy little harbour where the River Stinchar flows into the sea. From the harbour there are boat trips to **Ailsa Craig**, a large rock some 10 miles off shore which is actually the plug of an extinct volcano. In medieval times, offending monks from Crossraguel Abbey were sent here to contemplate their sins; its only residents nowadays are thousands of gannets, one of the largest colonies in the British Isles.

This pretty seaside village is located near the place where the River Stinchar, well known for its trout and salmon fishing, runs into the sea; inland stretch the wide open spaces of the south Ayrshire hills, grand country for walkers.

BRODICK

The comings and goings of the ferries which link Brodick on the Isle of Arran to the mainland at Ardrossan provide constant activity in this large village overlooking a broad, sandy bay and backed by granite mountains. Brodick's development as a tourist resort was obstructed for many years by the Dukes of Hamilton, who owned the village and much of the surrounding land. Their ancestral home, **Brodick Castle** (National Trust for Scotland), stands to the north of the village, crowning a steep bank. The oldest parts date back to the 13th century, with extensions added in 1652 and 1844, the latter in the familiar Scottish Baronial style. The interior contains some fine period furniture, notable paintings (by Watteau, Turner and Richardson among others), and important collections of silver and porcelain. The castle grounds are particularly attractive. There's a formal walled garden which was first laid out in 1710, and a woodland garden covering some 60 acres, which was established in 1923 by the Duchess of Montrose, daughter of the 12th Duke of Hamilton. The magnificent collection of rhododendrons is widely regarded as one of the finest in Britain. The two gardens form part of **Brodick Country Park** which also includes the mountain of **Goat Fell** (2,866 feet): a popular walk is the path leading to its summit where the views are quite staggering. The castle is open daily from Easter to October; the grounds are open daily throughout the year, from 10 a.m. to dusk.

In Brodick itself, the **Arran Heritage Museum** is housed in an 18th century crofter's farm and among its exhibits are a working smithy, an Arran cottage and a wide range of agricultural tools. The museum is open weekdays from Easter to October.

DALMELLINGTON

Dalmellington lies in the heart of the Doon Valley, once the industrial heartland of Ayrshire. The area's industrial heritage is explored in the **Cathcartston Interpretation Centre** which contains a working loom and interesting displays on weaving, mining and other local industries. **Chapel Row Cottage** has been carefully reconstructed and furnished to reflect the austere lifestyles of iron workers during the years of the First World War.

Dalmellington is set beside the River Doon, whose source is **Loch Doon** about two miles to the south, a delightful place for walks and picnics. On its shore stand the impressive ruins of **Loch Doon Castle** with walls up to 9 feet thick and 26 feet high. Dating back to the early 14th century, the castle was originally built on an island in the loch; when the Galloway hydroelectric scheme raised the water level in the 1930s, the castle was dismantled stone by stone and re-erected on the shore. The island can still be seen from time to time when water levels are low.

FAIRLIE

This picturesque village boasts a sandy beach, a pier and not just one but two castles. Standing in a glen to the east, **Fairlie Castle** was built in 1521 and is now a ruin. **Kelburn Castle & Gardens**, two miles north of the town, is very much lived in, the historic home of the Earls of Glasgow. The castle has a late 16th century tower attached to a house of 1700 and is open to visitors during the summer months. The park is open from Easter to October and offers woodland walks, pony treks, a secret forest, crocodile swamp and much more.

GALSTON

Lying in wooded country in the valley of the River Irvine, Galston has a thriving textile industry established in the 17th century by Dutch and Huguenot immigrants. Visitors can see lace tablecloths and curtains being made at some of the mills. Nineteenth century designs are still in production and visitors are welcome to purchase souvenirs from the factory shops.

On the edge of the town, **Loudoun Gowf Club** is unique in retaining the game's old Scots

spelling. The course is open to visitors on weekdays. Nearby **Loudoun Castle** is notable as the location where the Act of Union between Scotland and England was signed in 1707. Most of the present building is 19th century, although a 15th century tower has survived. The castle's 500-acre grounds are now home to the **Loudoun Castle Theme Park** which claims to be the largest in Scotland. Along with stomach-churning roller coaster rides, the park also offers a wide variety of amusements for all the family, including pony rides, a kids' farm, log flume and much more. There's an à la carte restaurant in the former coachhouse, and fast food outlets such as the William Wallace Food Court, named after the Scottish patriot who won a resounding victory over the English in 1297 at nearby Loudoun Hill.

IRVINE

The largest town in North Ayrshire, Irvine used to be the main port for Glasgow and those busy days are recalled at the **Scottish Maritime Museum** beside the old harbour. Visitors can board the world's oldest Clipper ship, as well as vintage Clyde "puffers" and tugs. Nearby, the **Magnum Centre** is one the largest sports and leisure complexes in Europe, a 250-acre site complete with swimming pools, theatre, cinema, ice rink, bowls hall and much more.

Naturally, the town has connections with Robert Burns. He lived here between 1781 and 1783 at **No. 4 Glasgow Vennel** while learning to dress flax at No.10 in the same street, one of the few old streets in the town to have survived. The town boasts the oldest continuous Burns Club in the world, founded in 1826. At the **Burns Club & Museum** you can see a collection of original manuscripts prepared for the famous Kilmarnock Edition of his poems. There's also an impressive 9 foot high statue of the poet on the banks of the River Irvine.

Mary Stuart stayed at Irvine in 1563; her visit is celebrated each year with a week-long **Marymass Festival** in August.

KILMARNOCK

It was back in 1820 that a Kilmarnock grocer named Johnnie Walker began blending his own whisky at his shop in King Street. Today, the whisky bottling business he founded is the largest in the world and one of Kilmarnock's major

60

industries along with the manufacture of carpets and footwear.

The town also has strong connections with Robert Burns. The first edition of his poems was published here in 1796. An original copy is on display in the museum attached to the red-sandstone **Burns Monument** in Key Park. Among other memorabilia is the announcement of the poet's death on 21 July 1796 as printed in the *Kilmarnock Standard*.

A short walk from the Monument, the **Dick Institute** is noted for its impressive geology, Scottish archaeology and natural history collections and reminders of bygone history. The Institute also offers a varied programme of contemporary art and other exhibitions.

On the northern edge of the town **Dean Castle Country Park** extends to 200 acres. Facilities include a ranger service, children's zoo, riding centre and visitor centre. The massive 14th century Castle Keep houses an excellent collection of armour, tapestries and early European musical instruments. Children love exploring the dingy dungeons. Guided tours of the Keep and the adjacent 15th century Palace are available, culminating in superb views from the battlements.

KIRKOSWALD

Two of Burns' best-loved characters lie buried in the churchyard at Kirkoswald. Douglas Graham of Shanter was the model for Tam O'Shanter, and his crony, the village cobbler John Davidson, inspired the character of Souter Johnnie in the same poem. **Souter Johnnie's Cottage** (National Trust for Scotland), built in 1785, stands across the road from the churchyard and has been furnished with contemporary furniture, including items used by the Souter family, a cobbler's chair that was almost certainly his, and various bits of Burns memorabilia. In the garden are life-size stone figures of a jovial-looking Souter Johnnie and other characters from *Tam O'Shanter*. They were carved in 1802 and exhibited around Scotland and England before being brought to the house in 1924.

LAMLASH

The second largest village on the Isle of Arran after Brodick, Lamlash enjoys an unusually mild climate. Its mainly Edwardian architec-

ture bestows a pleasing kind of period charm. The village's curious name is actually a corruption of *Eilean Mo-Laise*, or St Molaise's Island; originally the name applied to what is now called **Holy Island**, where the 6th century St Molaise lived in a cave. St Molaise's Island, two miles from Lamlash, is currently owned by a group of Scottish Buddhists who have established a meditation centre there, but visitors are welcome to the island and there are regular ferries during the season.

LARGS

Set against a spectacular backdrop of spreading woodland and hills rising up to 1,500 feet, Largs has been a popular seaside resort for many years and has in recent times been voted Scotland's Top Tourism Town. Just a few yards from the harbour, the superb **Skelmorlie Aisle** (Historic Scotland, free) is all that remains of the former parish church. In 1636 the aisle was converted into a mausoleum for Sir Robert Montgomerie; its elaborately painted barrel-vaulted ceiling and Montgomerie's intricately carved tomb are masterpieces of Renaissance art.

Among the town's many visitor attractions, a relative newcomer is **Vikingar!** which with state-of-the-art multi-media technology tells the story of the Vikings from their first raids in west Scotland to their defeat at the Battle of Largs in 1263. That victory is celebrated every year with a Viking Festival held during August and September. To the south of Largs, the site of the battle is marked by the elegant **Pencil Monument**, reached by a coastal footpath.

Just five minutes by ferry from Largs, **Great Cumbrae Island** is worth visiting for its fine beaches, splendid views and peaceful countryside. Rather surprisingly the island, just four miles long and two miles wide, boasts a **Cathedral of the Isles**, located in its one and only town, Millport. Completed in 1851 to a design by the Gothic revival architect William Butterfield, it is the smallest cathedral in Europe. Another major attraction on Great Cumbrae is the **Marine Life Museum**, operated by Glasgow and London Universities, which houses a magnificent aquarium.

MAUCHLINE

This little town is still vibrant with memories of Robert Burns. Following the death of his father in 1784, the 25-year-old Burns took a lease on nearby Mossgiel Farm which is still a working farm to this day. Robbie was hopelessly in-competent as a farmer and his financial prob-lems with the farm were compounded by a roller-coaster emotional relationship with Jean Armour, a sparky Mauchline lass. Despite these dual tensions, this was a period of extraordi-nary creativity for Burns and in 1786 his first volume of poems was published. The book be-came a best-seller and, after savouring his liter-ary triumph in the salons of Edinburgh, Burns returned to Mauchline in 1788 to marry Jean.

They set up home in a single room in a house in Castle Street which is now the **Burns House Museum** where a rather meagre collection of memorabilia will enthuse only the most de-voted of his fans. Much more rewarding is a visit to the poet's favourite "howff", or water-ing-hole, **Poosie Nansie's Tavern**, the setting for his cantata *The Jolly Beggars* and still a popu-lar pub in the town. To the north of Mauchline stands **The National Burns Memorial Tower**, an impressive three-storey tower whose first and second floors house an interpretation centre and from whose roof there are panoramic views of the surrounding countryside.

Burns' residence in Mauchline has rather over-shadowed the town's two other claims to fame: the

production of Curling Stones, made from Ailsa Craig granite, and Mauchline Ware - highly collectable small boxes and other items made from plane or sycamore wood, hand-painted with local scenes and varnished.

MAYBOLE

Maybole is the fifth largest town in Ayrshire and formerly the capital of the Carrick area. It is notable for its restored 17th century **Maybole Castle**, a picturesque building with turrets and oriel windows. It was formerly the town house of the Earls of Cassillis, leaders of the powerful Lowland Kennedy family, who now live at Cassillis House (private) about four miles north-east. It was the Kennedys who established a **Collegiate Church** at Maybole in 1371; the roofless ruin of the 15th century church can be seen in the old graveyard in Abbot Street.

In the High Street, a clock tower is all that remains of the ancient **Tolbooth** which was originally the town house of the Lairds of Blairquhan. It stands next door to Maybole's 19th century Town Hall, forming the Town Buildings.

About four miles west of Maybole, **Culzean Castle** (National Trust for Scotland) is Ayrshire's premier tourist attraction. Magnificently fur-

Culzean Castle

nished, the castle was designed by Robert Adam in 1777 and built around an ancient tower of the Kennedys. The work took 15 years to com-

National Burns Memorial Tower

62

plete but the result is one of Adam's finest creations, marked by dazzling features such as the oval staircase and circular saloon. A small exhibition commemorates the life and times of Dwight D. Eisenhower, who stayed here several times during the Second World War. The top floor was presented to him for life by the castle's owners at that time, the Kennedys.

Culzean overlooks the Firth of Clyde and stands in 565 acres of grounds set alongside the shore. Guided tours are available, there's a Reception & Interpretation Centre, swan pond, deer park, picnic sites, restaurant and tea rooms. Definitely not to be missed.

Two miles southwest of Maybole, the substantial ruins of **Crossraguel Abbey** (Historic Scotland) include a mighty gatehouse and a sturdy tower house. Founded in 1244, the remains date mostly back to 1400s and are a fine example of that glorious period of church architecture. The Abbey's funnel-shaped **Dovecote** is remarkably well-preserved, with 240 nesting boxes for the birds which provided the monks with a reliable year-round source of food.

PATNA

About a mile south of Patna, at Waterside, **The Dunaskin Experience** stands on the site of the former Dalmellington Iron Works Company. An open-air living museum, The Dunaskin Experience contains Europe's best remaining example of a Victorian Ironworks with more than half its 110 acres listed as a Scheduled Ancient Monument. Attractions include an audio-visual recreation of Ayrshire life in the late 19th century, a period cottage, Furnace Play Tower, walks through Dunaskin Glen, gift shop and coffee shop

SALTCOATS

In the 1500s, King James V dipped into his own pocket to establish the salt panning industry here from which the town takes its name. Saltcoats nowadays is much better known for its picturesque harbour and golden, sandy beaches set around Irvine Bay. Visitors interested in the history of the area will find a comprehensive overview at the **North Ayrshire Museum** which is well worth visiting.

With its superb position on the promenade at Saltcoats, the **Bay Hotel** provides its guests with fantastic views over the Firth of Clyde to Arran.

TARBOLTON

Anyone following the Burns Trail will want to seek out this small village in order to visit the charming 17th century house known as the **Bachelors' Club** (National Trust for Scotland). Between 1777 and 1784, the Burns family lived at **Lochlea Farm** near Tarbolton and during these years Burns was a leading light of the Bachelors' Club, a debating society where his ardent republican views ensured that discussions were never less than lively. As well as debating, drinking and the pursuit of pretty women, another of Rab's passions was dancing. It was in this house that he attended dancing lessons and in 1781 was initiated as a freemason. The thatched, white-washed building contains a small museum of material relating to Burns' life in the area.

TROON

As far back as the early 1700s the attractions of coastal towns like Troon were becoming clear to those who lived in the cities and industrial areas. Troon was considered at the time to possess *"an excellent situation for sea bathing"*. In this respect the town has changed little - it's still a small fishing town boasting two miles of soft, sandy beaches stretching from either side of the harbour.

The harbour itself is always busy with yachts arriving and berthing, anglers trying their luck, and children exploring all the nooks and crannies of the countless rock pools.

Troon's municipal Golf Club offers no fewer than 3 separate courses.

About five miles northeast of Troon, the ruins of **Dundonald Castle** (Historic Scotland) loom over the pretty village of the same name. This hilltop site was occupied well before 2000 BC and a hill fort stood here between 500 and 200 BC. The present castle was built in 1390 by Robert II, the first of the Stuart line of kings who were to rule Scotland and then England for more than three centuries. There's a visitors' centre with a coffee shop, grand views, and an exhibition outlining the castle's history.

Allandale House | 63

Brodick,
Isle of Arran
KA27 8BJ
Tel/Fax: 01770 302278

Directions:

Brodick is the terminus of the ferry from Ardrossan on the mainland. Allandale House is close to the ferry terminal - turn right towards Lamlash and take the second left. The hotel stands on this corner

Conveniently close to the ferry terminal, **Allandale House** occupies a superb site standing in a lovely mature garden and enjoying entrancing views over the surrounding countryside. Built in 1920, the house is an imposing villa with spacious rooms, all beautifully furnished in soft, pastel shades and immaculately maintained. Your hosts, Valerie and Muriel Young, have an established reputation for providing a warm, friendly welcome, personal attention and good food. The latter is outstanding, concentrating on good home Scottish cooking using the best meat and fish available. The hotel is licensed so you can enjoy a drink with your meal. Afterwards, settle down in the inviting lounge with its large windows overlooking the garden, perhaps with a favourite book or enjoy a chat and an after dinner drink. Allandale has 6 guest bedrooms, all beautifully appointed and with the added convenience of private facilities, colour television and tea/coffee making facilities. Not surprisingly, Allandale is the kind of place where guests wish to return year after year. Whatever your particular interest - hill walking through the spectacular countryside, playing on one or all of the island's 7 golf courses, or just relaxing amidst outstanding scenery, Allandale provides a perfect base. As Valerie and Muriel put it, "Allandale is your place in the country!"

Opening Hours: Hotel open all day

Food: Hours vary according to the season

Credit Cards: All major cards except Amex & Diners

Accommodation: 6 rooms, all with private facilities

Facilities: Restaurant; residents' lounge; ample parking

Local Places of Interest/Activities:
Brodick Castle, Brodick Country Park, Arran Heritage Museum, all in Brodick; Holy Island, by ferry (summer only) from Lamlash, 4 miles; Machrie Moor Stone Circles, 8 miles

64 The Annfield House Hotel

6 Castle Street, Irvine,
Ayrshire KA12 8RJ
Tel: 01294 278903
Fax: 01294278904

Directions:

Irvine is off the A78/A71 about 12 miles north of Ayr. In the town, continue north along the High Street into Eglinton Street. Castle Street is the second road on the left. Turn here and Annfield House Hotel is a short way along this road, on the right

'A Country House in Town' is how Peter Battison describes **Annfield House Hotel**, his welcoming hotel and restaurant set on the banks of the River Irvine. Although only a few minutes walk from the town centre, the hotel is wonderfully secluded. It's set in 2 acres of conservation land, with caringly tended gardens where visitors could be forgiven for thinking they were in the heart of the countryside. This relaxing haven with its homely Scottish atmosphere is well known for its good food and service, complemented by tasteful and comfortable furnishings. Friendly and approachable staff add to the pleasure of staying here.

The hotel's bar and restaurant enjoy an excellent local reputation for high quality cuisine and are both open throughout the day for lunches. Evening meals in the restaurant are always something special since fresh Scottish produce is delivered daily to be prepared by expert chefs. Meals can be taken on the riverside gardens which are a delight in the summer months. At night, guests ascend an original 19th century staircase to one of the 9 country house style bedrooms, each en suite with satellite TV, modem socket, direct dial telephone and hospitality tray. Irvine itself offers visitors a wide choice of attractions ranging from the Magnum Centre, one of the largest sports and leisure complexes in Europe, to links with Robert Burns who lived here between 1781 and 1783. The Burns Club, which is open to visitors, is the oldest continuous such club in the world, founded in 1826.

Opening Hours: Hotel: all day. Restaurant/Bar: 12.00-14.15; 17.00-20.30

Food: Bar lunches; Restaurant lunches & evening meals

Credit Cards: All major cards accepted

Accommodation: 9 rooms, all en suite

Facilities: Riverbank gardens; ample parking

Local Places of Interest/Activities: Scottish Maritime Museum, 1 mile; Magnum Leisure Centre, 1 mile; Burns Club & Museum, 1 mile; Eglinton Country Park, 3 miles

The Bank 65

111 Main Street, Prestwick,
Ayrshire KA9 1LA
Tel/Fax: 01292 471113

Directions:
Prestwick is on the A79, about 4 miles north of Ayr. The Bank pub is on the main street

Occupying a prime location on a corner of the main street, **The Bank** was originally just what its name suggests, although now it looks much more appealing with its colourful hanging baskets and flower tubs. Inside, some of the old bank features have been retained - marble walls and wood panelling, for example, but nowadays there are comfy armchairs and highly polished tables. The old bank counter is still in place in the traditional bar with its cosy atmosphere - it is now the serving area. The owners of this inviting hostelry, Irene and Tom Jones, took over here in 1999 when, after some 20 years in the hospitality business, they decided to go on their own to offer customers quality food. The pub's charming internal decor is their work and their welcoming personalities have made The Bank one of the most popular venues in the area. One of the attractions is undoubtedly the appeal of the food on offer - all based on top quality produce, served with fresh vegetables and always cooked to order. In addition to the regular menu, there are specials which change every week. The menu has something for everyone and at prices to suit everyone's pocket.

Opening Hours: 11.00-24.00

Food: Quality food lunchtimes & evenings

Credit Cards: Delta, Visa, Switch

Local Places of Interest/Activities: Sandy beaches & many golf courses nearby;

Wallace's Tower, Ayr, 4 miles; Burns Cottage & Burns Monument, both at Alloway, 7 miles; Dundonald Castle, 8 miles; Bachelors Club (NTS), Tarbolton, 10 miles;

66 The Boswell Arms

Main Street,
Auchinleck,
Ayrshire
KA18 2AA
Tel/Fax:
 01290 421886

Directions:

Auchinleck is 2 miles NW of Cumnock, off the A76. The Boswell Arms is on the B7083 Cumnock to Auchinleck road

Built some 200 years ago in the attractive local red sandstone, **The Boswell Arms** is a handsome looking structure with some interesting architectural features. To one side is a circular tower with a "witch's hat" turret crowned by a weathervane while the front gable is topped by a stone thistle. An impressive-looking crest hangs over the front door bearing the arms of the Boswell family. Their most famous son, James, later achieved eternal fame as the biographer of Dr Samuel Johnson.

Inside, the two bars are very inviting and the tavern's owner, Douglas Aitken, is a welcoming and genial host. Another good sign is that the Boswell Arms is very popular with local people, attracted no doubt by the informal and relaxed atmosphere but also by the hearty fare on offer at lunchtimes from Thursday to Saturday, and throughout the day on Saturday and Sunday. The menu offers something for everyone, served in generous helpings and at sensible prices. The bar is well-stocked with all the leading brands and the pub's pool table is a well-used amenity.

Opening Hours: Mon-Thu: 11.00-24.00; Fri-Sat: 11.00-01.00; Sun: 12.30-24.00

Food: Thu-Sat: 12.00-14.00; Sat-Sun: available all day. (No food Tues-Wed)

Credit Cards: Cash only

Facilities: Pool table; parking

Entertainment: Occasional live music

Local Places of Interest/Activities: Burns House Museum, National Burns Memorial Tower, Poosie Nansie's Tavern, all at Mauchline, 6 miles; Bachelors Club (NTS), Tarbolton, 10 miles

Catacol Bay Hotel

*Catacol, Isle of
Arran KA27 8HN
Tel: 01770 830231
Fax: 01770 830350*

Directions:

Catacol is on the
northwest corner of
the island, about 16
miles from the ferry
terminal at Brodick

Geologically, the
northwestern area of
Arran is part of the spectacular Scottish Highlands and in this gloriously unspoilt part
of the island the **Catacol Bay Hotel** nestles amongst the hills with grand views across
Kilbrannan Sound. This small and friendly hotel, originally a church manse, has been
owned and run by Dave Ashcroft for more than 21 years. During that time he has
established a solid reputation for providing excellent food and ales, comfortable accommodation and a wonderfully friendly atmosphere. The extensive menu is available throughout the day, from noon until 10pm, offering a wide choice of main meals
and bar snacks as well as a "Small Bites" menu which is ideal for children or anyone
with a small appetite. Take away meals are available and your hosts will be delighted
to arrange special meals for special occasions. There's also a special Sunday buffet each
week, between noon and 4pm, and every Thursday from October to June special Over
60s lunches are served at top value for money prices. The hotel is open all year, except
Christmas Day, and if you would like to stay in this very special place, there's a choice
of either bed & breakfast accommodation in the hotel itself or self-catering accommodation in a modern, split level bungalow just 200 yards away. The bungalow can sleep
up to 7 people in three bedrooms (1 double, 1 twin and 1 family), has a well appointed, spacious kitchen, dining area and a large lounge with colour TV and an open
fire. Ideal for an "away from it all" holiday.

Opening Hours: Hotel open all day

Food: Daily 12.00-22.00. Also take away
meals

Credit Cards: All major cards accepted

Accommodation: Either in the hotel or in
a self-catering bungalow

Facilities: Beer garden; children's play area

Entertainment: Pool table; quiz night,
Saturday; occasional live music

Local Places of Interest/Activities:
Lochranza Distillery, 2 miles; Ferry to the
Kintyre Peninsula (summer only), 2 miles;
Brodick Castle & Country Park, 16 miles

Internet/Website: www.catacol.co.uk
e-mail: davecatbay@lineone.net

68 Clachan Bar

14 Bath Street,
Largs,
Ayrshire KA30 8BL
Tel: 01475 672224

Directions:

Largs is on the A78, about 19 miles north of Irvine. The Clachan Bar is on the main road at the northern end of the street

Located in one of the town's most attractive streets, the **Clachan Bar**, unusually for a pub, has a very inviting window display. The interior is just as appealing, very smartly furnished and decorated. There's a stylish lounge and a large public bar, both modern and with an extremely well thought out design. Mine host at the Clachan is Linda Maxwell, a charming lady whose personality has no doubt been one of the major ingredients in establishing the pub's popularity. Another is the occasional live music sessions although, as Linda says, "generally the regulars are entertainment enough!"

Also important for the Clachan's regulars is the appetising home cooked food on offer - served in generous portions at value for money prices. The well stocked bar has all the popular brands of beverage and there are often promotional evenings with selected drinks at discount prices. Largs itself is set against a spectacular backdrop of woodland and hills rising to 1500ft. It has been a favoured holiday resort for many years and its traditional seaside attractions have in recent years been expanded by the arrival of Vikingar!, a state-of-the-art museum detailing the story of the Vikings from their first forays into southwest Scotland to their defeat at the Battle of Largs in 1263.

Opening Hours: Mon-Wed: 11.00-24.00. Thu - Sat: 11.00-01.00. Sun: 12.30-24.00

Food: Home cooked, value for money cuisine

Credit Cards: Cash only

Entertainment: Live music every Friday, "generally the regulars are entertainment enough"

Local Places of Interest/Activities: Skelmorlie Aisle (HS), Vikingar!, both in Largs; Great Cumbrae Island, Marine Life Museum, (by ferry), 1.5 miles; Fairlie Castle, 3 miles

The Coylton Arms 69

Low Coylton,
nr Coylton,
Ayrshire KA6 6LE
Tel: 01292 570320

Directions:
From Ayr, take the A70 towards Cumnock. About 6 miles along this road, turn right on the B742, then left into Low Coylton

A striking building with thick walls painted a brilliant white, **The Coylton Arms** is a beautiful country pub built some time in the early 1800s. Inside, the walls are smothered with old photographs of the village and although at the time of writing the inn is being refurbished by the time you read this all will be spick and span again. There are two bars, a separate restaurant and a games room with pool and darts. The best entertainment though is when the local farmers, with whom the Coylton Arms is very popular, burst into song.

The tavern is run by Jeanette and Lindsay Wilson, with Lindsay looking after the food. Based on local produce, the appetising menu is available throughout the day. In good weather, you can enjoy your refreshments in the pleasant Beer Garden at the front and watch village life pass by. If you plan to stay in this part of Burns Country, the inn has two guest bedrooms available on a bed & breakfast basis. Jeanette hails from Sunderland but has fallen in love with Ayrshire and its countryside. There's a delightful walk from the inn itself and Burns' lovers will also want to visit the Trysting Thorn which is situated close by.

Opening Hours: Mon-Fri: 12.00-24.30; Sat: 11.00-24.30; Sun: 12.30-24.00

Food: Available all day

Credit Cards: Cash only

Accommodation: 2 rooms

Facilities: Beer garden; large car park

Entertainment: Games room with pool & darts

Local Places of Interest/Activities: Bachelors' Club (NTS), Tarbolton, 6 miles; Burns Monument, Burns Cottage & Museum, Tam O'Shanter Experience, all at Alloway, 9 miles

Internet/Website: e-mail: wilsonjeanette@talk21.com

70 The Crown Hotel

The Crown Hotel,
24 Cunningham Street,
Tarbolton,
Ayrshire
Tel: 01292 541222

Directions:

From the A77, about 4 miles north of Ayr, take the A719 towards Galston. About 4 miles along this road, turn right on the B730 to Tarbolton (1.5 miles). The Crown Hotel is on the main street of the village

For anyone following the Burns Trail, there are two very good reasons for seeking out this small village. The first is the charming 17th century house known as the Bachelors' Club. Between 1777 and 1784 the Burns family lived at nearby Lochlea Farm and during these years Burns was a leading light of the Bachelors' Club, a debating society where his ardent republican views ensured that discussions were never less than lively. As well as debating, drinking and the pursuit of pretty women, another of Rabbie's passions was dancing. It was in this house that he attended dancing lessons and in 1781 was initiated as a freemason. The thatched, whitewashed building contains a small museum of material relating to Burns' life in the area.

When visiting Tarbolton, Rabbie would often stable his horse at **The Crown Hotel** and landlady Zandra Edgar can show you the very spot. This handsome old inn, dating back to the early 1700s, has recently been comprehensively refurbished and its interior is a delight to the eye. Outside, there's peaceful courtyard beer garden ablaze with flowers where customers can enjoy the hotel's appetising fare of main meals or bar snacks which are available every lunchtime and evening. For special occasions, there's a spacious function room on the first floor. Burns followers especially will be interested in staying at this outstanding hostelry but all will appreciate the comfortable, attractively furnished rooms some of which are en suite.

Opening Hours: 11.00-24.00

Food: Main meals & bar snacks every lunchtime & evening

Credit Cards: Cash only

Accommodation: 7 rooms, 3 en suite

Facilities: Courtyard beer garden; large function room

Entertainment: Occasional live music

Local Places of Interest/Activities: Bachelors' Club (NTS), nearby; National Burns Memorial Tower, Mauchline, 4 miles; Ayr, 8 miles

The Harbour Bar   **71**

*169/173
Templehill,
Troon,
Ayrshire
KA10 6BH
Tel: 01292 312668*

Directions:

From Ayr, take the A79 north, then the A78. At the first roundabout, turn left for Troon (3 miles). The Harbour Bar is on the main road from Troon town centre to the harbour

As far back as the early 1700s, Troon was considered to possess "an excellent situation for sea bathing". In this respect the town has changed little - it's still a small fishing town boasting 2 miles of soft, sandy beaches stretching from either side of the harbour. The harbour itself is always busy with yachts arriving and berthing, anglers trying their luck, children exploring all the nooks and crannies of the countless rock pools.

Overlooking this bustling scene is **The Harbour Bar**, well known for its good, wholesome Scottish fare. The inn's seasoned chef offers a tempting menu of dishes prepared from fresh local produce, and what's more it's available throughout the day, every day, until 21.00. Families are welcome and there are special dishes for children. The Harbour Bar is a free house so there's a wide choice of all the best-selling brews and the excellent draught Guinness is said to be the best around. The bar has a games room with darts and a pool table, and mine host Dave Nelson lays on live blues and jazz sessions on Tuesday evenings and Quiz Nights on Wednesdays. Originally from Co. Antrim where pub entertainment is a well-established tradition, Dave has ambitious plans to develop this side of the business.

Opening Hours: Mon-Sat: 11.00-00.30; Sun: 12.30-24.00

Food: Available all day, every day, until 21.00

Credit Cards: Cash only

Entertainment: Games room with pool & darts; live music, Tues; Quiz Night, Wed

Local Places of Interest/Activities:
Excellent beaches nearby; 6 golf courses within a few miles radius; Dundonald Castle (HS), 5 miles

Internet/Website:
e-mail: dave@harbourbar.freeserve.co.uk

72 The Lochside House Hotel

nr New Cumnock,
Ayrshire
KA18 4PN
Tel: 01290 333000
Fax: 01290 333002

Directions:

New Cumnock is on the A76 about 38 miles northwest of Dumfries. The Lochside House Hotel is located about half a mile south of New Cumnock

The Lochside House Hotel dates back to the late 1800s when it was built for the Marquis of Bute as a shooting lodge. If that sounds rather modest, you'll be surprised by the scale of the building which today offers 16 guest bedrooms, all beautifully furnished and decorated and all enjoying a 4-star rating. The house occupies a lovely site, surrounded by magnificent rolling countryside, and the interior is just as grand as the outside leads you to expect. Fine ornate woodwork, quality furniture (sumptuous leather couches, for example) and elegant fittings (such as deep pile tartan pattern carpets) are enhanced by state-of-the-art concealed lighting.

The owner, Robert Kyle, also runs a thriving hair salon and it was by listening to his customers that he determined what visitors want most from a good hotel and went ahead to provide exactly what they had specified. Naturally, a good restaurant was an essential feature and there's also a lounge bar serving lighter meals. At the time of writing the refurbishment is still under way but by the time you read this everything should be in place.

Opening Hours: Mon-Thu; 11.00-24.00, Fri-Sat; 11.00-00.45. Sun; 12.30-24.00

Food: Available all day until 21.00

Credit Cards: Access, Mastercharge, Visa

Accommodation: 16 rooms, all 4-star rated

Facilities: Boating & fishing lake; large function room

Entertainment: Occasional live music & dances

Local Places of Interest/Activities: 9 hole golf course next door

Scoretulloch House 73

Darvel,
Ayrshire KA17 0LR
Tel: 01560 323331
Fax: 01560 323441

Directions:

From the M74 at Junction 8, take the A71 westbound and follow the signs for Kilmarnock. Ten miles beyond the town of Stratheven you will see signs for Scoretulloch House on the A71 immediately at the eastern boundary of the hamlet of Priestland

Exceptional cuisine and all the peace and tranquillity of the tranquil Scottish countryside are just a few of the attractions that make Scoretulloch House such a memorable place to eat. The house stands high on a green hillside by the edge of the grouse moor where in late summer a cloak of purple heather spreads as far as the eye can see. Scoretulloch is a gourmet's delight. The Loudoun Room is one of the west of Scotland's premier restaurants and its head chef, Annie Smith, has won 2 rosettes for the exceptional quality and style of her cuisine. It veers sharply away from nouvelle cuisine both in approach and quantity. The hotel smokes all its own salmon, using staves from old whisky barrels, cures it own meats, and the Scotch fillet steaks from Aberdeenshire are just the best! And the chips are real chips, cooked in dripping. Scoretulloch's own herb garden furnishes the kitchen with flavours as fresh as can be. The food served in Oscar's Brasserie might be called bar meals but the dishes are prepared and cooked to the same high standard as for the Loudoun Room although being individually and modestly priced. Part of the brasserie is a conservatory overlooking the patio and gardens where on fine days it's a delight to enjoy the food from Oscar's in the open air.

The gardens themselves are very special. In summer they are a riot of flower from plants which come from all over the world. Donald and Annie Smith, the owners of Scoretulloch, have a passion for nature. An internationally respected naturalist, wildlife photographer and author, Donald will be delighted to guide you to the best sites for seeing birds such as peregrines, merlins and hen harriers - altogether 111 species have been recorded around the house.

Opening Hours: 12.00-14.30 (last orders), Wed-Sun; 19.00-21.30 (last orders), Wed-Sat

Food: A la carte restaurant; brasserie

Credit Cards: All major cards accepted

Facilities: Spacious gardens; function room; covered barbecue area; adventure activities

Local Places of Interest/Activities: Loudoun Castle, 6 miles; Ayrshire coast, 20 miles; City of Glasgow, 30 miles

Internet/Website:
e-mail: scotel@btinternet.com

74

The Ship Inn

120/122 Harbour Street,
Irvine, Ayrshire
KA12 8PZ
Tel/Fax: 01294 279722

Directions:

Irvine is off the A78/A71, about 12 miles north of Ayr. In the town, follow the signs to Harbourside

Dating back to 1597 and licensed as a hostelry in 1754, **The Ship Inn** is, unsurprisingly, the oldest pub in Irvine. Long and low, this inviting free house is owned by Iain Murray who has retained as many of the old features as possible. There are stone floors, linked by thick tartan carpets, low ceilings and all kinds of interesting nooks and crannies. Iain has decorated the interior with a nautical theme incorporating some fascinating prints, pictures and memorabilia. The Ship is well known locally for the quality of the food on offer here.

There are two restaurants, both non-smoking, and an extensive menu with something to please everyone. Amongst the starters, there's naturally Haggis, Neeps and Tatties but also dishes such as poached mushrooms in a wine and garlic sauce, or homemade paté with oatcakes. Amongst some 20 main courses are old favourites such as Steak Pie (served in a pottery dish: "Big Wan" £5.55; "Wee Wan" £4.55), along with less familiar dishes like Brie & Broccoli Pancakes in a wine and peanut sauce. The regular selection of delicious desserts is supplemented by a choice of daily specials. And to complement your meal, The Ship offers you a huge selection of quality wines.

Opening Hours: Mon-Fri: 12.00-15.00 & 17.00-23.00; Sat: 12.00-23.00; Sun: 12.30-23.00

Food: Mon-Fri: 12.00-15.00 & 17.00-23.00; Sat: 12.00-22.00; Sun: 12.30-21.00

Credit Cards: All major cards except Amex & Diners

Facilities: Beer garden; parking

Local Places of Interest/Activities: Scottish Maritime Museum, 1 mile; Magnum Leisure Centre, 1 mile; Burns Club & Museum, 1 mile; Eglinton Country Park, 3 miles

Internet/Website: www.shipinn.co.uk

The Stair Inn

75

The Stair Inn,
Stair, Mauchline,
Ayrshire
KA5 5HW
Tel: 01292 591650

Directions:

From Ayr take the A70 towards Cumnock. Seven miles along this road turn left onto the B730. Stair is 1½ miles along this road.

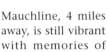

Mauchline, 4 miles away, is still vibrant with memories of Robert Burns who at the age of 25 in 1784 took a lease on nearby Mossgiel Farm which is still a working farm today. Rabbie was hopelessly incompetent as a farmer and his financial problems were compounded by a roller-coaster emotional relationship with a sparky Mauchline lass, Jean Armour, whom he eventually married in 1788. They set up home in a house in Castle Street which is now the Burns House Museum. To the north of Mauchline stands the National Burns Memorial Tower, an impressive 3-storeyed tower whose first and second floors house an interpretation centre and from whose roof there are panoramic views of the Ayrshire countryside.

Scotland's greatest poet may well have supped a dram or two at **The Stair Inn** which opened for business a few years before Rabbie was born. In those days, it would have been a simple 'howff' or alehouse; today, it's a popular venue noted for its excellent food as much as for its quality ales. Three specialist chefs combine their skills to present an imaginative and appetising menu.

For anyone exploring Burns Country, the Stair Inn provides an ideal place to stay. There are 6 guest rooms (3 with bath & shower; 3 with power showers). **They are furnished and equipped to the standard of a 3-star hotel** and have a separate entrance from the inn itself.

Opening Hours: Daily 11.00-23.00

Food: Available Mon-Sat: 12.00-14.30 & 18.00-21.00. Sun: 12.00-20.00

Credit Cards: Access, Visa, Mastercard, Switch

Accommodation: 6 rooms, all en suite

Facilities: Riverside beer garden; parking

Local Places of Interest/Activities: Several 'Burns Trail' locations in Mauchline; Bachelor's Club, Tarbolton, 2 miles; Golf at Royal Troon 9 miles, Turnberry 20 miles; Walking, many interesting walks

76   The Wheatsheaf Inn

*3, Main Street
Symington,
Ayrshire KA1 5QB
Tel/Fax:
 01563 830307*

Directions:

The Wheatsheaf Inn
sits about halfway be-
tween Kilmarnock
and Ayr, just off the
A77 in the village of
Symington

Any visit to Ayrshire should include a trip to the picturesque village of Symington. It lies close to the county's great golfing area, with no fewer than 6 golf courses within a few miles of each other. Amongst them is the famous Royal Troon Championship Course and many leading players on the course such as Seve Ballasteros have made their way to Symington to enjoy the excellent fare on offer at **The Wheatsheaf Inn**. Other celebrity visitors who have experienced its internationally renowned food and service include Tom Lehman, Craig Brown and Colin Montgomery.

The inn is a charming 17th century building with a wonderful olde-worlde atmosphere. A hostelry has been here since the 1500s and in the days of stage coaches the inn was an important posting stage. For the last 20 years it has been run by the father and son team of Martin and Milton Thompson who offer their customers an extensive menu of dishes prepared with care and imagination. A typical menu lists more than a dozen starters, (how about Haggis, Neeps & Tatties in Drambuie and Onion Cream?), a wide choice of fish, meat, poultry and vegetarian dishes, and a large selection of home made sweets. An outstanding choice of wines is available to complement your meal. In good weather, you can enjoy your meal in the superb beer garden which is also the only one for miles around.

Opening Hours: Daily 11.00-24.00

Food: Extensive menu available from 12.00-21.30

Credit Cards: All major cards accepted except Diners

Facilities: Beer garden; ample parking

Local Places of Interest/Activities: Dundonald Castle, 3 miles; Bachelors' Club, Tarbolton, 6 miles; Maritime Museum, Irvine, 7 miles

4 Central Scotland

PLACES OF INTEREST:

Arniston 80
Balquhidder 80
Biggar 80
Blantyre 80
Callander 81
Dalkeith 81
Dirleton 81
Dumbarton 81
Dunbar 82
East Linton 82
Edinburgh 82
Falkirk 84

Glasgow 85
Haddington 86
Hamilton 86
Killin 87
Lanark 87
Linlithgow 88
North Berwick 88
Paisley 89
Roslin 89
South Queensferry 89
Stirling 90
Tyndrum 91

PUBS AND INNS:

The Beech Tree Inn, Dumgoyne 92

Bird in the Hand Hotel,
  Johnstonebridge 93

The Bridgend Hotel, East Linton 94

The Burgh, Musselburgh 95

The Cardwell Inn, Gourock 96

The Crooked Arm, Bridge of Allan 97

Devon Park Inn, Devonside,
  by Tillicoultry 98

Goblin Ha' Hotel, Gifford 99

Golfer's Rest, North Berwick 100

Jameshaven Inn, Auldhouse,
  East Kilbride 101

The Lorne Taverna, Dollar 102

Lugton Inn Motel, Dalkeith 103

Masonic Arms, Longcroft,
  by Bonnybridge 104

Oak Tree Inn, Balmaha,
  by Loch Lomond 105

The Plough Tavern, Haddington 106

Roslin Glen Hotel, Roslin 107

The Royal Hotel, Bonnybridge 108

Tantallon Inn, North Berwick 109

Tyneside Tavern, Haddington 110

Waterside Bistro & Restaurant,
  Haddington 111

Wee Bush Inn, Carnwath 112

West Barns Inn, West Barns,
  nr Dunbar 113

The Hidden Inns of Central and Southern Scotland

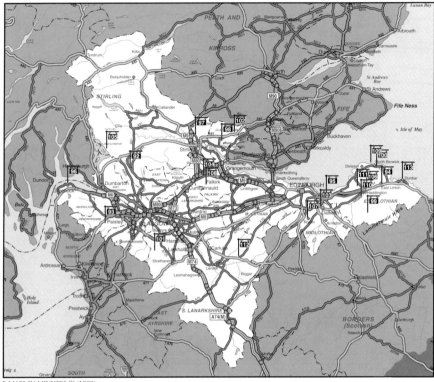

© MAPS IN MINUTES ™ (1999)

92 The Beech Tree Inn, Dumgoyne		**103** Lugton Inn Motel, Dalkeith	
93 Bird in the Hand Hotel, Johnstonebridge		**104** Masonic Arms, Longcroft, by Bonnybridge	
94 The Bridgend Hotel, East Linton		**105** Oak Tree Inn, Balmaha, by Loch Lomond	
95 The Burgh, Musselburgh		**106** The Plough Tavern, Haddington	
96 The Cardwell Inn, Gourock		**107** Roslin Glen Hotel, Roslin	
97 The Crooked Arm, Bridge of Allan		**108** The Royal Hotel, Bonnybridge	
98 Devon Park Inn, Devonside, by Tillicoultry		**109** Tantallon Inn, North Berwick	
99 Goblin Ha' Hotel, Gifford		**110** Tyneside Tavern, Haddington	
100 Golfer's Rest, North Berwick		**111** Waterside Bistro & Restaurant, Haddington	
101 Jameshaven Inn, Auldhouse, East Kilbride		**112** Wee Bush Inn, Carnwath	
102 The Lorne Taverna, Dollar		**113** West Barns Inn, West Barns, nr Dunbar	

Please note all cross references refer to page number

Central Scotland

Scotland's most populous region by far, the area around the Firths of Forth and Clyde contains the country's largest city, Glasgow, one of its most atmospheric, Stirling, and the cosmopolitan capital, Edinburgh. It was in this region that the 14th century struggle for independence raged, culminating in Robert the Bruce's decisive victory at the Battle of Bannockburn near Stirling in 1327.

The area boasts a wealth of castles, palaces and stately houses: Linlithgow Palace, where Mary, Queen of Scots was born; Stirling Castle, set on a soaring crag high above the central lowlands; and Hopetoun House, a William Adam masterpiece, are just a few of the places that should figure on every visitor's itinerary.

Both Edinburgh and Glasgow offer an incredible range of cultural attractions, with the treasures of Glasgow's Burrell Collection alone sufficient to occupy several days. And the countless events staged during Edinburgh's famed International Festival will satiate even the most voracious culture vulture.

"The River Clyde" still conjures up an outdated image of interminable miles of shipbuilding yards and multi-storey warehouses. In fact, for most of its 106 miles the river passes through unspoilt countryside. There's a particularly lovely stretch near Lanark where the river drops 250 feet in four miles over a spectacular series of waterfalls, the **Falls of Clyde**.

Glasgow itself vies with Edinburgh for the title of cultural capital of Scotland. Glasgow's claim is greatly strengthened by being the home town of Charles Rennie Mackintosh, whose Art Nouveau architecture provides some of the city's most distinctive buildings. It is also home to the stupendous Burrell Collection, a dazzling assemblage of works of art from all around the world.

Among the many places of historic interest in the area, two in particular stand out. One is the humble tenement at Blantyre in which David Livingstone spent his childhood years; the other, the fascinating community of **New Lanark** where, in the early 19th century, Robert Owen managed to translate his Utopian ideas of a socialist "village of unity" into practice.

East of Loch Lomond lies the area known as the **Central Lowlands**. It is certainly central but not all that low-lying. Some 700 years ago, this was the cockpit in which Scottish folk-heroes such as William Wallace and Robert the Bruce fought ferociously against the English to establish the independence of their homeland, an ambition they finally achieved with the decisive defeat of Edward II at the Battle of Bannockburn, near Stirling, in 1314.

Echoes of that epic struggle still resound. Mel Gibson's 1997 film, Braveheart, displayed the customary Hollywood disregard for historical facts in telling the story of William Wallace but his well-crafted film brought many Scottish cinema audiences to their feet, applauding, and the film has been credited with boosting the triumphs of the Scottish Nationalist Party in elections.

ARNISTON

Standing just outside this small village, **Arniston House** is by common consent one of William Adam's finest buildings. It's a noble and dignified house built in a local sandstone that blushes pink in the clear Midlothian sun. The mansion was commissioned by Robert Dundas, Lord President of the Court of Session, and a singularly unprepossessing person *"with small, ferret eyes, round shoulders, and a harsh croaking voice"*. But Dundas was also a fine example of that 18th century ideal - a Man of Taste and Judgement. Building at Arniston began in 1726, but four years later financial problems brought the work to a halt with one third of the house unfinished. More than 20 years passed before a judicious marriage to an heiress allowed it to be resumed, by which time both Dundas and William Adam were dead. The building was eventually completed in 1754 by William's son, John.

Most of William Adam's glorious interiors have survived intact, along with some excellent period furniture. One of the most appealing features of the house is its comprehensive collection of family portraits, including several by Allan Ramsay.

BALQUHIDDER

Here in the attractive little village of Balquhidder, the "Highland Rogue" himself, Rob Roy, is buried alongside his wife and two of his sons in the graveyard of the ruined church. The **Grave of Rob Roy** is marked by a rough-hewn stone on which is carved a sword, a cross and a man with a dog. Despite a sometimes violent career - at one point there was a Government bounty of £1,000 on his head - Rob Roy died peacefully in his bed at Balquhidder in 1734, at what was in those days the ripe old age of 65.

The outlaw's story is well told at the Rob Roy Centre in Callander, so the **Bygones Museum & Balquhidder Visitor Centre** concentrates instead on a collection of everyday items and curios from the past, all displayed in a former Laird's mansion which is also home to the **Clan Ferguson Centre**.

Four miles southeast of Balquhidder, Strathyre - the name means "sheltered valley" - is home to **Strathyre Forest**. Walter Scott wrote appreciatively about the area and his enthusiasm is shared by modern visitors who come to this quiet resort close to Loch Lubraig for its lovely scenery and tranquil walks.

BIGGAR

This colourful market town boasts no fewer than six museums featuring a wide diversity of interests. They range from the history of Upper Clydesdale at the **Moat Park Heritage Centre** through the **Greenhill Covenanters' Museum** to the **Biggar Puppet Museum** which puts on large scale puppet shows in its Victorian-style 100-seat theatre. **Gladstone Court Museum** contains a "real" Victorian street complete with bootmaker's, dressmaker's and even a schoolroom, while at the **Biggar Gasworks Museum** in the town's former gasworks visitors can follow the process of extracting gas from coal.

Just outside the town is the *but an ben* (two-room cottage) in which the Scottish poet Hugh MacDiarmid lived with his wife Valda from 1951 until his death in 1978. The cottage has been restored to exactly as it was and is now the base for a writer-in-residence. As the house is very small it can be visited by appointment only.

BLANTYRE

Blantyre is now a suburb of Hamilton, but was just a quiet village beside the River Clyde when David Livingstone was born here in 1813. His family lived in a one-room apartment in a tenement block which is now the spruce white-painted **David Livingstone Centre**. Visitors can see the cramped room in which he was brought up; other rooms have displays on the great explorer and missionary's life and work, including of course the legendary meeting with Henry Stanley. Outside there's a themed garden, African playground and riverside walks.

About a mile north of Blantyre, **Bothwell Castle** is considered by many to be the finest 13th century fortress in Scotland. The mighty

Bothwell Castle

ruin stands dramatically on a hill above a loop in the river, its walls 15 feet thick. Built in the 1200s by the Douglas family, the oldest part is the great circular donjon, or keep, 65 feet in diameter and 90 feet tall.

CALLANDER

This popular holiday centre has Sir Walter Scott to thank for putting Callander on the map. He first visited the town in 1806 when he rode through the dramatic **Pass of Leny** and gazed entranced at the raging **Falls of Leny**. He travelled westwards to **Loch Katrine** whose mystical beauty inspired his best-selling poem, *The Lady of the Lake*. And Scott absorbed like a blotter the colourful stories of Rob Roy Macgregor, cattle rustler, freebooter and local folk hero. He romanticised the latter-day Robin Hood in his novel *Rob Roy* (1818), a book which prompted an immediate tourist interest in Rob Roy's home territory, the Trossach Hills. The novelist's championing of the area is reflected in the naming of the vintage steamship, the **SS Sir Walter Scott**, which has been navigating the waters of Loch Katrine since 1900 and still sails forth three times a day during the season.

Rob Roy's chequered career is explored at the **Rob Roy & Trossachs Visitor Centre** in Callander, which poses the question "Rob Roy - hero or villain?" and presents a wealth of evidence on either side, inviting visitors to decide for themselves. In the mid-20th century, Callander benefited from the work of another popular author, A. J. Cronin, whose books about a local GP named Dr Finlay cast Callander in the starring role of "Tannochbrae".

DALKEITH

This busy little town has an unusually wide High Street at the eastern end of which are the

gates of **Dalkeith Country Park**. This lovely wooded estate surrounds Dalkeith Palace, home of the Dukes of Buccleuch, a fine early 18th century mansion which can only be seen from the outside. Its former chapel, built in 1843 and now the parish **Church of St Mary**, is open, however, and well worth visiting to see its exceptionally fine furnishings and the only water-powered Hamilton organ in Scotland!

About a mile to the south of Dalkeith, the former Lady Victoria Colliery has been converted into the **Scottish Mining Museum** which offers guided tours by former miners, award-winning "talking tableaux", a visitor centre, tea room and gift shop. Visitors can also marvel at the massive proportions of the largest steam engine in Scotland. It used to power the winding machinery which lowered workers down the mine shaft, 1,625 feet deep.

DIRLETON

Many visitors consider Dirleton the prettiest village in Scotland. It is certainly a charming sight. Mellow 17th century cottages with red pantiled roofs nestle in well tended gardens, there's a pretty, corbelled church, and the ruins of the 13th century **Dirleton Castle** provide a romantic backdrop to its own herbaceous borders and carefully tended gardens first laid out in the 1500s. An unusual, honeypot-shaped dovecot built with 1,100 nests stands beyond the colourful borders, and the geometric gardens provide a wonderful summer display.

DUMBARTON

A mile or so southeast of this rather unremarkable town, **Dumbarton Castle** stands proudly atop a volcanic plug guarding the Clyde estuary. For 2000 years this strategic site has been fortified and the present castle's remarkably well-preserved medieval structure provides visitors with superb views across the Firth of Clyde.

A few miles to the north of Dumbarton, the beauty of **Loch Lomond**, the largest expanse of fresh water in Britain, just about manages to survive the busy A82 which runs along its western shore. There are much more peaceful views of the famed loch from the **Balloch Castle Country Park** which is owned and run by Glasgow City Council.

82

DUNBAR

A Royal Burgh since 1370, Dunbar has a broad High Street, a ruined Castle, picturesque harbour, excellent beaches and more sunshine hours to enjoy them than anywhere else in Scotland. One of the oldest buildings in Dunbar is the 16th century **Town House**, once a prison but now housing a small museum of local history and archaeology. Americans especially will be interested in **John Muir House** in the High Street, where the explorer, naturalist and founder of the American conservation movement was born in 1838. His family emigrated to America when John was 11 years old and he was later instrumental in the establishment of the Yosemite National Park, the first in the United States. Appropriately, Dunbar commemorates its most famous son with the **John Muir Country Park**, located on a beautiful stretch of coastline.

Preston Mill, East Linton

Some 10 miles further north, Luss is a 19th century estate village with a fine beach and mesmerising views over Loch Lomond. The **Loch Lomond Park Centre** offers audio-visual presentations on both the natural and human influences on the area and has a gift shop selling locally-produced crafts.

EAST LINTON

This pleasant little town is well known because of **Preston Mill and Phantassie Doo'cot** (National Trust Scotland, free). Standing picturesquely beside its duck pond, the 18th century Mill has been carefully restored and visitors can watch one of the oldest mechanically intact water-driven meal mills at work. A short walk away, Phantassie Doo'cot, or dovecote, was once home to 500 birds. Just outside the town, **Hailes Castle** is a beautifully sited ruin incorporating a 13th century fortified manor. Mary Stuart was brought here by the Earl of Bothwell, her 3rd husband, on her flight from Borthwick Castle in 1567.

In the old days, East Linton was a regular resting-point for drovers herding their prime Scottish cattle southwards to the markets of northern England.

About four miles northwest of East Linton, the **Museum of Flight** houses a massive collection of aircraft and related items. Displayed in cavernous Second World War hangars, the planes on show include a Tigermoth, a Spit-

fire, a Comet and a Vulcan bomber. The museum is open daily during the season.

EDINBURGH

One of the world's great cities, Edinburgh is also one of the most attractive. Dramatically sited overlooking the Firth of Forth, like Rome the city drapes itself across seven hills. The most prominent of these is **Castle Rock**, a craggy outcrop which has been fortified since Stone Age times.

The present **Castle** dates back to 1230 although there have been many additions and alterations. The oldest part is **St Margaret's Chapel**, an austere Norman place of worship which for 300 years was used as a powder magazine. Its original purpose was recognised in 1845 and the chapel was finally re-consecrated in 1924. The castle is part fortress, part Renaissance palace. In the palace visitors can see the room in which Mary, Queen of Scots gave birth to James VI (later James I of England), and view the **Honours of Scotland**, the Scottish equivalent of England's Crown Jewels. The dazzling display includes the Crown, Sceptre and Sword of State and, lying rather incongruously in the midst of such splendour, the **Stone of Destiny**, the plain sandstone slab on which 47 kings of Scotland were crowned.

The Castle stands at the western end of the **Royal Mile**, the backbone of the medieval city.

83

In herringbone fashion, narrow wynds and alleys skitter off this main road which is stacked for most of its length with lofty tenements. One of these, the six-storey **Gladstone's Land** (National Trust Scotland), is a splendid and authentic example of an early 17th century merchant's house. The Gladestan family occupied part of the tenement and rented out the remainder. If you are looking for a rather unusual holiday location, it's still possible to rent one of the floors.

Allow plenty of time for exploring the Royal Mile. Its places of interest are too numerous to detail here, but not to be missed are the **High Kirk of St Giles** with its magnificent spire, **Outlook Tower** whose *camera obscura* has been delighting visitors ever since it was installed in 1853, **John Knox's House** where the fiery reformer lived for a while, and the **Museum of Childhood** which, paradoxically, was created by a man who hated children. He dedicated his museum to King Herod.

At the eastern end of the Royal Mile stands the **Palace of Holyroodhouse**, most of which was built in the 1660s as a Scottish residence for Charles II, who never in fact visited his elegant northern home. Of the medieval palace, only the Tower House remains, ingeniously incorporated into the present building. Here visitors can see Mary, Queen of Scots' private rooms, among them the study in which her private secretary, David Rizzio, was murdered. A group of Scottish noblemen, incited by Mary's husband, Lord Darnley, burst into the study, stabbed Rizzio 56 times, and dragged his body through her bedchamber.

Within the Palace grounds stand the romantic ruins of **Holyrood Abbey**, founded by David I in 1238. Most of it was destroyed in 1547 by English troops on the orders of Henry VIII when the Scots refused his demand to hand over the infant Mary, Queen of Scots.

When King David built his Abbey here, it was surrounded by open countryside. Astonishingly, it still is. **Holyrood Park** covers five square miles of fields and lochs, moorland and hills, all dominated by **Arthur's Seat**. The crest of an extinct volcano, Arthur's 823 feet are easily scaled and the views from the summit are breathtaking.

By the 1790s the old town, or "Royalty", had become so grossly overcrowded, decayed and dangerously unsanitary that a New Town was started on land to the north. With its leafy squares and handsome boulevards, Edinburgh's New Town was an inspired masterpiece of town planning. Stately neo-classical public buildings blend happily with elegant Georgian terraces and the main thoroughfare, Princes Street, was deliberately built up along one side only so as not to obstruct the dramatic view of the Castle, high above. Some 40 years later, the town's planners even managed to make the huge expanse of Waverley railway station almost invisible by tucking it against the hillside.

A stroll along Princes Street begins at **Register House** (free), a noble neo-classical building designed by Robert Adam in the 1770s to house Scotland's historic documents and records. It still does. A little further west, the 200-foot high **Scott Monument** celebrates the country's greatest novelist with the largest memorial to a writer anywhere in the world. The monument's Gothic details echo the architecture of Scott's beloved Melrose Abbey.

High Kirk of St Giles

84

The **Royal Scottish Academy** is a grand Doric building which hosts temporary art exhibitions throughout the year and the annual Academy Exhibition from April to July. The Academy was designed by William Playfair who was also the architect for the nearby **National Gallery of Scotland** (free) which houses a mouth-watering display of masterworks. They range from Hugo van der Goes' lovely mid-15th century altarpiece, the "Trinity Panels", through exquisite Renaissance and 17th century European works, to a com-

Greyfriars Churchyard

prehensive collection of Scottish paintings. Adding to the charm of this famous street (also renowned for its shopping opportunities) are the green open spaces of the extensive gardens which border its length. There always seem to be public entertainers here, especially during August when the **Edinburgh Festival** attracts around one million visitors to the city. If you plan to be one of those visitors, book your accommodation well in advance.

As in the old town, the New Town has too many attractions to list in full here. But you certainly shouldn't leave the city before sampling the **Scottish National Portrait Gallery** (free), housed in a curious building modelled on the Doge's Palace in Venice, and the **Georgian House**, restored by the National Trust for Scotland to its late-18th century elegance, complete with furniture of that time and some fine paintings by Ramsay and Raeburn.

Several of the city's most popular attractions are to be found in the suburbs. **Edinburgh Zoo** is Scotland's top wildlife venue, home to some 1,500 animals, many of them endangered species, and the world's largest number of penguins in captivity.

Also well worth a foray into the suburbs are the **Royal Observatory Visitor Centre** on Blackford Hill for an informative introduction to the mysteries of the skies, and the **Royal Botanic Gardens** (free), within whose 70 acres of beautifully landscaped grounds you will find the largest collection of Chinese wild plants outside China itself.

Another suburb, **Leith**, was formerly Scotland's major east coast port. Most of that maritime traffic has long since moved elsewhere, but Leith's harbour area has been regenerated in the past few years and is now busy with potential patrons sussing out its stylish cafés, bistros and restaurants. In 1997, against fierce competition, Leith also managed to acquire a prime attraction, the former **Royal Yacht Britannia**. Visitors to the Britannia follow an audio-led tour around its four main decks which, as you might expect, reveals a distinct difference between the royal apartments and those accorded to the crew.

Finally, and rather unexpectedly, Edinburgh also has a beach, at **Portobello**, once a stylish seaside resort but now somewhat down at heel.

FALKIRK

Around AD 140 the Romans made a doomed attempt to quell the rebellious Picts by building the **Antonine Wall** which ran through Falkirk. They abandoned the enterprise some 20 years later, but stretches of the brick and turf construction can be seen in the grounds of **Callendar House** and, five miles to the west at Bonnybridge, **Rough Castle** is a well-preserved example of one of the forts established along the wall at two-mile intervals. Callendar House was the home of the Livingston family, loyal Jacobites, and is notable for its marvellous Georgian kitchens complete with steaming cauldrons, a mechanised spit, and a kitchen maid in costume who explains it all. Falkirk boomed during the Industrial Revolution when a network of canals was constructed linking the town to Edinburgh and Glasgow. These provide plenty of scope for walks, boating and canoeing. A major millennium project, currently under way, will eventually restore the old canal routes providing a through route from the North Sea to the Atlantic.

GLASGOW

With its traditional industries of iron, steel and shipbuilding no longer significant, Glasgow has re-invented itself as a vibrant, self-confident city. High points in the process came in 1990

Glasgow Waterfront

when it enjoyed the year-long title of European City of Culture, and most recently in 1999 with its designation as City of Architecture and Design.

At the time, Glasgow's role as City of Culture provoked amused comment from those who only knew the city as the home of the Gorbals (one of the worst slums in Europe) and as the originator of the "Glasgow Kiss" (a head butt). In fact, Glasgow has enjoyed a long history of cultural vitality, most notably during the Art Nouveau period when the architect and interior designer Charles Rennie Mackintosh

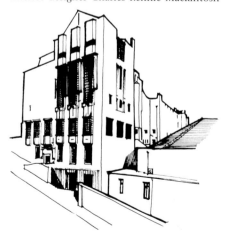

Glasgow School of Art

(1868-1928) brought great prestige to the city.

His career took off in 1896 when he won a competition to design the **Glasgow School of Art**, generally considered one of Mackintosh's most impressive buildings. (Student-led guided tours are available.) His most popular creation though was the **Willow Tea Rooms** in Sauchiehall Street, for which he also designed the furniture, fixtures and fittings, cutlery and even the menu cards. The original building of 1908 closed in

Burrell Museum

1930, but half a century later Mackintosh enthusiasts funded a reconstruction faithful in every detail and standing on the original site. Mackintosh was also the architect for the Glasgow Herald building off Argyle Street, the **Queens Cross Church** in the northwest of the city, and **Scotland Street School** which stands near another of Glasgow's premier attractions, **The Burrell Collection** (free).

The shipping magnate Sir William Burrell (1861-1958) was a lifelong collector of works of art and his interests ranged from 4,000-year-old antiquities such as the splendid Mesopotamian lion's head, through Oriental art to mainstream European painting. Unlike his close contemporary William Randolph Hearst, Burrell was a discriminating collector, acquiring pieces because he admired them rather in deference to current fashion. In 1943, Burrell offered his

86

fabulous collection to the city stipulating only that it should be housed in a rural setting, away from the then heavily polluted city centre. It was only in 1983 that the purpose built gallery was opened. For many, the Burrell Collection is in itself worth a journey to Glasgow.

Art lovers will find it easy to overdose in the City of Culture. In addition to the inexhaustible treasures of the Burrell Collection, there are also outstanding collections at the **Kelvingrove Museum & Art Gallery** (free), a huge Victorian pile containing a wide range of European paintings, and at the **Hunterian Museum & Art Gallery** which majors on Scottish painters and the work of the US-born James McNeill Whistler.

It may seem that Glasgow is just one huge art gallery, but there are, of course, many other places of interest. **Glasgow Cathedral** is a splendid Gothic building dating in parts to the 12th century. Here in a superb medieval tomb lie the remains of St Mungo, the 6th century evangelist and reputed founder of the city. Adjoining the Cathedral, the **Necropolis** is a wonderfully atmospheric wonderland of funerary extravagances. It was designed in 1833 by John Strong who modelled it on the Père Lachaise cemetery in Paris.

Across from the Cathedral, in Cathedral Square, stands the oldest house in the city, **Provand's Lordship** (free), built around 1470 and originally a clerical residence. The rooms contain furniture of the period and outside there's a fragrant medieval herb garden, a peaceful retreat from the busy city.

Glasgow's visitor attractions are too numerous to detail in full here, but two more must be mentioned. **The People's Palace** (free) opened as a social history museum as long ago as 1898 and, more than a century later, remains as innovative as ever with inventive interactive displays and lively exhibits evoking the city's colourful story. Also not to be missed is the time capsule of **Tenement House** (National Trust Scotland). Agnes Toward moved in here with her mother in 1911 and for more than half a century its decor and furnishings remained unchanged. Agnes was something of a magpie, so the rooms contain a marvellously random collection of ephemera such as ration books, framed religious mottoes and monochrome holiday snaps.

HADDINGTON

Fortunately, the A1 by-passed Haddington as long ago as 1920, and so allowed its picturesque market place, elegant streets and dignified buildings to remain unspoilt. More than 200 buildings in the town centre are listed ones. The classical **Court House**, designed by William Burn, dominates Court Street and, close by, the **Jane Welsh Carlyle House** was the childhood home of the girl who later married Thomas Carlyle. Only the dining-room and garden are open to the public; both have been preserved much as she would have known them.

Jane's sudden death in 1866 left Carlyle grief-stricken. His touching words mourning the loss of *"the light of his life"* can be seen on a plain slab in the choir of **St Mary's Church**. The largest parish church in Scotland, the "Lamp of Lothian" is also notable for the sumptuous alabaster tombs in the Lauderdale Aisle, for its concerts and art exhibitions of international standard and for providing the unusual amenity of an excellent tea-room.

Also well worth seeking out is **Mitchell's Close**, a picturesque 17th century corner of the town where the houses with their crow-stepped roofs and cramped staircases have recently been restored.

A mile south of the town, **Lennoxlove House**, home of the Dukes of Hamilton, is an impressive sight with its 14th century tower house. The interior is equally splendid. The Hamilton collection of fine and applied art includes some striking family portraits, French furniture, and porcelain. One of the Maitland family was secretary to Mary Stuart at the time of her execution and it was he who obtained a death mask of the Queen and one of her rings, both of which are on display. Lennoxlove House acquired its name from one of its former owners, the Duchess of Lennox, otherwise known as *La Belle Stewart*. An outstanding beauty, the Duchess was the model for the figure of Britannia on British coinage. On her death in 1672 she bequeathed the house to Lord Blantyre, stipulating that it should be re-named in memory of her love for her husband.

HAMILTON

This former coal mining town is mostly notable for the colossal **Hamilton Mausoleum**, burial place of the Dukes of Hamilton. It was built by the eccentric 10th Duke in the 1850s

Hamilton Mausoleum

and cost the huge sum of £150,000. A large portion of this sum was spent on the floor alone, a wheel mosaic containing almost every known variety of marble. The building is famous for its 15-second echo which made using it as a chapel, the original intention, impossible.

Hamilton's other historic building of interest is **Chatelherault**, a former hunting lodge designed by William Adam in 1732, also for the Hamilton family. The lodge is set in the beautiful surroundings of Chatelherault Park (free) where there are some pleasant riverside walks.

KILLIN

At the western end of Loch Tay, the Breadalbane Mountains provide a spectacular backdrop to the picturesque little town of Killin where the River Dochart rushes through its centre, tumbling on its way down the foaming **Falls of Dochart**. Opposite the Falls, the **Breadalbane Folklore Centre** presents the old tales and legends of Breadalbane, (pronounced *Bread-al-bane*), which was one of the country's founding earldoms. Its Gaelic name means "High Country of Scotland".

A couple of miles northeast of Killin, the village of Morenish sits beside Loch Tay with Perthshire's loftiest mountain, **Ben Lawers** (3,980 feet) looming over its shoulder. The Visitor Centre here provides copious information about the natural history of the area. From its doorstep, a quite strenuous trail leads to the summit where the dedicated hill-walker will be

rewarded with views which, on a clear day, extend from the North Sea to the Atlantic.

LANARK

Lanark is one of the original four Royal Burghs of Scotland created by David I, who also built a castle here in the 12th century. It was at Lanark Castle that William Wallace began the war of independence by successfully attacking the English garrison here. Wallace is commemorated by a statue in front of St Nicholas' Church, which is itself notable for possessing the world's oldest bell, cast in 1130.

Lanark sits on hills high above the Clyde; in the valley below is the fascinating village of **New Lanark**, a nominated World Heritage Site. This model village was founded in 1785 by David Dale and Richard Arkwright for their cotton-spinning business. The Palladian-style mills and the workers' houses, by the standards of the time, approached the luxurious. But it was Dale's son-in-law, Robert Owen who had the vision of creating a "village of unity". Fair wages, decent homes, health care, free education for adults and children, a co-operative shop, and even the world's first day nursery would prove that a happy workforce was a productive workforce.

Visitors can wander through the three huge mills, take a chair-ride through the **Annie McLeod Experience** - which re-creates the life and times of a young mill girl in 1820 - and see Robert Owen's house with its Georgian-style furnished rooms. The focus of the village in Owen's time was the neo-classical building of 1816 he called The Institute for the Formation of Character, now the Visitor Centre. The high-minded name didn't exclude the provision of a dance hall along with its library, chapel and meeting rooms.

Also within the village, housed in the former dyeworks, The **Scottish Wildlife Trust Visitor Centre** has copious information about the nearby **Falls of Clyde** Wildlife Reserve. A lovely riverside walk from the village leads to the famous Falls of Clyde, a series of picturesque waterfalls with drops ranging from the 30 feet fall at Bonnington, to Cora Linn's 90 foot descent in three scenic cascades.

88

LINLITHGOW

The glory of this little town is the partly-ruined **Linlithgow Palace**, whose origins go back to the 1200s. The oldest surviving parts date from 1424 when James I began rebuilding after a catastrophic fire; his successors continued to extend the palace over the next two centuries. The palace has many royal associations. Mary, Queen of Scots was born here in 1542, and her father, James V, was married to Mary of Guise in a sumptuous ceremony during which the elaborate octagonal fountain in the inner court flowed with wine. Cromwell made Linlithgow his headquarters for a while, and Bonnie Prince Charlie visited during the rebellion of 1745. The cavernous medieval kitchen is still in place, as is the downstairs brewery which must have been a busy place: old records show that an allowance of 24 gallons per day per person was considered just about adequate in the 1500s.

Adjoining the palace, **St Michael's Church** is a splendid medieval building, one of the largest in Scotland. Inside there is some outstanding woodcarving around the pulpit.

In the town itself, the **Linlithgow Story** tells the story of its royal, industrial and social past, while the **Canal Museum** (free) presents the history of the Union Canal, built in 1822 to link Edinburgh to the Forth-Clyde canal near Falkirk. The museum is located at the Manse Road Basin, where you can also board a replica Victorian steam packet for trips along the canal.

A few miles outside the town, the **House of the Binns** (National Trust Scotland) has been occupied by the Dalyell family for more than 350 years. It was built in the early 1600s by Tam Dalyell, one of the band of "hungrie Scottis" who accompanied James VI southwards to his coronation as James I of England. Less than a decade later, Tam returned to Scotland an exceedingly wealthy man.

The outstanding feature of the tall, grey three-storey house he built is the artistry of the ornate plaster ceilings. They were created in 1630 when it was hoped that Charles I would stay at The Binns before his coronation at Holyrood as King of Scotland.

It was Tam's son, General Tam Dalyell, who added the four corner turrets, a design feature apparently instigated by the Devil. The fearsome General was reputed to have frequent

"trookings [dealings] wi' the deil". During one of these trookings, the Devil threatened to *"blow down your house upon you"*, to which Tam retorted *"I will build me a turret at every corner to pin down the walls."*

One of the great charms of the House of the Binns is the wealth of family memorabilia which has been amassed over the years and displayed informally around the house. Outside there are extensive grounds and a folly tower affording panoramic views over the Forth Valley.

NORTH BERWICK

For grand views across North Berwick and the Firth of Forth, follow the undemanding path to the top of **North Berwick Law** (612 feet). On top of this prominent hill stands a watchtower built during the Napoleonic wars and an archway made from the jawbone of a whale which was first set up in the early 1700s.

A few miles offshore rises the towering bulk of the **Bass Rock**, a volcanic outcrop which is now home to millions of seabirds, mostly gannets but with colonies of puffins, fulmars, terns and razorbills. During the season, weather permitting, there are regular boat trips around the rock, but be prepared for the noise. Some 500 years ago the poet William Dunbar described the air near the rock as dark with birds that came *"With shrykking, shrieking, skymming scowlis/And meikle noyis and showtes"*.

North Berwick town, which likes to describe itself as the *"Biarritz of the North"*, is a popular family resort with safe, sandy beaches and a rather genteel atmosphere inherited from the mid-1800s when it was first developed as a holiday destination. Down by the shore stand the ruins of **Old Kirk**, where in 1590 a gathering of witches and wizards negotiated with the Devil (actually the Earl of Bothwell in disguise) to bring about the death of James VI. Despite completing the ceremony by kissing the Devil's bare buttocks (*"as cold as ice and hard as iron"*), the coven's efforts were in vain. Ninety-four witches and six wizards were tried and tortured. They were not executed, however, James taking the view that their failure, even when in league with the Devil, demonstrated his invincibility.

Tantallon Castle, three miles to the east of North Berwick, is spectacularly sited on a sheer-sided crag and surrounded by the sea on three sides. Tantallon was a fortress of the Douglas family for centuries until it was destroyed by

General Monck in 1651. Only an imposing 50 foot high tower and a curtain wall 14 foot thick have survived. Together with the dramatic location and the Bass Rock in the background, Tantallon provides a good photo opportunity but otherwise there is little to see within the ruins.

PAISLEY

This famous textile manufacturing town grew up around its 12th century **Abbey** which was destroyed by Edward I in 1307 but rebuilt seven years later after the Scottish victory at the Battle of Bannockburn. Victorian restorers gave the Abbey a mauling, but the interior with its beautiful stained glass and fine stone-vaulted roof, is still impressive.

Victorian builders made a much better job of the **Thomas Coats Memorial Church**, a grand red sandstone masterpiece which is generally considered the finest Baptist church in Europe. The Coats family, local textile magnates, also furnished the town with the **Coats Observatory** (free) where, on winter evenings, visitors can use its 10-inch telescopes to view the night sky.

The colourful Paisley "tear-drop" design is known around the world and one of the displays at the town's **Museum & Art Gallery** follows its development from simple design to the elaborate pattern now so familiar.

ROSLIN

This quiet village in the Esk Valley is notable for the unique **Rosslyn Chapel**, a fantastic medley of pinnacles, towers, flying buttresses and gargoyles. The chapel is best known for the number and quality of the stone carvings inside. Among allegorical figures such as the Seven Deadly Sins are carvings of plants from the New World which pre-date Columbus' arrival in America by more than a century. These tend to confirm the legend that the daring navigator Prince Henry of Orkney, grandfather of the Prince of Orkney who founded the chapel, did indeed set foot in America. The most famous of the carvings is the **Prentice Pillar**, which tradition asserts was crafted by an apprentice. When his master saw the finished work he murdered the lad in a fit of jealousy.

SOUTH QUEENSFERRY

At times, South Queensferry lies literally in the shadow of the mighty **Forth Rail Bridge** which

passes directly overhead. Completed in 1890, the cantilevered bridge is one of the greatest engineering triumphs of the Victorian age. A mile and a half long and 360 feet high, its construction absorbed more than 50,000 tons of steel. Close

Forth Bridge

by, the **Forth Road Bridge** is a graceful suspension structure whose opening in 1964 put an end to the ferry service which had operated from here for almost a millennium. But there are still regular boat trips from Hawes Pier along the Firth of Forth and to the little island of **Inchcolm** with its lovely ruined Abbey.

About three miles east of South Queensferry, **Dalmeny House** has been the home of the Primrose family, Earls of Rosebery, for more than three centuries. The splendid Tudor Gothic house seen today was built in 1815 by the English architect William Wilkins. Along with a hammerbeam roofed hall, vaulted corridors and classical main rooms, the interior also features some excellent family portraits, works by Reynolds, Gainsborough and Lawrence, tapestries, fine 18th century French furniture, porcelain from the Rothschild Mentmore collection and Napoleonic memorabilia. In the grounds there's a delightful four-mile walk

90

along the shoreline.

Flanking South Queensferry to the west, **Hopetoun House** lives up to its claim of being "Scotland's Finest Stately Home". Back in the late 1600s the 1st Earl of Hopetoun built a grand house overlooking the Forth, and a mere 20 years later commissioned William Adam to extend it enormously. Adam rose to the challenge magnificently, adding a colossal curved façade and two huge wings. The interior, completed after William Adam's death by his two sons, has all the elegance and panache one associates with this gifted family. Their ebullient decor is enhanced by some superb 17th century tapestries, Meissen porcelain, and an outstanding collection of paintings which includes portraits by Gainsborough, Ramsay and Raeburn. The grounds are magnificent too.

STIRLING

Stirling is one of the most atmospheric of Scottish towns. Its imposing **Castle** (National Trust Scotland) gives the appearance of having grown naturally from the 250 foot high crag on which it stands. Long before the present castle was built, this bottleneck in the only feasible route in ancient times between southern and north-

Stirling Castle

ern Scotland across the River Forth demanded a military presence. Iron Age warriors established a garrison at Stirling: the Stuart kings of Scotland from James I onwards also recognised the importance of the town's dominating position.

So did the English. During the 13th and 14th centuries, the neighbour nations fought sav-

agely for control of this crucial river-crossing. In a famous victory in 1297, William Wallace recaptured Stirling from the English. Edward I seized it back in 1304, and the aggressive to-and-fro ended only when Robert the Bruce finally routed the English army at the **Battle of Bannockburn** in 1314. **Bannockburn Field**, to the east of the town and now in the care of the National Trust for Scotland, is dominated by a striking equestrian statue of the Bruce; an audio-visual interpretation of the battle can be seen in the **Heritage Centre**.

Stirling Castle enjoyed its greatest glory during the reigns of the Stuart monarchs. The castle's magnificent 125-foot long **Great Hall**, one of the finest medieval structures in Scotland, was built by James IV between 1500 and1503. James V added the superb **Renaissance Palace** with its exterior of richly carved figures, while James VI had the old chapel demolished and replaced in 1594 by the sumptuously decorated **Chapel Royal**. In the restored **Castle Kitchens** there is a fascinating re-creation of the lavish banquet given by Mary Stuart to celebrate the baptism of her son, James VI (later James I of England).

The castle also houses the **Regimental Museum of the Argyll & Sutherland Highlanders** which explores the annals of the 200-year-old regiment, while outside on the Castle Esplanade, the **Royal Burgh of Stirling Visitor Centre** offers a multi-lingual audio-visual tour through 1,000 years of the town's history.

Just outside the castle gates stands the fine medieval Church of the Holy Rude where Mary, Queen of Scots and, later, her son James VI were crowned, both of them babies at the time.

A short walk from the castle, **Argyll's Lodging** (Historic Scotland) is a charming 17th century building, once the home of the Marquis of Argyll. A prominent Scottish nobleman, it was Argyll who in 1651 crowned Charles II as King of Scotland nine years before he was restored to the English throne.

Darnley Coffee House, situated in the heart of Stirling's Old Town, enjoys a unique setting - the barrel-vaulted cellars of the 16th century "Darnley's House". According to tradition, these were the cellars of the Town House of Lord Darnley, husband of Mary, Queen of Scots, and the nursery home of their son, James VI.

Before leaving the Old Town, a visit to the forbidding **Old Town Jail** provides a chilling experience, with presentations by costumed actors of old-style prison life. Stirling's medieval hangman is on site to explain the mysteries of his craft, and the displays include such correctional hardware as the "Crank", a lever which prisoners had to turn pointlessly 14,400 times a day.

To the north of town rises the extraordinary, many-turreted **Wallace Monument**, erected in the 1860s during a surge of Scottish nationalism. Commemorating Wallace's victory over

the English at the Battle of Stirling Bridge in 1297, the tower stands on top of 360-foot high Abbey Craig and is itself 220 feet high. Inside, the exhibits include what is claimed to be Wallace's own sword, and the **Hall of Heroes** features models of famous Scotsmen ranging from Adam Smith to John Knox.

Another unusual structure can be seen at Dunmore Park, about eight miles southeast of Stirling. If you enjoy curiosities you will really relish **The Pineapple** (National Trust Scotland, free). This extraordinary folly, 37 feet high, was erected in 1761 as a wedding present from the 4th Earl of Dunmore to his new bride. If you fancy spending more time close to the exotic fruit, the attached outhouse, which sleeps four, can be rented from the Landmark Trust.

TYNDRUM

Surrounded by the sky-scraping summits of Beinn Odhar, Ben Lui and Ben Udlaidh, this modestly-sized village has been described as a "fulcrum of Highland communications". In other words, two main roads strike off from the village: the A85 westwards to Oban, and the A82 northwestwards to Fort William or southwards to Glasgow. Two railway lines, with two separate stations, also set off in different directions to these same destinations. Both railway lines are adored by lovers of Great Railway Journeys. (The two routes have, in fact, been featured in the television series of the same name.)

The Pineapple

92 The Beech Tree Inn

Dumgoyne,
Stirlingshire
G63 9LA
Tel: 01360 550297
Fax: 01360 550008

Directions:

Dumgoyne is on the A81 about 15 miles north of Glasgow. The Beech Tree Inn is about 2 miles north of the village, on the left

Since it was built more than a century ago **The Beech Tree Inn** has been extended several times, most recently with the addition of an elegant conservatory restaurant. At the time of writing, further extension work is in progress and by the time you read this the inn will comprise two restaurants and two large bars. The Beech Tree's two restaurants offer a good choice of wholesome traditional Scottish food with dishes based on fresh local produce such as venison and beef. Outside, there's a pleasant beer garden and a children's play area. The inn is run by Joan Brechin and her husband, Crawford, whose family has been in the hospitality business since 1792.

Walkers will be pleased to know that the West Highland Way passes by the rear of the Beech Tree Inn. The 95-mile walk runs from Milngarvie on the outskirts of Glasgow to Fort William and was the first long-distance path to be designated in Scotland. From Dumgoyne the route passes through woodland to the lovely shores of Loch Lomond.

Opening Hours: 11.00-24.00, daily

Food: Available in the Conservatory Restaurant & The Butterfly Room

Credit Cards: All major cards except Amex & Diners

Facilities: Beer garden; conservatory restaurant; children's play area

Local Places of Interest/Activities: The West Highland Way runs past the inn; Glencoyne Distillery, ¼ mile; Mugdock Country Park, 8 miles; Loch Lomond, 10 miles

Bird in the Hand Hotel

93

Beith Road,
Johnstone,
Renfrewshire
PA5 9LQ
Tel: 01505 329222
Fax: 01505 324770

Directions:

From Exit 29 of the M8, take the A737 to Johnstone (4 miles). Continue through Johnstone towards Beith and the Bird in the Hand Hotel is about 1 mile beyond the town

The Bird in the Hand Hotel is a striking building, sturdily constructed in attractive Scottish sandstone and with interesting features like the half-timbered first floor and a tower-like structure to one side. It was originally built in 1883 and extended around 1910 by the local procurator fiscal - the Scottish equivalent of the English public prosecutor. The interior is spacious and pleasantly furnished and the 6 bedrooms provide value for money accommodation for those travelling on a budget. All the rooms are equipped with television and tea/coffee making facilities and guests share the 2 bathrooms.

Mine host, Denis McNally, managed a 5-star hotel in the Highlands before buying the Bird in the Hand in partnership in 1999. The hotel is highly regarded locally for the quality and value of the food on offer. The lunch menu is supplemented by an excellent children's menu; there are special rates for Early Bird diners (those who eat before 19.00); an à la carte dinner menu and a popular Sunday lunch. In good weather visitors can enjoy their refreshments at one of the picnic tables overlooking the courtyard. The hotel's location makes it a convenient base for exploring either the unspoilt Ayrshire countryside or the metropolitan attractions of the City of Glasgow just 12 miles away.

Opening Hours: Sun-Thu: 11.00-24.00; Fri-Sat: 11.00-01.00

Food: Available daily 12.00-14.30; 17.00-21.00

Credit Cards: All major cards except Amex & Diners

Accommodation: 6 rooms sharing 2 bathrooms

Facilities: Patio; function room; parking

Local Places of Interest/Activities: Weavers Cottage (NTS), 2 miles; Castle Semple Country Park, 6 miles; City of Glasgow, 12 miles

94   The Bridgend Hotel

East Linton,
East Lothian EH40 3AF
Tel: 01620 860202

Directions:

From the A1, 6 miles west of Dunbar, turn right on the B1377. The Bridgend Hotel is just over the River Tyne, on the right

A striking stone building dating from the 1870s, **The Bridgend Hotel** stands at the southern end of the bridge over the Tyne. The hotel has a friendly public bar where most weekends traditional Scottish music is performed - with landlord Les Orde often joining in on the bagpipes! There's a lounge where lunches are served every day and evening meals at the weekend, and also a function room which can accommodate parties of up to 70. The hotel has 5 en suite twin bedrooms and a 4-bed family room - all the rooms have colour TV and tea/coffee making facilities. Les Orde and his staff are always on hand to cater for your requirements whether it's just for a friendly chat, for information on local history, or for booking golf, fishing or excursions. Only a 30-minute drive from Edinburgh, The Bridgend Hotel is the perfect place to base yourself during your visit to the area.

East Linton is a pleasant little town, well known because of Preston Mill and Phantassie Doo'cot. Standing picturesquely beside its duck pond, the 18th century mill has been carefully restored and visitors can watch one of the oldest mechanically intact water-driven mills at work. A short walk away, Phantassie Doo'cot, or dovecote, was once home to 500 birds. Just outside the town, Hailes Castle is a beautifully sited ruin incorporating a 13th century fortified manor. Mary, Queen of Scots was brought here by the Earl of Bothwell, her third husband, on her flight from Borthwick Castle in 1567.

Opening Hours: Mon-Thu: 11.00-14.00; 19.00-23.00. Fri-Sun: 12.00-24.30

Food: Available at lunchtimes, daily; evening meals at weekend

Credit Cards: Access, Mastercharge & Visa

Accommodation: 6 rooms, all en suite (5 twins; 1 family room)

Facilities: Function room; parking

Entertainment: Pool table; live Scottish traditional music most weekends

Local Places of Interest/Activities: Preston Mill & Phantassie Doo'cot, nearby; Hailes Castle, 2.5 miles; Museum of Flight, 4 miles

Internet/Website: www.scoot.co.uk/bridgend_hotel/

The Burgh

95

83 High Street, Musselburgh,
East Lothian EH21 7DA
Tel: 0131 665 3367
Fax: 0131 530 6494

Directions:

Musselburgh is about 6 miles east of Edinburgh, on the A199. The Burgh is located in the High Street

A hostelry that was Regional Winner in the Scottish Pub Food Operator of the Year 1999 clearly has to be sampled. Especially when it won the award in

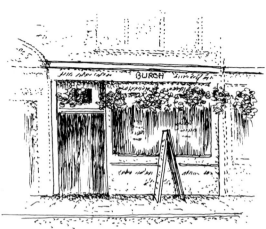

2000 as well. The pub so honoured is **The Burgh** which is easily found in Musselburgh's High Street. It's owned and run by Linda Tweedie who is also the chef whose cooking has received such acclaim. Her lunchtime menu, served between noon and 2pm, offers some tempting starters (Jalapenos & Salsa, for example), a good choice of main courses ranging from Steak Pie to a Scampi Platter, and a fabulous range of specially made desserts. There's also a remarkably reasonably priced 'Kids Stuff' menu.

The evening menu is titled 'Bit on the Side' and Linda has enjoyed herself dreaming up some witty names for the appetising dishes on offer. Amongst the starters there's 'Prawn to be Wild', or 'Wings of Fire' (heaps of sticky fiery chicken wings with a hot sweet & sour dip). Main dishes include 'Good Cod Almighty', 'A Dig in the Ribs' and perhaps best of all, 'Double Breasted. Suits you? - A double breast of chicken cooked to perfection in a creamy brandy and mushroom sauce'. Vegetarians are well catered for and so are those with mighty appetites. The Burgh Mixed Grill is not for the faint-hearted - a 7oz steak, gammon steak, sausages, bacon and black pudding is just the start of it. There's so much to eat that the fries come on a separate plate. In addition to the atmospheric restaurant and bar area, in good weather customers can enjoy a peaceful beer garden at the rear of this outstanding pub.

Opening Hours: Mon-Wed: 11.00-23.00; Thu: 11.00-24.00; Fri-Sat: 11.00-01.00; Sun: 12.30-24.00

Food: Breakfast from 09.00. Lunch: Mon-Sat: 12.00-14.00; Sun: 13.00-16.00; Evening meals: 18.00-21.30, daily

Credit Cards: Cash only

Facilities: Beer garden; parking

Entertainment: Full programme of entertainment

Local Places of Interest/Activities: Musselburgh race course, nearby; Inveresk Lodge Garden (NTS), 1 mile; Dalkeith Country Park, 5 miles; City of Edinburgh, 6 miles

96   The Cardwell Inn

The Cardwell Inn,
49 Cardwell Road,
Gourock,
Renfrewshire PA19 0XG
Tel: 01475 631281

Directions:

From Exit 31 of the M8, continue along the A8 to Greenock and then take the A770 to Gourock (3 miles). The Cardwell Inn is on the main through road

Gourock has been a popular holiday spot with Glaswegians for generations and the regular ferries to Dunoon on the Cowal peninsula attract another swathe of visitors. The town looks across the Firth of Clyde to Holy Loch and the spectacular mountains of Argyll - if you're prepared to make the steep climb up Tower Hill the view is even more breathtaking.

Located in the heart of the town, **The Cardwell Inn** is a modern building, long and low with something of the appearance of a Spanish hacienda. Tubs of flowers and hanging baskets add to the appeal and the interior, which is much more spacious than the outside leads you to believe, has a welcoming atmosphere. Low lighting and comfortable well-upholstered furnishings create a very relaxing ambience. You'll quickly realise that this is where the locals come to eat - always a sure indication of good dining at value for money prices. The varied menu is supplemented by daily specials and the owners, Ian Jewer and his wife Linda, proudly boast that "no one leaves the Cardwell Inn hungry!" At one time they just managed the inn but now they own it and their friendly, relaxed manner contributes greatly to its success. It's just the kind of place you would like to have as your own local.

Opening Hours: Sun-Wed: 11.00-23.00;
Thu-Sat: 11.00-24.00

Food: Available every lunchtime &
evening

Credit Cards: Access, Mastercharge, Visa &
Switch

Local Places of Interest/Activities: Ferries
to Dunoon; Newark Castle (HS), 7 miles;
Cornalees Bridge Visitor Centre, 9 miles

The Crooked Arm

Allan Vale Road,
Bridge of Allan,
Stirlingshire FK9 4NU
Tel: 01786 833830

Directions:

From Exit 11 of the M9 Stirling to Perth road, take the A9 south to Bridge of Allan (1 mile). The Crooked Arm stands at the top of the main street

Beautifully set with the Ochil Hills rising to the east, Bridge of Allan was a popular Victorian spa town and it still has a dignified and elegant air about it. On a quiet backwater on the west side of the town stands **The Crooked Arm**, a welcoming, traditional inn which is well worth a visit. Unimposing from the outside, this is a cosy old inn with a charming basement bar which is owned and run by Stuart Galloway, assisted by his friendly staff. Together, they have created a warm relaxed atmosphere which makes the tavern a popular venue with visitors and locals alike. (The unusual name, incidentally, was given to the inn by Stuart who has a crooked arm himself).

The inn dates back to 1783 and it still has the original thick walls and low ceilings creating an olde worlde atmosphere enhanced by the open fire. From noon until 6pm, a wide range of tasty home cooked bar meals are available - wholesome traditional Scottish fare at value for money prices. In addition to the menu there's a regularly changing selection of blackboard specials. To accompany your meal, choose from the fine range of ales served here which always includes 2 real ales that are regularly changed.

Opening Hours: Mon-Thu: 11.00-24.00; Fri-Sat: 11.00-01.00; Sun: 12.30-24.00

Food: Available 12.00-18.00, daily

Credit Cards: Access, Mastercard, Visa & Switch

Entertainment: Large screen TV; Quiz night, Tuesdays

Local Places of Interest/Activities: golf, nearby; Ochil Hills to the east; Wallace Monument, 2 miles; Dunblane Cathedral, 3 miles; Stirling Castle, Chapel Royal, Church of the Holy Rude, Old Town Jail, all at Stirling, 4 miles; Blair Drummond Safari Park, 4 miles; Castle Campbell (NTS), 13 miles

98 Devon Park Inn

*27/29 Alexander
Street,
Devonside,
by Tillicoultry,
Clackmannanshire
FK13 6HR
Tel: 01259 751492*

Directions:

From Stirling take the
A91 west towards
Tillicoultry.   At
Tillicoultry, turn right
on A908 to Devonside
(0.5 miles)

The little village of
Devonside enjoys a
pleasant position beside the River Devon, with the Ochil Hills rising to the north.
Here you'll find the **Devon Park Inn**, built in the late 1800s in typical Scottish style
and with an attractive frontage - before you enter, turn and take a look at the spectacular mountain panorama filling the horizon. The inn is owned and run by the husband
and wife team of John and Elizabeth Grant, a warm and welcoming couple whose
friendly personalities have made the hostelry very popular with local people and visitors alike. They took over here in 1998 and have fallen in love with this scenic corner
of Clackmannanshire.

They offer their customers a wide choice of quality ales and ciders, and although
they do not serve food on a daily basis, they are happy to provide meals at weekends
for groups which have booked ahead. They specialise in family menus and the appetising food is freshly prepared and very reasonably priced. If you would like a meal at
other times, please ask and if the Grants can possibly, they surely will!

Opening Hours: Mon-Thu: 12.00-24.00;
Fri-Sat: 12.00-01.00; Sun: 12.30-24.00

Food: Sat-Sun: on request for groups

Credit Cards: Cash only

Entertainment: Pool; darts; karaoke, Fri-
Sat; quiz night, Tuesday

Local Places of Interest/Activities:
Riverside walks, nearby; Ochil Hills to the
north; Castle Campbell (NTS), 6 miles;
Wallace Monument, 8 miles; Stirling
Castle, Chapel Royal, Church of the Holy
Rude, Old Town Jail, all at Stirling, 10
miles; Dunblane Cathedral, 13 miles; Blair
Drummond Safari Park, 16 miles

Goblin Ha' Hotel 99

Main Street,
Gifford,
East Lothian
EH41 4QH
Tel: 01620 810244
Fax: 01620 810718

Directions:

Gifford is about 4½ miles south of Haddington, on the B6369 and B6355

Nestling at the foot of the Lammermuir Hills, the charming village of Gifford was mostly laid out in the 1700s when the Earl of Tweeddale began building a new residence, Yester House. The settlement of Bothans lay too close to the Earl's new home for his liking so all the inhabitants were relocated in the hamlet of Gifford. At the heart of the village stands the **Goblin Ha' Hotel**. It's unusual name goes back to the 14th century and the War of Independence. In 1311, the Castle of Yester was recaptured from the English and the Scots then demolished the keep, leaving the Ha' (Hall) intact. Later, when the site was being restored, the rubble from the keep was used to level off the site leaving the basement of the keep underground. This became known as the Goblin Ha'.

Since 1960, the hotel has been in the ownership of the Muir family who like to think that the atmosphere is exceptionally friendly, that the table consists of the best of food, well cooked, with home baking and their own garden produce being a speciality of the hotel. Guests have a choice of 7 rooms, six with full en suite and one with shower only, all having TV, tea/coffee making facilities and hair dryers. There's a large garden to the rear of the hotel which has a patio area, boule court and children's play area. Goblin Ha' is a delightful place to spend a quiet restful holiday. A 9-hole golf course and bowling club are within easy walking distance and there are many beautiful walks in the immediate area of the hotel. Although in the heart of the country, Goblin Ha' is only 20 miles from Edinburgh and 12 miles from Gullane and North Berwick which not only have good beaches but also probably the finest seaside golf courses on Britain's east coast.

Opening Hours: Every day, 12.00-14.00,18.00-21.00

Food: Available 12.00-14.00 & 18.00-21.00

Credit Cards: All major cards except Diners

Accommodation: 7 rooms, all en suite

Facilities: Beer Garden; children's play area

Entertainment: Occasional folk music & jazz nights

Local Places of Interest/Activities: Golf, bowling, walking, all nearby; Lennoxlove House, 4 miles; Lammermuir Hills to the south: City of Edinburgh, 20 miles

100 — Golfer's Rest

High Street, North Berwick,
East Lothian
EH39 4HD
Tel: 01620 892320
Fax: 01620 892641

Directions:

North Berwick is on the A168 coastal road, east of Edinburgh. The Golfer's Rest is on the main street of the town

North Berwick, which likes to describe itself as the "Biarritz of the North", is a popular family resort with safe, sandy beaches and a rather genteel atmosphere inherited from the mid-1800s when it was first developed as a holiday destination. **The Golfer's Rest** dates back to those days of Victorian prosperity. It's a handsome and sturdily built structure with an impressive red sandstone double frontage. Looking through the bow windows, customers can watch the boats bobbing in the nearby sea. The interior is very spacious indeed with high ceilings and large alcoves, creating a very relaxed and welcoming atmosphere.

Eric and Anne took over here in the summer of 2000 and they have made customers new and old feel that they are genuinely welcome. Food is available Mon-Sat lunchtime - simple and wholesome, and all home cooked. To accompany your meal, real ales are available along with all the familiar brands of beverages. Since Eric and Anne took over, the Golfer's Rest has become a lively place. There are quiz nights, live music evenings, and do feel free to go along and display your vocal skills on the karaoke nights!

Opening Hours: Sun-Wed: 11.00-23.00; Thu-Fri: 11.00-01.00; Sat: 11.00-24.00

Food: Mon-Sat lunchtimes 12.00-14.30

Credit Cards: Cash or cheque with card only

Entertainment: Free quiz nights; Prize karaoke nights; live music

Local Places of Interest/Activities: Dirleton Castle, 3 miles; Tantallon Castle, 4 miles; Museum of Flight, 6 miles; Gosford House, 10 miles; Myreton Motor Museum, 10 miles; John Muir Country Park, 12 miles. Boat trips to Bass Rock, 5 miles

Jameshaven Inn & Auldhouse Arms | 101

2/12 Langlands Road,
Auldhouse, East
Kilbride G75 9DW
Tel/Fax:
01355 231068

Directions:

From East Kilbride take the A726 towards Strathaven. At Torrance roundabout take right turn then straight on across two roundabouts. At the third turn left, then left at fork junction to Auldhouse Village (1 mile)

The Jameshaven Inn & Auldhouse Arms has a long history that stretches back to the late 1700s when it opened for business as an alehouse. In those days, cattle drovers still used the road through Auldhouse on their way to the more prosperous markets in the south. The Auldhouse Arms provided them with basic accommodation, food and drink. The inn has come up in the world since then although it has retained a wonderful olde-worlde atmosphere. Oak tables and chairs, open log fires, gleaming copperware and a fascinating array of old pictures, prints and photographs all add to the charm.

Your hosts, Diane and Archie Young, have run this welcoming old inn for more than 30 years. Archie was born in the area and has great knowledge of bygone days in East Kilbride, the surrounding countryside and local worthies. Diane is the chef for the Jameshaven restaurant where she creates outstanding meals from fresh Scottish produce, using local sources whenever possible. Good wines and real ales are available to complement your meal. Smoking is permitted in the public bar, but not in the restaurant. lounge or bedrooms. If you are planning to stay in the area, the inn has 5 traditional cottage style guest bedrooms, with en suite facilities (one has an adjoining private bathroom). The rooms have their own private entrance and have been recently refurbished to the highest standards, all having relaxing countryside views, for your enjoyment.

Opening Hours: 12.00-00.00

Food: Available from 18.00-22.00; lunches by request

Credit Cards: Access, Mastercharge, Visa & Switch

Accommodation: 5 rooms, 4 en suite

Facilities: Ample parking

Entertainment: Scottish folk music evening with live music

Local Places of Interest/Activities: Calderglen Country Park, 2 miles, Museum of Country Life , Hunter Museum, cinema,swimming, golf, ice skating and Shopping Mall, all within 3 miles.

102 The Lorne Taverna

17 Argyll Street, Dollar,
Clackmannanshire FK14 7AR
Tel: 01259 743423
Fax: 01259 743065

Directions:

From Stirling take the A91 west. Dollar is on the A91, about 11 miles west of Stirling. The Lorne Taverna stands just off the High Street

Beautifully located in a fold of the Ochil Hills, and set beside the River Devon, Dollar is perhaps best known for its famous Academy, a handsome building in the Classical style erected in 1820. It's estimated that the Academy's pupils and staff make up one third of the population of this attractive little town. Dollar can also boast the only Greek restaurant for miles around. **The Lorne Taverna** began life as an alehouse in the early 1800s but in recent years has established a reputation for fine home cooking, offering both Scottish and Greek dishes, including a vegetarian menu, prepared by chef Giorgios Patelaros and Gregorio Fikouras. Only the freshest local produce is used, with the taverna's own award-winning olive oil providing the secret ingredient. The bar stocks a large selection of beers, real ales, aperitifs and spirits from around the world with, naturally, wines from Greece taking pride of place.

The taverna also caters for weddings, christenings and other special occasions. And if you are planning to stay in this glorious part of the country, the inn has 4 guest bedrooms available all year round. With the Lorne Taverna as your base, you are well placed to explore the Dollar Glen, a spectacular ravine surmounted by Castle Campbell. It was once known as Castle Gloume, stands beside the Waters of Griff (Grief) in the Glen of Care from which the Burn of Sorrow runs to the town of Dollar (Dolour). Fortunately, the lovely scenery is much more inspiriting than the names!

Opening Hours: All day, every day

Food: Available Wed-Sun. 18.00-22.00

Credit Cards: All major cards except Amex or Diners

Accommodation: 4 standard rooms

Facilities: Parking

Entertainment: Pool table; - and the locals!

Local Places of Interest/Activities: golf, 1 mile; Dollar Glen & Castle Campbell (NTS), 1.5 miles; Gartmorn Dam Country Park, 6 miles; Wallace Monument, 12 miles; Stirling Castle, 14 miles; Loch Leven & Loch Leven Castle, 14 miles

Internet/Website:
e-mail: jim@lornetavern.co.uk

Lugton Inn Motel 103

16/18 Bridgend,
Dalkeith,
Midlothian
EH22 1JU
Tel: 0131 663 2115
Fax: 0131 6632135

Directions:
Dalkeith is on the A68, about 7 miles south-east of Edinburgh.

The oldest part of the **Lugton Inn Motel** dates back to 1847 but this small stone building has been extended over the years to provide comfortable and attractive accommodation. There are 6 guest bedrooms, all of them en suite, smartly furnished and decorated, and each equipped with TV and tea/coffee-making facilities. Guests also have the use of a spacious lounge/dining room with its own small bar. Food is available here from noon each day and the ever changing menu is supplemented by a further choice of half a dozen daily specials. The motel was acquired in the summer of 2000 by Dave and Annette Knox who made significant improvements to the interior and have introduced entertainment in the form of Quiz and Folk Music evenings.

Dalkeith is a busy little town with an unusually wide High Street. At the eastern end of the street are the gates of Dalkeith Country Park. This lovely wooded estate surrounds Dalkeith Palace, hereditary home of the Dukes of Buccleuch, a fine early-18th century mansion which can only be viewed from the outside. Its former chapel, built in 1843 and now the parish Church of St Mary, is open however and well worth visiting to see its exceptionally fine furnishings and the only water-powered Hamilton organ in Scotland!

Opening Hours: 11.00-24.00 every day

Food: Available from 12.00, all day

Credit Cards: Access, Mastercharge, Visa, Switch

Accommodation: 6 rooms, all en suite

Facilities: Parking

Entertainment: Quiz nights; folk music nights

Local Places of Interest/Activities: Golf, Dalkeith Country Park, both nearby; Scottish Mining Museum, 2 miles; Arniston House, 5 miles; City of Edinburgh, 7 miles

104 Masonic Arms

224 Glasgow Road,
Longcroft, by Bonnybridge,
Stirlingshire FK4 1QP
Tel: 01324 840236

Directions:

From the A80/M80 interchange, 9 miles south of Stirling, take the A830 east to Bonnybridge (3.5 miles). Longcroft is on the outskirts of Bonnybridge

Conveniently located a few minutes drive from the M80, the **Masonic Arms** is a hostelry with a very long history. Title deeds dated 1831 have survived but there was an inn here long before that, serving the drovers herding their cattle to the richer markets of the south. Today, the exterior of the Masonic Arms is rather unassuming but once you step inside you'll find attractively designed and decorated rooms which have all been recently upgraded. Customers will immediately appreciate the very relaxed and welcoming atmosphere. Mine host, Robert Heeps, who has been here for some 12 years, says that he tries to make his pub accessible to everyone, from students to sportsmen, from businessmen to old age pensioners. He certainly seems to have succeeded to judge by the Masonic Arms' wide range of customers.

The inn serves food every lunchtime and evening - appetising traditional Scottish fare at very sensible prices. All the leading brands of beverages are available as well as an outstanding choice of wines. For special events or parties, the inn has a function room, The Shedding Lounge, which can accommodate up to 70 guests.

Opening Hours: Mon-Thu: 11.00-23.00; Fri-Sat: 11.00-01.00; Sun: 12.30-23.00

Food: Available Mon-Fri: 12.00-14.30; 18.30-21.00; Sat-Sun: 12.00-14.30; 16.30-21.00

Credit Cards: Access, Visa, Switch

Facilities: Function suite; massive car park

Local Places of Interest/Activities: Rough Castle, 1.5 miles; Colzium House & Walled Garden, 6 miles; Stirling Castle, Chapel Royal, Old Town Jail, Church of the Holy Rude, all at Stirling, 9 miles

Oak Tree Inn 105

Main Street, Balmaha,
Loch Lomond G63 0JQ
Tel: 01360 870357
Fax: 01360 870350

Directions:

From the A811 about 20 miles north of Glasgow, turn left at Drymen on to the B837 which leads directly to Balmaha (5 miles)

Standing in the shade of a magnificent 500-year-old oak tree, the **Oak Tree Inn** provides a focal point in this peaceful village which enjoys panoramic scenic views across Loch Lomond. The inn is a striking building with an unusual history. In a remarkable architectural salvage operation, timbers and panelling were dismantled from a neighbouring country house dating from 1864, a local slate quarry was re-opened for this one building. The material was brought to the site by hand and painstakingly cut and constructed over a period of 12 months using traditional building methods to give the Oak Tree Inn its authentic rustic appeal. Similar care was taken over the interior with its extensive use of natural oak - note especially the bar area, constructed from a 300-year-old oak tree.

The attractive oak beamed dining room serves as a traditional tea room during the day, serving teas, coffees and light refreshments. In the evening, a full restaurant menu is available, offering traditional Scottish cuisine using only the finest and freshest local produce. Bar meals are also served all day in the bar area. With its relaxed friendly atmosphere, the Oak Tree Inn is a place where you will want to linger. Overnight guests can enjoy well-appointed, en suite accommodation with full facilities or, if preferred, there is equally comfortable bunk accommodation available. The surrounding area offers a wide range of activities for all the family - Forest Trail walks, coarse fishing and boating on the loch, golf and much, much more.

Opening Hours: 08.00-22.30 every day

Food: Breakfast, bar meals all day; tea room; full restaurant menu every evening

Credit Cards: All major cards except Amex & Diners

Accommodation: En suite rooms or bunk accommodation

Facilities: Beer Garden & patio overlooking Loch Lomond; disabled access & toilet; ample parking

Entertainment: Live bands Fri & Sat evenings

Local Places of Interest/Activities: Fishing & boating on Loch Lomond; West Highland Way passes nearby; Queen Elizabeth Forest Park, 5 miles

106   The Plough Tavern

Haddington,
East Lothian EH41 3DS
Tel: 01620 823326

Directions:
Haddington is just off the A1, about 18 miles east of Edinburgh. The Plough Tavern is on the main street

Located on the main street of this unspoilt market town, **The Plough Tavern** is a fine old Victorian building with lots of atmosphere and charm. It's owned and run by Mike Chitty, a hands-on landlord who takes great care of the premises - and of his customers. He offers them a good choice of home cooked traditional Scottish food, available every lunchtime and evening, along with a selection of daily specials. The evening menu changes regularly. In good weather you can enjoy your refreshments in the beer garden at the front and currently a conservatory is being completed which should be up and running by the time you read this. If you are planning to stay in Haddington, The Plough has 5 comfortable rooms, all en suite and provided with TV and tea/coffee-making facilities.

Haddington is a charming little town which boasts more than 200 listed buildings so there's plenty to interest the visitor. The most glorious of them is unquestionably St Mary's Church with its magnificent tombs, but the Jane Welsh Carlyle House, childhood home of the wife of Thomas Carlyle, is also well worth a visit. Mitchell's Close is a picturesque 17th century corner of the town where the houses with their crow-stepped roofs and cramped staircases have recently been restored. And just to the south of the town, Lennoxlove House, home of the Dukes of Hamilton, is an impressive sight with its 14th century tower house and the interior contains an outstanding collection of French furniture and porcelain.

Opening Hours: Sun-Thu: 11.00-23.00; Fri-Sat: 11.00-24.00

Food: Available 12.00-14.00, daily; 17.30-20.30 Sun-Thu; 18.00-21.00 Fri-Sat

Credit Cards: Access, Mastercharge, Visa & Switch

Accommodation: 5 rooms, all en suite

Facilities: Beer Garden; conservatory; parking

Local Places of Interest/Activities: St Mary's Church, Jane Welsh Carlyle House, Court House, all nearby; Lennoxlove House, 1.5 miles; Museum of Flight, 6 miles

Roslin Glen Hotel **107**

2 Penicuik Road, Roslin,
Midlothian EH25 9LH
Tel: 0131 440 2029
Fax: 0131 440 2229

Directions:

From the Edinburgh by-pass take the
A701 towards Penicuik & Peebles.
About 2.5 miles along this road, turn
left on the B7006 to Roslin (1.5 miles)

The quiet conservation village of Roslin is famed for its unique Rosslyn Chapel, a fantastic medley of pinnacles, towers, flying buttresses and gargoyles. The most astonishing work though is the Prentice Pillar which tradition asserts was crafted by an apprentice. When his master saw the finished work he murdered the lad in a fit of jealousy. Amongst the wealth of other stone carvings inside the chapel are allegorical figures such as the Seven Deadly Sins and carvings of plants from the New World which pre-date Columbus' arrival in America by more than a century. They tend to confirm the legend that the daring navigator Prince Henry of Orkney, grandfather of the founder of the chapel, did indeed set foot in America.

Only a short walk from the chapel, nestling at the foot of the Pentland Hills, sits the **Roslin Glen Hotel**, an impressive and spacious mid-Victorian building. It's run in a friendly and professional manner by Archie and Jenny Mears who are dedicated to making their visitors' stay comfortable and memorable. For formal or casual dining, the restaurant and lounge bar provide an imaginative menu using fresh, top quality ingredients prepared by experienced chefs. There are 7 guest bedrooms, all en suite and well equipped with telephone, television and tea/coffee making equipment. An apartment sleeping 4 is also available and this can be rented on a self-catering basis if required. The room prices include a full English or Scottish breakfast cooked to order and just the thing to set you up for a busy day. Roslin Glen Hotel is the ideal base for anyone visiting Edinburgh who also enjoys the tranquillity of the countryside - from the hotel's front door it's just seven miles to the city's Princes Street. Also nearby, as well as the famous chapel, are scenic walks through the glen beside the River Esk, a route that takes you past Rosslyn Castle, another local attraction.

Opening Hours: Bar: Sun-Thu: 11.00-23.00; Fri-Sat: 11.00-24.00

Food: 12.00-14.00; 18.00-21.00

Credit Cards: Amex; Mastercharge; Visa; Switch

Accommodation: 7 rooms, all en suite; 1 apartment sleeping 4 & also available as self-catering

Facilities: Parking

Local Places of Interest/Activities:
Rosslyn Chapel nearby; golf, 2 miles; Dalkeith Country Park, 6 miles; City of Edinburgh, 7 miles

Internet/Website:
e-mail: roslinglenhotel@bigfoot.com
website: www.roslinhotel.co.uk

108　The Royal Hotel

High Street, Bonnybridge,
Stirlingshire FK4 1DA
Tel: 01324 812324
Fax: 01324 811433

Directions:

From the A80/M80 junction about 8 miles south of Stirling, take the A803 west to Bonnybridge (3 miles). The Royal Hotel is located on the town's main street (the A803)

Located in the heart of this ancient settlement which was an important garrison in Roman times, **The Royal Hotel**

is an imposing 3-storey building with walls painted a cheerful custardy-yellow. Built in 1787, it stands boldly at the top of the town, dominating the smaller buildings around. The hotel is owned and run by the husband and wife team of Brendan and May Devaney. Brendan hails from Ireland; May is a local girl. They bought the Royal in 1998 and their outgoing personalities have made it a lively place which attracts locals and visitors alike. The hotel's decor was a tad dowdy when they took over but they've put that right with a comprehensive refurbishment worthy of being featured on one of BBC-TV's Changing Rooms programmes.

Another good reason for the Royal's popularity is the excellent food on offer. Everything is home cooked, based on fresh, locally-sourced ingredients, the appetising dishes served in generous portions and at remarkable value for money prices - at the time of writing, main courses start at £3.95.

Bonnybridge provides a perfect base for exploring southern Scotland. It stands almost halfway between Edinburgh and Glasgow, and good roads lead north to Stirling and the Fair City of Perth. If you want to take advantage of this convenient location, The Royal Hotel offers 7 comfortable and attractive guest bedrooms, all of them en suite and equipped with TV and tea/coffee-making facilities.

Opening Hours: Mon-Thu + Sun: 11.00-00.00; Fri-Sat: 11.00-01.00

Food: Wed-Sat: 12.00-14.30, 17.00-21.00; Sun: 14.00-20.00

Credit Cards: Access, Delta, Visa, Switch

Accommodation: 7 rooms - en suite rooms are due for completion in the near future

Facilities: Restaurant; lounge bar; public bar

Local Places of Interest/Activities: Rough Castle, nearby; Callendar Park, 5 miles; The Pineapple (NTS), 9 miles; Stirling Castle, Church of the Holy Rude, Old Town Jail, all at Stirling, 10 miles

Tantallon Inn

Marine Parade,
North Berwick,
East Lothian EH39 4LD
Tel: 01620 892238
Fax: 01620 895313

Directions:

North Berwick is on the A198 coastal road, east of Edinburgh. In the town itself, make for the sea front

The only beach front hotel in North Berwick is the **Tantallon Inn**, a sturdy Victorian building of 1860 whose frontage provides stunning views of the ancient Bass Rock with its world-famous gannet colony. Colin and Karen Chalmers bought the hotel in 1994 and have built up an enviable reputation for their freshly prepared and exquisitely cooked local produce. Colin has been a top class chef for almost three decades and has had the honour and experience of working with a Culinary Olympics Gold Medal Chef. His outstanding cuisine is served in the attractive wood-panelled restaurant which is candlelit in the evenings. Karen has some 20 years experience in hotel management and "front-of-house" organisation, ensuring that guests receive a warm welcome and courteous, efficient service.

The hotel lounge bar, with its open log fire and relaxed atmosphere, provides an inviting resting place at the end of a tiring day and the hotel's 4 guest bedrooms, 3 of them en suite, complete the sense of peace and tranquillity. The Tantallon enjoys an ideal location. Step from the hotel in one direction and you are on the beach; in another on the first tee of the Glen Golf Course; and finally step out onto two 18-hole putting greens, two petanque pitches and six of the best blaes tennis courts in Scotland. Boat trips, including circuits of the famed Bass Rock, operate from the nearby harbour and the town itself boasts a new indoor heated swimming pool and sports centre.

Opening Hours: Tue-Sun: 12.00-14.00, 18.00-21.00

Food: Available lunchtimes Tue-Sun: 12.00-14.00; Evenings Tue-Sat: 18.00-21.00; Sun: 18.00-20.30

Credit Cards: All major cards except Amex & Diners

Accommodation: 4 rooms (3 en suite)

Facilities: Beachside location; parking

Local Places of Interest/Activities: Dirleton Castle, 3 miles; Tantallon Castle, 4 miles; Museum of Flight, 6 miles; Gosford House, 10 miles; Myreton Motor Museum, 10 miles; John Muir Country Park, 12 miles. Boat trips to Bass Rock, 5 miles

110   Tyneside Tavern

10 Poldrate,
Haddington,
East Lothian EH41 4DA
Tel: 01620 822221
Fax: 01620 825877

Directions

Haddington is just off the A1, about 18 miles east of Edinburgh. The Tyneside Tavern is 400 yards from the High Street

Located close to the historic St Mary's Church and the scenic Riverside Walk beside the Tyne, the **Tyneside Tavern** is a traditional Scottish hostelry where a warm welcome awaits all. The tavern has been offering hospitality since it was first built in 1819 as an alehouse and there's a fascinating list of all the landlords since then displayed near the entrance. Mine hosts today are Ann and Paul Kinnoch, an energetic and enthusiastic couple whose motto is "Tell us what you want. If we can do it: NO PROBLEM!" This customer-friendly inn is open all day, every day, for ales (including real ales), wines, spirits, tea and coffee, and on Friday and Saturday evenings doesn't close until a quarter to one in the morning. The Kinnochs pride themselves on providing good, wholesome food at reasonable prices. Food is available every lunchtime and evening with a menu that offers traditional pub fare along with vegetarian options, daily specials and a children's menu. Weather permitting, enjoy your meal in the patio garden.

If you want to watch your favourite sports programme on Sky TV, there are 6 large screens available. No problem. The pub also hosts regular promotions and quiz nights, as well as special promotions on various drinks. And if you are planning your own celebration, the Kinnochs can provide an Outside Bar Service. No problem at all!

Opening Hours: Mon-Wed: 11.00-23.00; Thu: 11.00-12.00; Fri-Sat: 11.00-24.45; Sun: 12.30-24.00

Food: Mon-Sat: 12.00-14.00; 17.00-20.00. Sun: 12.30-14.30; 17.00-20.00

Credit Cards: Switch, Solo, Visa

Facilities: Patio Garden; wheelchair access; ample parking nearby

Entertainment: Sky TV; Regular promotions

Local Places of Interest/Activities: St Mary's Church, Jane Welsh Carlyle House and Poldrate Mill are all nearby; Lennoxlove House, 1.5 miles; Museum of Flight, 6 miles

Waterside Bistro & Restaurant | 111

1-5 Waterside, Nungate,
Haddington,
East Lothian EH41 4BE
Tel: 01620 825674
Fax: 01620 825607

Directions:

Haddington is just off the A1, about 18 miles east of Edinburgh. The Waterside Bistro & Restaurant stands beside the bridge in the High Street

Occupying a lovely position near the bridge is the **Waterside Bistro & Restaurant**. It was originally the Weir House and along with 5 adjacent cottages has been thoughtfully refurbished to retain its olde worlde charm, complete with some attractive antique furnishings. The proprietor, Jim Findlay, offers his customers excellent food in the two restaurants and in good weather you can also eat at the tables on the riverside terrace. There's an extensive choice that ranges from an à la carte menu in the silver service restaurant to a selection of appetising bar meals and snacks. If you're planning to stay in this attractive old town, Jim has 7 guest bedrooms, all en suite and all provided with TV and tea/coffee making facilities. Recently converted, the rooms are set around a picturesque courtyard. Jim is a hospitable host and his customer care even extends to running a courtesy bus which will pick you up and drop you off without charge.

Haddington itself, with its more than 200 listed buildings, is well worth exploring. The classical Court House, designed by William Burn, dominates Court Street and close by is the Jane Welsh Carlyle House, childhood home of the girl who later married Thomas Carlyle. Her sudden death in 1866 left Carlyle grief-stricken. His touching words mourning the loss of "the light of his life" can be seen on a plain slab in the choir of St Mary's Church, the largest parish church in Scotland. "The Lamp of Lothian" is notable for the sumptuous alabaster tombs in the Lauderdale Aisle and also for its concerts and art exhibitions of international standard. It also provides an amenity unusual in ecclesiastical buildings - an excellent tea-room.

Opening Hours: Bistro, Mon-Fri: 11.30-14.00; Sat-Sun: 11.30-14.30. Restaurant, Mon-Sat: 12.00-14.00; Sun: 12.30-14.30

Food: A la carte restaurant and bar meals

Credit Cards: All major cards accepted

Accommodation: 7 rooms, all en suite

Facilities: Riverside terrace; parking

Entertainment: Occasional live jazz

Local Places of Interest/Activities: St Mary's Church, Jane Welsh Carlyle House, Court House, all nearby; Lennoxlove House, 1.5 miles; Museum of Flight, 6 miles

112 Wee Bush Inn

Main Street,
Carnwath,
Lanarkshire
ML11 8HH
Tel: 01555 840587
Fax: 01555 841233

Directions:

Carnwath is 26 miles
SW of Edinburgh, on
the A70/A721

The Wee Bush Inn has the unique distinction of being the only thatched pub in Scotland. This charming traditional inn dates back to 1750 and it was still a relatively new hostelry when one of its regular patrons was Scotland's national poet, Robert Burns, a man with a knack for finding excellent taverns. In fact, the inn takes its name from one of his lines, "Better a Wee Bush than Nae Bield (shelter)". The inn is owned and run by Helen C. Wilson who can often be seen in her beloved 1971 Morris Minor pickup, a splendid vintage vehicle which has often made its way to the Winner's Circle at Morris Minor Owners' Club rallies.

Helen has been here since 1985 and, together with her daughter, offers customers a good choice of appetising home cooked food every lunchtime and evening. It's all freshly prepared from prime local produce - and the sweets are to die for! Look out too for the Wee Bush's own label whisky and own label chocolate.

Helen and her daughter have won a Conservation Award for their loving restoration of the old inn. It's an absolute delight, with its stone floors and small-paned windows. Although only 26 miles from Edinburgh, the Wee Bush Inn has the authentic atmosphere of a genuine country pub and is a hostelry that should definitely not to be missed.

Opening Hours: Mon-Fri: 11.00-15.00, 18.00-23.00; Sat: 11.00-15.00, 17.00-23.45; Sun: 12.30-15.00, 17.00-23.00

Food: Mon-Sat: 12.00-15.00 & 18.00-21.00. Sun: 12.30-15.00 & 18.00-21.00

Credit Cards: Access, Mastercard, Visa, Switch

Local Places of Interest/Activities: Walking in the Pentland Hills to the northeast; New Lanark Mills, 7 miles; Six (!) Museums at Biggar, 9 miles;

Internet/Website:
website: www.weebush.co
e-mail: mail@weebush.com

West Barns Inn

113

5 Duke Street, West Barns,
Dunbar,
East Lothian EH42 1UR
Tel: 01368 862314

Directions:

From the A1, about 24 miles east of Edinburgh, turn left on the A1057 towards Dunbar. The village of West Barns is about 1 mile along this road

The original **West Barns Inn** was built in 1836 and that old structure still stands although this charming old hostelry has been extended over the years and now stretches along the street. The very spacious interior is decorated with a maritime theme, appropriately enough since Bellhaven Bay is just yards away and landlord Tug Wilson is a seafarer who spent many years in the Royal Navy. Good food is a priority here and that's the responsibility of Tug's wife, Fred, whose appetising menu of freshly prepared home cooking is based on local produce. A speciality is smoked trout - the fish come the nearby river and the village also boasts its own seafood shop, but there's also a good choice of meat and vegetarian dishes. At lunchtimes, a selection of snacks and light meals is available. Complement your meal with a selection from the wine list or perhaps sample the local ale from Bellhaven brewery.

The inn has a game room with darts and pool table and on Sunday evenings the bar resounds to the strains of Scottish country music. There are regular karaoke evenings and occasionally other kinds of live music. For special occasions or celebrations a function room is available and in good weather customers can take advantage of the peaceful beer garden at the rear.

A short walk from West Barns Inn brings you to the John Muir Country Park, located on a beautiful stretch of coastline. John Muir was born at nearby Dunbar in 1838 and his family emigrated to America when he was 11 years old. He was later instrumental in the establishment of the Yosemite National Park, the first national park in the United States.

Opening Hours: Mon-Wed 11.00-23.00; Thu 11.00-24.00; Fri - Sat 11.00-01.00; Sun 12.30 - 24.00

Food: Available daily (except Wednesday) from 12.00-15.00; 18.00-21.00

Credit Cards: Access, Mastercharge, Visa

Facilities: Beer garden; function room; ample parking

Entertainment: Games room with pool and darts; Scottish country music, Sunday evenings; karaoke evenings; live music every Sat night

Local Places of Interest/Activities: John Muir Country Park, 1 mile; Preston Mill and Phantassie Doo'cot, East Linton, 5 miles; Tantallon Castle, 12 miles

The Hidden Inns of Central and Southern Scotland

5 Argyll and Bute

PLACES OF INTEREST:

Cairndow 118
Campbeltown 118
Carsaig 119
Craignure 119
Dervaig 119
Dunoon 120
Fionnphort 121
Glenbarr 121
Inveraray 121
Kilmartin 122

Kilmun 122
Lerags 122
Lochgoilhead 122
Oban 123
Port Appin 124
Rest and Be Thankful 124
Rothesay 124
Tarbert 125
Tobermory 125

PUBS AND INNS:

Ardbrecknish House, South Lochaweside, nr Dalmally 126

Ardfillayne Country House Hotel, West Bay, nr Dunoon 127

The Auld Hoose Restaurant, Dunoon 128

The Boat, Rothesay 129

Cairnbaan Hotel, Cairnbaan, by Lochgilphead 130

Colintraive Hotel, Colintraive 131

The Cot House Hotel, Sandbank, nr Dunoon 132

Cuilfail Hotel, Kilmelford 133

Furnace Inn, Furnace 134

The Horseshoe Inn, Bridgend, nr Lochgilphead 135

Kilmartin Hotel, Kilmartin, nr Lochgilphead 136

The Kilmun House Hotel, Kilmun, nr Dunoon 137

Kingarth Hotel, Kingarth, Isle of Bute 138

Knipoch Hotel, Knipoch, by Oban 139

The Lochnell Arms Hotel, North Connel 140

The Lorne, Ardrishaig 141

The Oyster Inn, Connel, nr Oban 142

The Regent Hotel, Rothesay 143

St Catherine's Old Ferry Inn, St Catherine's, nr Cairndow 144

The Stagecoach Inn, Cairndow 145

Tayvallich Inn, Tayvallich 146

The Hidden Inns of Central and Southern Scotland

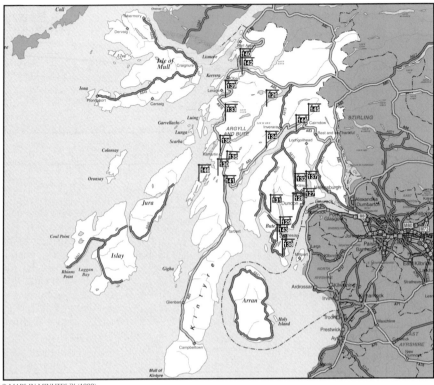

© MAPS IN MINUTES ™ (1999)

126 Ardbrecknish House, South Lochaweside, nr Dalmally

127 Ardfillayne Country House Hotel, West Bay, nr Dunoon

128 The Auld Hoose Restaurant, Dunoon

129 The Boat, Rothesay

130 Cairnbaan Hotel, Cairnbaan, by Lochgilphead

131 Colintraive Hotel, Colintraive

132 The Cot House Hotel, Sandbank, nr Dunoon

133 Cuilfail Hotel, Kilmelford

134 Furnace Inn, Furnace

135 The Horseshoe Inn, Bridgend, nr Lochgilphead

136 Kilmartin Hotel, Kilmartin, nr Lochgilphead

137 The Kilmun House Hotel, Kilmun, nr Dunoon

138 Kingarth Hotel, Kingarth, Isle of Bute

139 Knipoch Hotel, Knipoch, by Oban

140 The Lochnell Arms Hotel, North Connel

141 The Lorne, Ardrishaig

142 The Oyster Inn, Connel, nr Oban

143 The Regent Hotel, Rothesay

144 St Catherine's Old Ferry Inn, St Catherine's, nr Cairndow

145 The Stagecoach Inn, Cairndow

146 Tayvallich Inn, Tayvallich

Please note all cross references refer to page numbers

Argyll and Bute

This huge area has a smaller population than the City of York. It attracts large numbers of visitors in the summer months, but apart from a few "honey-pot" centres Argyll is wonderfully empty and peaceful. Oban is the undisputed holiday centre, with generally excellent road and rail communications and a generous choice of regular car and passenger ferries serving the main islands of the Inner Hebrides, as well as seasonal day trips to many of the smaller islands. The town stands at the heart of what was the 5th century Kingdom of Lorn, supposedly founded by the legendary Irish Celt of that name. Lorn later formed part of the great early Kingdom of Dalriada, whose kings were crowned at Dunstaffnage Castle, just north of Oban, on the hallowed "Stone of Destiny", later known as the Stone of Scone.

The area's main attraction, of course, is its magnificent coastal and mountain scenery, but the formidable Duart Castle on the Isle of Mull should be on every visitor's itinerary. For 10 months of the year, from September until June, the 3,000 residents of Mull virtually have its 370 square miles to themselves - a spectacular landscape of moorland dominated by the massive bulk of **Ben More** (3,170 feet), with a west coast gouged by two deep sea-lochs, and an east coast unusually well-wooded for the Hebrides. During July and August it's quite a different story, as visitors flock to this unspoilt island. Its charming "capital", the little port of Tobermory, becomes crowded and the narrow roads congested. But as always in the Highlands, one only has to travel a mile or so from the popular venues to find perfect peace and quiet. Getting away from the pestilent swarms of summer midges may not be quite so easy.

Some 200 years ago there were more than three times as many permanent residents on the island, but the infamous Highland Clearances of the early 19th century saw a constant stream of the destitute and dispossessed pass through Tobermory, boarding ships which would take them to an uncertain future in Glasgow or on the distant shores of America, Canada, and Australia. The island is still littered with the ruins of the crofts from which these refugees were driven or, quite often, even smoked out.

Today Mull is well-served by vehicle and passenger ferries from Oban, either by the 40-minute crossing to Craignure on the southeastern tip of the island, or to Tobermory in the northeast.

The holy island of Iona has a very special mystical charm, and anyone with an interest in Scotland's industrial heritage will want to visit the Bonawe Iron Furnace near Taynuilt.

Bounded by Loch Long and Loch Fyne, the Cowal Peninsula is like a three-taloned claw with the Isle of Bute clutched in its grip. (The name Cowal is believed to come from an old Norse word meaning a forked piece of land.) In this comparatively small area there's a wide variety of scenery, from the extensive forests smothering the Highland peaks of the north to the low-lying coastline of the southwest. Apart from the area around Dunoon, where two-third's of the peninsula's 16,500 population live, Cowal is sparsely populated with an abundance of wildlife untroubled by too much human disturbance. The area is particularly popular with bird-watchers. In addition to the prolific variety of indigenous species, including hawks, buzzards and eagles, there are even more exotic birds to be seen at the Cowal Bird Garden, near Dunoon.

118

A short ferry crossing from Colintraive will take you to the Island of Bute, an island which displays something of a split personality. Its sheltered east coast has been a popular holiday venue for Clydesiders since Victorian times; the west coast, however, never more than five miles distant, is sparsely populated, its most northerly minor road coming to a halt some eight miles short of the northern tip of the island. Fortunately there's no difficulty in getting to the mile-long sands of Ettrick Bay, regarded by many as the most beautiful place on the island.

PLACES OF INTEREST

CAIRNDOW

Standing at the head of Loch Fyne, Cairndow on the Cowal Peninsula is a small village with a curiously shaped white-washed church. Built in 1816, the church is hexagonal in shape with Gothic-style windows in pairs and a tower crowned by an elaborately carved parapet and four turrets. Just behind the village, **Ardkinglas Woodland Garden** boasts the tallest trees in Britain - conifers more than 200 feet high, and hundreds of other attractive trees and shrubs, including many exotic rhododendrons. Dominating a promontory overlooking Loch Fyne, **Castle Lachlan** was first mentioned in a charter of 1314 and was the ancient home of the MacLachlan of MacLachlan. Today the clan Chief, Madam Maclachlan of Maclachlan, lives in a nearby 18th century castle/mansion and if you are a member of the MacLachlan clan you are welcome to visit by appointment.

CAMPBELTOWN

Campbeltown enjoys a very scenic position at the head of a deep bay sheltered by Davaar Island and surrounded by hills. In its 19th century heyday, when Campbeltown boasted a large fishing fleet and a thriving shipbuilding industry, it was said that there were 34 distilleries and almost as many churches in the town. A glance at the skyline here shows that most of the churches seem to have survived, although not necessarily for religious purposes. The former Longrow Church, for example, is now the **Campbeltown Heritage Centre** - where the altar once stood there's now a beautifully crafted wooden skiff constructed in 1906. There are displays on the area's whisky industry, and exhibits relating to the 6th century St Kieran, the "Apostle of Kintyre". Kieran lived in a nearby cave which can still be visited at low

tide. The saint believed in self-abnegation of an extreme kind. His food consisted of three equal parts of bread, herbs and sand; he heaped his body with heavy chains, and slept in the open air with a flat stone for his pillow. One is not surprised to learn that, after sleeping outside during a snowfall, St Kieran died of jaundice at the age of 33.

Of Campbeltown's numerous distilleries which, it was claimed, produced such a powerful aroma that boats could find their way through thick fog to the harbour by following its bouquet, only two remain: Glen Scotia and Springback. They produce a malt which is quite distinctive from those made at nearby Islay or at any other of the Highland and Lowland distilleries. The family-owned **Springback Distillery** has tours by appointment.

The most striking feature of the town is the **Campbeltown Cross** overlooking the harbour. The 15th century cross is carved with highly intricate ornamentation of biblical figures and Celtic designs.

A popular outing from Campbeltown is to **Davaar Island**, which at low tide is linked to the mainland by a mile long causeway. The uninhabited island is used for grazing (so no dogs are allowed), and its main attraction is a cave in which a wall painting of the Crucifixion mysteriously appeared in 1887. Years later, in 1934, a local artist, Archibald MacKinnon, admitted that the painting was his work, and in the following year, at the age of 85, he returned to renovate it.

Ten miles south of Campbeltown, **Keil**, just to the west of Southend, is best known as the spot where St Columba first landed in Scotland, in AD 563. It's claimed that two footprints carved into a rock mark his first steps ashore, and that the ruined medieval chapel stands on the site of the one he founded here.

Beyond Keil, a minor road leads to the most southwesterly point of the peninsula, the **Mull of Kintyre**. The road ends a mile short of the lighthouse of 1788 which stands 300 feet above sea level, exposed to the full force of Atlantic gales. It's a bleak, wild spot, but on a clear day worth the trek for the views across to Ireland, just 12 miles away.

CARSAIG

Carsaig is a small village noted for its scenic setting, picturesque old stone pier, and the **Carsaig Arches**, dramatic columns of basalt some 750 feet high which have been sculpted by the sea into fantastic caves and arches. On the A849 southwestwards, you pass the **Angora Rabbit Farm** (seasonal) where children can stroke these appealing floppy-eared creatures and watch their fur being clipped and then spun.

CRAIGNURE

As one approaches Craignure on the east coast of Mull on the ferry from Oban, the great fortress on *dubh ard*, the "black height", becomes ever more imposing. **Duart Castle**, with its huge curtain wall 30 feet high and 10 feet thick, was built in the 13th century by the Macleans of Duart to protect them from their inveterate enemies, the Campbells. A century later, around 1360, they added the massive Keep that still stands today.

Like most of the clans at that time, the Macleans were a pretty blood-thirsty bunch, but the behaviour of one of their early 16th century chiefs appalled even his contemporaries. Lachlan Maclean had taken as his second wife Catherine, sister of the powerful Earl of Argyll. When Catherine failed to produce an heir, Lachlan decided to dispose of her. One night, he bound her, took her to a rock in the Sound of Mull which becomes submerged at high water, and abandoned her there. The next day, he informed her brother of Catherine's death by drowning. In fact, she had been rescued by fishermen and taken to the Earl's castle at Inverary. A few days later the grieving Lachlan arrived at the castle with his "late" wife's coffin and was ushered into the Great Hall to find Catherine sitting at the head of the table. Throughout the meal that followed no one made mention of her amazing resurrection, but later that year, 1523, Catherine's family had their revenge. Lachlan was visiting Edinburgh when he was surprised by her uncle, the Thane of Cawdor, and stabbed to death in his bed.

At low water the skerry on which Catherine was marooned, now known as **The Lady Rock**, can be clearly seen from the Sea Room at Duart Castle. The splendid vista takes in Lismore lighthouse, the town of Oban and, on a clear day, the lumpy profile of Ben Nevis, some 30 miles distant.

In the Macleans' long connection with the castle there is a huge gap of more than 200 years. In 1691, Duart was sacked by their relentless enemies, the Campbells; after the Battle of Culloden the Maclean estates were confiscated by the Crown and the castle was allowed to become increasingly dilapidated. Then in 1911, Sir Fitzroy Maclean, 10th Baronet and 26th Chief of the Clan Maclean, was able to buy Duart and begin the daunting work of restoration. To his eternal credit Sir Fitzroy disdained any fake medieval additions - none of the extraneous castellations and pepper-pot turrets favoured by most Victorian and Edwardian restorers. When he died here at the age of 101 in 1936, he left behind a castle that was faithful in essentials to the uncompromising spirit of his forefathers who had laid its foundations some 700 years earlier.

Craignure village itself offers a number of guest-houses, an inn, and a part-time Tourist Information Centre, but perhaps its most popular attraction is the **Mull and West Highland Railway**, a miniature-gauge line which runs southwards for a couple of miles to **Duart Bay** and **Torosay Castle**. The ancestral home of the Guthrie family, Torosay Castle is an extravagant 19th century mansion, a full-blooded example of the Scottish Baronial style of architecture. The opulent Edwardian interior contains an interesting collection of family portraits by artists such as Sargent and de Laszlo, and wildlife paintings by Landseer, Thorburn and Peter Scott. Even more impressive are the magnificent terraced gardens, which include a Japanese garden area and an avenue lined with 19 elegant life-size statues by the 18th century Venetian sculptor, Antonio Bonazza.

DERVAIG

From Tobermory on the Isle of Mull, the B8073 to Dervaig follows a tortuously twisting route through dramatic scenery - one of the more

120

demanding stretches of the annual round-the-island **Mull Rally** held in October.

Nestling at the head of Loch a'Chumhainn, Dervaig itself is a pretty village of white-washed houses set in pairs along the main road. It is perhaps best known for being the home of the **Mull Little Theatre**. Housed in a former cow byre, this is the smallest professional theatre in Britain with just 43 seats for the audience. Each season, nevertheless, it stages a varied programme of plays, some of which have to be adapted for the small number of resident actors.

About a mile south of Dervaig, **The Old Byre Heritage Centre**, housed in a lovely old building of variously-coloured stone, has become an essential stop on any visitor's tour of the island. The Centre explores the history of the island's inhabitants and dwellings, from the first settlers to the present day, with the help of over 25 specially created models. These striking models also feature in a 30-minute film presentation, "The Story of Mull and Iona", with a commentary accompanied by specially composed music played on the Clarsach, or Celtic harp.

Five miles west of Dervaig, still on the B8073, the tiny village of **Calgary** has one of the best sandy beaches on the island and enjoys enchanting views across to Coll and Tiree. Calgary has been known as an ideal holiday spot for generations, and one of its earliest visitors was a certain J. F. McLeod. Later, as a Colonel in Canada's North West Mounted Police, he founded what later became the capital of the province of Alberta and christened the new settlement with the name of this remote Scottish village. Twenty miles further along this road, just after it joins the B8035 at Gruline, another famous founder is commemorated at the **Macquarie Mausoleum** (National Trust Scotland). This is the burial place of Lachlan Macquarie, the "Father of Australia", who served as Governor of New South Wales for 12 years from 1809 when he was appointed to succeed the highly unpopular William Bligh, former captain of *HMS Bounty*. Macquarie's simple tomb looks across Loch na Keal to the island of Ulva where he was born in 1761.

Travelling southwestwards along the B8035, there is a spectacularly scenic drive as the road runs between the edge of the loch on one side, and mighty **Ben More** (3,170 feet), an extinct volcano, rises in terraced slopes on the other. Then, as the road swings south, it passes beneath the formidable, overhanging **Gribun Rocks**. Some years ago one of these rocks tumbled down the hillside and smashed through the hamlet of Gribun, demolishing one of the houses. The boulder is still there.

After another eight miles or so, the B8035 joins the A849. Turn right here, and you now enter the **Ross of Mull**, a 20-mile narrow, rocky promontory.

DUNOON

A popular resort in the 19th century for Glaswegians (it was, and still is, linked to Clydeside by a regular ferry), Dunoon on the Cowal Peninsula is by far the largest town in Argyll, with some 13,000 inhabitants. In the years following the Second World War, the town benefited greatly from the establishment of a US nuclear submarine base on nearby Holy Loch, and later suffered badly from the economic effects of the base's closure in 1992. But Dunoon is once again a lively resort, well-known for the **Cowal Highland Games**, Scotland's largest, which take place on the last Friday and Saturday of August and completely take over the town. Upwards of 150 bands and more than 2,000 pipers and drummers take part, and some 40,000 visitors come to watch the spectacle.

On Castle Hill are some sparse remains of the 12th century **Dunoon Castle**, notorious as the setting for a grisly massacre in 1646 when the Marquis of Argyll had scores of his Lamont prisoners hanged from "a lively, fresh-growing ash tree" and their bodies tossed into a shallow communal grave. The grave was rediscovered in the 19th century during construction of a new road; a memorial now marks the site. Forty years after that massacre, the castle was burnt down and remained derelict until 1822 when James Ewing, Provost of Glasgow, cannibalised its stone to build **Castle House**, a castellated "marine villa" which is currently used as council offices.

At the foot of Castle Hill is an appealing **Statue of Mary Campbell**, the Dunoon-born lass who became one of Robert Burns' many lovers. It was an intense affair and, despite being already married, Burns became engaged to Mary. At that time he was obsessed with the idea of emigrating to the West Indies; poems such as *Will you go to the Indies, my Mary?* make it clear that the poet's then-pregnant wife was not his preferred partner in the enterprise. Mary died at the age of 22, officially of a fever, but there has been persistent speculation that she died giving birth to a stillborn baby.

Dunoon Grammar School merits a special mention since it is second only to Eton in the number of its former pupils who have become Members of Parliament, among them Ken Livingstone, Virginia Bottomley, Brian Wilson and the late leader of the Labour Party, John Smith.

Less than a mile to the north of the town, on the A885, the **Cowal Bird Garden** makes an ideal venue for a family outing. Set in some 10 acres of oak and birch woods, this award-winning attraction is home to a fascinating variety of exotic birds, among them macaws and parrots who, if they're feeling like it, may well croak back a "Hello!" in response to yours; brightly-hued budgerigars; kakarikis from Australia, and many other species.

FIONNPHORT

Pronounced "Finnyfort", Fionnphort on the Isle of Mull is busy during the summer with ferries plying the one-mile crossing to the pilgrim island of Iona, or the 20-mile round trip to the Isle of Staffa to see the celebrated **Fingal's Cave**. In the village itself, the **St Columba Centre** has a small museum telling the story of the saint's life with the help of audio-visual effects and original artefacts. Opened in 1997 to celebrate the 1,400th anniversary of his death, the centre is open daily throughout the year. A mile or so south of Fionnphort there is a superb beach at **Fidden**, looking across to the Isle of Erraid where Robert Louis Stevenson stayed when he was writing *Kidnapped*. (He even had the hero of the book, David Balfour, shipwrecked here.)

GLENBARR

From Tarbert, the A83 skirts the rugged coastline, providing some excellent views of the islands of Jura and Islay, and if you are lucky, sightings of Atlantic grey seals, Britain's largest wild animals, draped across the offshore rocks. There are no settlements of any size along this route until you come to Glenbarr, which has been described as "the most pleasing village of south Kintyre".

Visitors to Scotland are understandably fascinated by the clan system, and at **Glenbarr Abbey** they can enjoy a privileged insight into this unique element of Scottish

121

society, as notable for its ferocious loyalties as for its sometimes barbarous feuds. The family seat of the Macalisters of Glenbarr, Glenbarr Abbey was built in the late 18th century and then greatly enlarged around 1815 with the addition of a striking west wing in the Gothic Revival style.

INVERARAY

A striking example of a planned "new town", Inveraray was built in the mid-1700s by the 3rd Duke of Argyll, chief of the powerful Clan Campbell. He demolished the old settlement to build his grand new Castle and rehoused the villagers in the attractive Georgian houses lining Main Street. The Duke also provided them with an elegant neo-classical church, **All Saints**, which was originally divided into two parts: one for services in English, the other for Gaelic speakers. A later addition, erected as a memorial to Campbells who fell in the First World War, is the free-standing **Bell Tower**, equipped with 10 bells which are reputedly the second heaviest in the world. During the summer season the tower is open to visitors and there are splendid panoramic views from the top.

One of the most popular attractions in the area is **Inveraray Jail**, yet another of the 3rd Duke's benefactions to the town. The stately Georgian courthouse and the bleak prison cells were last used in the 1930s and have since been converted into an award-winning and imaginative museum where costumed actors re-create the horrors of prison life in the past. Visitors can also seat themselves in the semi-circular courtroom and listen to excerpts from real-life trials that took place here.

A few minutes' walk from the Jail stands the grand neo-Gothic **Inveraray Castle**, still the family home of the Duke of Argyll whose ancestor, the 3rd Duke, began building it in 1746. Despite two major fires, in 1877 and 1975, the most important treasures survived and include portraits by Gainsborough, Ramsay and Raeburn, superb furniture, and a mind-boggling array of weaponry which includes the dirk, or traditional Highland dagger, used by Rob Roy. Outside, the grounds are extensive with many pretty walks, some by waterfalls on the River Aray, and the old stables now house the **Combined Operations Museum** which recalls the period leading up to the D-Day landings when some quarter of a million Allied soldiers were trained in amphibious warfare on Loch Fyne.

KILMARTIN

About 27 miles south of Oban, on the A816, **Carnasserie Castle** (Historic Scotland) is an outstanding example of a 16th century fortified house. Although the castle was sacked during the Monmouth rebellion of 1685, enough remains to give a good idea of what the house was like with features such as the huge open fireplace in the kitchen, large enough to roast a whole ox.

Two miles south of the castle, Kilmartin is well-known to archaeologists for the astonishing number of prehistoric chambered cairns, stone circles, burial cists and rocks inscribed with ritual cup-and-ring signs, all concentrated to the west and south of the village. The most ancient and impressive is the **Nether Lairg South Cairn**, some 5,000 years old, where visitors can enter the large chambered tomb with its stone-slabbed roof. A little further south, the two **Stone Circles** at Templewood, excavated as recently as the 1970s, appear to have been the main centre for burials from Neolithic times to the Bronze Age. The various sites are well-signposted, have useful information boards, and are normally open throughout the daylight hours. The village of Kilmartin is itself notable for the early Christian crosses in the church, some medieval grave slabs in the churchyard, and a ruined 16th century tower which was once the home of the rectors.

Kilmichael Glassary: and Lochgilphead

About five miles south of Kilmartin there are yet more prehistoric remains, some of the most important in the country. The rocky outcrop of **Dunadd Fort** was the seat of power in western Scotland from around AD 500 - the capital of the Pictish Kingdom of Dalriada. Here, generations of Scottish kings were crowned. One of them, Aidan, was crowned by St Columba; the ceremonies are recorded in some remarkable stone carvings along with an inscription in the ancient Irish language of Ogham. Dunadd thrived for nearly four centuries, until 873, when Kenneth McAlpin conquered the Picts and moved his capital to Scone, near Perth.

Kilmichael Glassary takes its name from yet another prehistoric survival, a rock inscribed with the typical cup and ring markings of that period.

Five miles further south, the little town of Lochgilphead overlooks Loch Gilp. Perhaps surprisingly, it is the administrative centre for the sprawling district of Argyll & Bute. The main visitor attraction is **Kilmory Woodland Park**, boasting gardens which were originally laid out in 1770. During the season the gardens delight the eye with a dazzling display of more than 100 varieties of rhododendrons.

KILMUN

Kilmun stands on the shore of **Holy Loch** which, according to tradition, was given its name when a ship carrying earth from the Holy Land, destined for the foundations of Glasgow Cathedral, was wrecked here. It was taken for granted that the exotic soil had sanctified the loch, hence its name. The village itself was an important early Christian site, with a chapel founded here around AD 620 by St Mun, a contemporary of St Columba. The present church was built in 1816, but looming behind it is the domed **Mausoleum** of 1794 which contains the earthly remains of all the Earls and Dukes of Argyll since 1442. Among them are the Earl Archibald, who died at the Battle of Flodden, and the 8th Earl who was beheaded in 1661. In the church's graveyard running up the hillside is the grave of Dr Elizabeth Blackwell (1821-1910), the first woman doctor registered in Britain. Just to the west of the village, the Forestry Commission's **Arboretum** will appeal to anyone who loves trees, and its Information Centre can provide copious details of the many forest walks throughout the Argyll Forest Park.

LERAGS

Lerags is a glen steeped in clan history, with the burial ground of the chiefs of the clan MacDougall, the ruins of Kilbride church, and the 16th century **Campbell of Lerags Cross** all within a one mile radius. The Cross, carved in 1526 with a depiction of the Crucifixion, was discovered centuries later lying in three pieces beside the ruined church. The figure of Christ escaped almost undamaged and is still a striking image.

LOCHGOILHEAD

From Rest-and-be-Thankful, the B828 climbs to almost 1,000 feet, drops sharply down into Glen

Mor and then passes through the **Argyll Forest Park** before reaching this little town set in a lovely position at the head of Loch Goil. The town is mostly a resort centre offering a wide range of watersport activities, but if you follow the lochside road southwards it will bring you to the ruins of **Carrick Castle**. A classic tower house castle, built around 1400, it was used as a hunting lodge by James IV. A stronghold of the Argylls, the castle was burned by their enemies, the Atholls, in 1685, but the lofty rectangular great hall is still imposing in its solitary setting beside the loch.

From Lochgoilhead, the last four miles of the route along the B839 to the A815 near Cairndow traverses the narrow **Hell's Pass**, a lonely, rockstrewn landscape ideal for the footpads and highwaymen who earned the pass its name. At the junction with the A815, look for the **Wedding Ring**, a group of inset white stones in the shape of a heart marking the spot where the gypsies of Argyll once solemnised their marriages. Southwestwards from this point, the A815 runs alongside Loch Fyne, where seals are a common sight, to Strachur, a straggling village where the road forks. The A886 runs down the western side of the peninsula, the A815 passes through more than 20 miles of the Argyll Forest Park before reaching the village of Kilmun. En route it passes the celebrated **Younger Botanic Gardens** at Benmore. They were established in the late 1800s by the Younger family, who bequeathed them to the Royal Botanic Gardens, Edinburgh, in 1928. The 120 acres of gardens contain a staggering collection of shrubs and trees, most notably some 250 species of rhododendron, azaleas, giant Californian redwoods, and more than 200 varieties of conifers, about one third of all those in existence. One of them, a fir tree, now stands at more than 180 feet high, (although there's an even loftier one near Cairndow which exceeds 200 feet).

Oban

The handsome and lively Victorian port of Oban is always busy with boat traffic criss-crossing between the islands of the Inner and Outer Hebrides. Protected by the length of the island of Kerrera, Oban's harbour is the finest on the west coast, with three piers and plenty of room for its still-active fishing fleet, a multitude of holiday craft, and the ever-busy ferries.

Tourism is by far Oban's most important industry, but the town does have its own distillery, founded in 1794, and the producer of the famous **Oban West Highland Malt**. Forty-minute tours of the distillery are available during the season. The tours conclude with a free dram and your admission fee is refunded if you buy a bottle of their product.

Another local industry is glass, and **Oban Glass**, part of the Caithness Glass group, also welcomes visitors to watch the process of glassmaking from the selection of the raw materials to finished articles such as elegant paperweights. Samples of their products are on sale in the factory shop. On the North Pier, **World in Miniature** displays some 50 minuscule "dolls' house" rooms in a variety of historical styles, including two furnished in the manner of Charles Rennie Mackintosh and, like the others, built to a scale of one-twelfth.

The most striking feature of Oban, however, is a completely unused building. High on the hillside overlooking the town stands one of Britain's most unforgettable follies, **McCaig's Tower**, erected by John McCaig between 1897 and 1900. On the foundation stone McCaig describes himself as "Art Critic, Philosophical Essayist, and Banker". He was motivated by a wish to provide work for unemployed masons in the area and, while a less romantic man might have built a Town Hall or a school, McCaig decided to build a replica of the Colosseum of Rome which he had admired on a visit there. His enormously costly project was designed from memory and its similarities to the original building are general rather than precise. McCaig had intended that a museum and

Oban Harbour

124

art gallery would also form part of the complex and that large statues of his family would be stationed around the rim. None of this came to pass. He died in 1902 and his sister Catherine, who inherited his fortune, didn't share her brother's taste for such a grandiose monument. John McCaig's Colosseum remained a dramatically empty granite shell, a wonderful sight when floodlit and adding an oddly Mediterranean aspect to this picturesque town.

The **Rare Breeds Farm Park**, two miles east of Oban, has been a winner of the Scottish Tourist Boards "Tourism Oscar" and is very popular as a family day out. In its 30 acres of attractive countryside, visitors can meet a large number of rare, but mostly indigenous, species of deer, goats, cattle and sheep. There's a children's corner where kids can meet the baby animals at close quarters, a woodland walk, conservation centre, and a tea room.

Just to the north of Oban stand the ruins of **Dunollie Castle**, much admired by both Sir Walter Scott and William Wordsworth. It was once the seat of the MacDougalls, Lords of Lorne, who still live nearby at Dunollie House (private), but little remains of the castle now apart from an impressive ivy-covered Keep rising majestically from a crag. **Dunstaffnage Castle** (Historic Scotland), a couple of miles further north, also sits atop a crag, and offers some superb views across the Lynn of Lorne to the island of Lismore. Substantial parts of the castle's 13th century fabric have survived, including walls 66 feet high and 10 feet thick in places, a curtain wall with three round towers, a large well surrounded by four small turrets, and a ruined chapel. As mentioned earlier, the castle was the original home of the Stone of Scone.

Over to the east, near Taynuilt, stands **Bonawe Iron Furnace** (Historic Scotland), the well-preserved remains of a charcoal furnace, or "bloomery", for iron smelting. Built in 1753, it was in operation until 1876, "the longest-lived blast furnace in the Scottish Highlands".

PORT APPIN

From Port Appin there are regular passenger-only ferries to the **Isle of Lismore**, 12 miles long and never more than two miles wide. (The island can also be reached by car ferry from Oban.) In Gaelic lios mor means "great garden" and indeed Lismore is one of the most fertile of the Inner Hebrides, albeit virtually treeless. In medieval times the island was the seat of the Bishops of Argyll, whose former cathedral has diminished in status to behind the parish church. With a population of around 150, Lismore is wonderfully peaceful, with gentle walks and cycle routes opening up exhilarating views across to the hills of Morven and the Isle of Mull.

REST AND BE THANKFUL

The modern A83 makes easy work of the pass through Glen Coe along which William and Dorothy Wordsworth struggled "doubling and doubling with laborious walk" in 1803. As they reached the summit, 860 feet above sea level, the Wordsworths noted with approval the plaque inscribed "Rest-and-be-thankful", placed here by the army troops when they repaired the old stone road in 1743. The viewpoint provides superb vistas of **Beinn an Lochain** (2,992 feet) to the west, and **Ben Ime** (3,318 feet) to the east.

ROTHESAY

The largest community on Bute is Rothesay, an attractive small town which displays its legacy as a popular Victorian resort for Clydesiders in its tall colour-washed houses, trim public gardens and pedestrianised esplanade. Long before the paddle-steamers brought 19th century holiday-makers here, Rothesay was a favourite refuge for Scottish kings in need of rest and recuperation. They would lodge at **Rothesay Castle** (Historic Scotland), built in the early 1200s and generally regarded as one of the finest medieval castles in the country. A picturesque moat surrounds the huge circular walls (unique in Scotland), which in turn enclose the well-preserved Great Hall built by James IV. The Argylls sacked the castle in 1685 but did a less thorough job than usual, leaving much of it intact. Some 200 years later the castle's hereditary guardians, the Marquesses of Bute, tidied the place up, opened it to the public, and Rothesay Castle has been one of the region's major tourist attractions ever since.

Rothesay has a definite taste for festivals. On the last weekend in August it hosts its own **Highland Games**, when the guest of honour may well be the Duke of Rothesay, a distinguished personage much better known as heir to the throne, Prince Charles. During the third weekend in July there's an **International Folk**

Festival, and on May Day Bank Holiday the town resounds to the upbeat rhythms of a **Jazz Festival**.

For a comprehensive insight into the island's history, archaeology and natural history, a visit to the **Bute Museum** across from the Castle in Stuart Street is essential and very rewarding. The museum houses exhibits from every period of Bute's history, from early stone tools to Clyde steamers.

Before you leave the town, do pay a visit to the celebrated **Victorian toilets** on the pier installed by Twyfords in 1899.

TARBERT

At Tarbert an isthmus, just one mile long, links the Kintyre Peninsula to the mainland. A venerable, but true, story recounts that in 1093 the wily Viking King Magnus Barefoot made a surprise attack on the west coast while the Scottish king, Malcolm Canmore, was away fighting the English. Malcolm was forced to cede the Hebrides, but seeking to keep Magnus off the mainland he stipulated that the 20-year-old invader might only retain any island he could navigate his ship around. Magnus coveted Kintyre, at that time much more fertile than the Hebridean islands, so he mounted his galley on wooden rollers and "sailed" his ship across the isthmus near Tarbert, thus claiming the whole of the peninsula.

More than three centuries later, Robert the Bruce performed an identical manoeuvre while establishing his supremacy over the region. The Bruce was also responsible for building a **Castle** at this strategic point, but today only the ivy-covered ruins of the Keep remain, standing atop a 100-foot mound. This appealing little town, backed by low green hills, was once a busy fishing port but nowadays it is pleasure craft which throng the harbour, particularly during the last week in May when the yacht races in the Rover series take place. They are followed the next week by the powerboat Grand Prix.

TOBERMORY

This picture-postcard little town (population 700) is set around an amphitheatre of hills which cradle one of the safest anchorages on Scotland's west coast. Oddly, Tobermory's potential as a port was not recognised until 1786 when the British Society for the Encouragement of Fisheries decided to develop the harbour and build a quay. Despite the Society's encouragement, the fishing industry never really prospered. (Lacking modern aids, the fishermen were baffled by the arbitrary movements of the herring shoals.)

The British Society's development of Tobermory port did, however, leave behind a charming legacy of (now) brightly-painted, elegant Georgian houses ranged along the quayside. Combined with the multi-coloured pleasure craft thronging the harbour, they help to create an atmosphere that is almost Continental: bright, cheerful and relaxed. The town's other attractions include its arts centre, **An Tobar**, which stages exhibitions and live events; the tiny **Tobermory Distillery** where visitors are offered a guided tour and a complimentary dram of its famed single malt whisky; and the **Mull Museum** on Main Street where one of the exhibits is devoted to the most dramatic incident ever recorded on the island.

This occurred in 1588 when a galleon of the routed Spanish Armada sought shelter in Tobermory harbour. The Spaniards were received with Highland courtesy; their requests for fresh water and victuals amply fulfilled. At some point, though, the people of Tobermory suspected that their guests intended to sail away without paying the bill for these provisions. Donald Maclean of Duart was deputed to go on board the Spanish ship and demand immediate payment. The Spaniards promptly locked him up and set sail towards their homeland. The ingenious Donald somehow managed to release himself, find his way to the ship's magazine, blow it up, and consign himself, the crew and the ship's rumoured cargo of fabulous amounts of gold bullion to the deep. Ever since then, strenuous efforts have been made to locate this watery Eldorado of Spanish gold. So far, all the divers have been rewarded with is a few salt-pocked cannon and a handful of coins.

During the summer months a vehicle ferry plies the 35-minute crossing from Tobermory to Kilchoan on the wild Ardnamurchan peninsula, famed for its abundance of birds, animals and wildflowers. From Kilchoan, with its ruined 13th century Mingary Castle dramatically sited on the cliff top, a five mile drive will bring you to **Ardnamurchan Point**, the most westerly point in mainland Britain, offering some grand views across to the islands of Coll, Mull and Tiree.

126 Ardbrecknish House

South Lochaweside,
by Dalmally,
Argyll PA33 1BH
Tel: 01866 833223/833242

Directions:

From Glasgow take the A82 north alongside Loch Lomond. At Tarbet, turn left on the A83 to Inveraray. At Inveraray, turn right on the A819 to Cladich (9 miles). At Cladich, turn left on the B840

Set in 20 acres of garden woodland on the south shore of spectacular Loch Awe, **Ardbrecknish House** dates back to the late 16th century when it was a fortified tower house. The house has been carefully converted to provide 10 delightful self-catering apartments, accommodating parties from 2 to 12 with facilities for larger groups. In the grounds are several custom designed holiday cottages, carefully spaced for optimum privacy and outlook, yet easily accessible to the central facilities. The house and grounds command breathtaking panoramic views over loch, mountain and glen.

Within the house is the Ardbrecknish Room, with a large open fire and wood-panelled ceiling, where visitors can enjoy an excellent home-cooked bar meal, sample the range of malt whiskies, play pool or darts and, on occasion, enjoy live music and dancing. Additionally, the house has a laundry/drying room and a library introducing the wealth of local history, attractions and wildlife. The beautiful grounds are ideal for woodland and waterside walks, and there's also a hard tennis court, children's play area, picnic and barbecue areas.

Opening Hours: Apartments & cottages accessible at all times

Food: Available 18.00-21.00, daily

Credit Cards: All major cards except Amex & Diners

Accommodation: 10 self-catering apartments; self-catering cottages

Facilities: Restaurant; library; laundry/drying room; hard tennis court, children's play area; picnic & barbecue areas

Entertainment: Pool; darts; quiz nights; occasional live music & dances

Local Places of Interest/Activities:
Fishing, boating, canoeing, steamer cruises on nearby Loch Awe; forest & hill walks, nearby; Kilchurn Castle, 6 miles; Inveraray Castle, Inveraray Jail, 12 miles; Cruachan Power Station, 13 miles; Argyll Wildlife Park, 14 miles

Internet/Website:
e-mail: ardbreck01@aol.com
website: www.ardbrecknish.com

Ardfillayne Country House Hotel | 127

West Bay, Dunoon,
Argyll PA23 7QJ
Tel: 01369 702267
Fax: 01369 702501

Directions:

The hotel is approximately 1 hour from Glasgow Airport. Take the M8 to the ferry at Gourock for Dunoon; or it can be reached by road from Glasgow via the A82, A83 and A815

Only a mile from the centre of Dunoon but set in 16 acres of natural woodland garden overlooking the Firth of Clyde, **Ardfillayne Country House Hotel** is a very special place. It was built in 1835 and there is an almost ethereal quality of the past at this compact comfortable country house. Visitors are instantly captivated by its period charm and the relaxed informal elegance of its eminently Victorian atmosphere. Fine furnishings and objets d'art enhance the affluent antiquity of the drawing rooms, all suggesting the gentler pace of the past. The intimate en suite bedrooms are unique peaceful havens individually designed with the guest's comfort in mind. The owner of Ardfillayne, Bill McCaffrey, has also added some homely touches - a rag doll in one room, a fluffy dog in another. As newspaper cuttings displayed in the elegant lounge testify, Bill is a leading figure in the spiritualist world and his work as a transmedium takes him around the world. Anyone with an interest in the spiritual world will find a conversation with him fascinating. But Bill is also an accomplished chef and his hotel is famous for the cuisine on offer - the proud holder of the Scottish Tourist Board's Dining Experience Award for 1997. The *fin de siecle* ambience of the hotel's Mackintosh-inspired dining room provides the setting for Beverley's Restaurant. It's the inspiration for exceptional food, helpful friendly service and fine wines from one of Scotland's most exclusive cellars. There are vintages of French wines here dating back to 1898 as well as superb malts, brandies and famous sherries. Classic cuisine and traditional Scottish dishes are carefully prepared and presented from fresh produce, game and fish originating locally from land, loch and sea. A stay at Ardfillayne is an experience to savour - locked in time it provides the key to a restful memorable break.

Opening Hours: Hotel open all day

Food: Quality cuisine available every evening

Credit Cards: All major cards accepted

Accommodation: 7 rooms, all en suite

Facilities: Beverley's Restaurant - ample parking

Local Places of Interest/Activities: Cowal Bird Garden, 1 mile; Golf, 1 mile; Arboretum, Kilmun, 7 miles; Argyll Forest Park, 7 miles; Younger Botanic Gardens, 11 miles

Internet/Website:
www.argyll- business-directory.com

128 The Auld Hoose Restaurant

Argyll Street, Dunoon,
Argyll PA23 7BH
Tel/Fax: 01369 701860

Directions:
Dunoon can be reached by ferry from Gourock or by road from Glasgow via the A82, A83 and A815

Unquestionably the best place to eat in Dunoon is The Auld Hoose Restaurant, conveniently located in the town's main street. Michael and Lorraine Lewis own and run this outstanding eatery where they serve good wholesome food at extraordinary value-for-money prices, (at the time of writing £3.95 for a 2-course lunch for example). The menu is excellent and very well-balanced, and everything, repeat everything, is freshly prepared and locally sourced. Well laid out and spotlessly clean, the restaurant is understandably popular with locals and visitors alike. Children are welcome and Michael and Lorraine make every effort to ensure that every customer is fully satisfied. The restaurant is fully licensed and offers a wide choice of wines, spirits and beers. Definitely not to be missed, but do remember that the Auld Hoose is closed on Sunday all day, and also on Monday evening.

Dunoon itself is the largest town in Argyll with some 13,000 inhabitants. It has been a popular resort since the 1800s with the people of Clydeside with which it is linked by a regular ferry. The town is perhaps best known for the Cowal Highland Games, Scotland's largest, which take place on the last Friday and Saturday of August and completely take over the town. Upwards of 150 bands, more than 2000 pipers and drummers take part in the centrepiece march past, and some 40,000 visitors come to watch the spectacle.

Opening Hours: 12.00-15.00; 17.00-22.30, daily except Sunday all day and Monday evening

Food: Value for money dishes based on local produce

Credit Cards: All major cards except Amex & Diners

Facilities: Parking nearby

Local Places of Interest/Activities: Cowal Bird Garden, 1 mile; Golf, 1 mile; Arboretum, Kilmun, 7 miles; Argyll Forest Park, 7 miles; Younger Botanic Gardens, 11 miles

The Boat 129

72 Victoria Street,
Rothesay,
Bute PA20 0AP
Tel: 01700 502938

Directions:

The Boat is on the sea front, just south of the ferry terminal

Built in the early 1900s, **The Boat** public bar occupies a convenient location on the sea front and close to the ferry terminal. At the time of writing, the inn is being completely refurbished by its new owner, Sara Goss, who took over here in August 2000. By the time you read this everything should be completed and in pristine condition. The new decor creates a warm and relaxing atmosphere which is enhanced by the strategically placed lighting. In this welcoming atmosphere, customers can enjoy the excellent food on offer every lunchtime - wholesome traditional Scottish fare, all home cooked and providing remarkable value for money. As well as the regular menu, there are daily specials adding to the choice. All the popular beverages are available and Sara also hosts occasional drinks promotions.

This lively hostelry maintains its own pool and darts teams, there's a pub quiz every Sunday evening and also occasional live music entertainment.

Opening Hours: Mon-Sat: 11.00-01.00; Sun: 12.30-01.00

Food: Mon-Sat: 12.00-14.00; Sun: 13.00-16.00

Credit Cards: Mastercard, Visa

Entertainment: Pool; darts; quiz night, Sunday; live music

Local Places of Interest/Activities: Rothesay Castle nearby; Mount Stuart, 5 miles; Ettrick Bay beach, 7 miles

Internet/Website: e-mail: theboat_bute@yahoo.com

130 Cairnbaan Hotel

Cairnbaan, by Lochgilphead,
Argyll PA31 8SJ
Tel: 01546 603668
Fax: 01546 606045

Directions:

From Glasgow take the A82 north to Tarbert. Turn left on the A83 to Cairndow and Lochgilphead. At Lochgilphead, turn right on the A816 towards Oban, About 3 miles along this road, turn left on the B841 into Cairnbaan. From Oban take the A816 south towards Lochgilphead. About 35 miles along this road, turn right on the B841 into Cairnbaan

Cairnbaan Hotel was built in the late 1700s as a coaching inn and to serve fishermen and 'puffers' trading on the newly-built Crinan Canal which runs past the front of the hotel. The 9-mile long waterway linked Loch Fyne at Ardrishaig with Crinan on the Sound of Jura, cutting out the long and often dangerous journey around the Mull of Kintyre. At Cairnbaan, the celebrated engineer, Thomas Telford, constructed a series of locks, 15 in all, on either side of the village. The canal towpath here provides pleasant, easy walking through picturesque countryside.

The Cairnbaan Hotel has recently been refurbished to a very high standard and along with quality cuisine and accommodation offers visitors the warm welcome typical of the West Coast. The 11 guest bedrooms are as individual as they are delightful, and equipped with all the facilities you would expect in a hotel of this quality. Guests at the Cairnbaan have a choice of dining. You can indulge yourself in the attractive à la carte restaurant which specialises in the use of fresh local produce - scallops, langoustine and game - or enjoy a lighter meal from the bistro-style menu in the relaxed atmosphere of the bar, Conservatory Lounge, or al fresco on the terrace overlooking the garden. Guests will find plenty to keep them occupied, whether they become involved in any of the host of outdoor activities available, in exploring the unique concentration of prehistoric sites around Kilmartin, sailing to the outer islands, or marvelling at the treasures on show in Inveraray Castle.

Opening Hours: Hotel open all day

Food: A la carte restaurant; bar meals & snacks

Credit Cards: All major cards except Amex & Diners

Accommodation: 11 rooms of 4-star quality

Facilities: Restaurant; bar; beer garden; parking

Local Places of Interest/Activities:
Canalside walks, nearby; Kilmory Woodland Park, Lochgilphead, 3 miles; Prehistoric stone circles, chambered tombs and cairns, around Kilmartin, 8 miles; Carnasserie Castle, 10 miles; Inveraray Castle, Inveraray Jail, 24 miles

Internet/Website:
e-mail: cairnbaan.hotel@virgin.net
website: www.cairnbaan.com

Colintraive Hotel

Colintraive,
Argyll PA22 3AS
Tel/Fax: 01700 841207

Directions:

From Dunoon, take the A815 north for about 5 miles, then turn left on the B836 towards Glendaruel. At the junction with the A886, turn left to Colintraive (7 miles)

No visit to the Cowal Peninsula would be complete without a drive around Loch Riddon from Tighnabruaich to Colintraive, a trip which opens up some of the most spectacular scenery in this land of breathtaking vistas. Colintraive sits beside the Kyles of Bute, the narrow strip of water that separates the Isle of Bute from the mainland. At its narrowest point the waterway is barely 200 yards wide and it is from here that the vehicle ferry operates. Right next to the ferry terminal stands the **Colintraive Hotel**, a handsome and substantial building where visitors will find good food and drink, quality accommodation and friendly hospitality.

The excellent food on offer is naturally strong on seafood but the menu also includes fabulous steak pies and a wide choice of other home cooked dishes. The hotel has 4 guest bedrooms, all of them en suite and equipped with TV and tea/coffee-making facilities. The rooms are spacious and the atmosphere very relaxing - an ideal place for those seeking peace and tranquillity.

Opening Hours: Hotel open all day

Food: Available 12.00-14.30; 18.00-21.00

Credit Cards: Mastercharge, Visa

Accommodation: 4 rooms, all en suite

Facilities: Ferry to Isle of Bute adjacent; ample parking

Local Places of Interest/Activities: Isle of Bute, Mount Stuart House via adjacent ferry; sailing in the Kyles of Bute; Kilmodan Sculptured Stones, Glendaruel, 7 miles

Internet/Website:
e-mail: kyleshotel@aol.com

132   The Cot House Hotel

by Sandbank, Kilmun,
Dunoon, Argyll PA23 8QS
Tel: 01369 840260
Fax: 01369 840689

Directions:

From Dunoon take the A815 north for 5 miles through Sandbank. The hotel is located behind the filling station on the right. From Glasgow follow signs for Dunoon. Past Kilmun turn off to filling station on left.

An attractive white-painted building with traditional crow-stepped gables, **The Cot House Hotel** occupies a superb position close to the shore of Holy Loch. It was originally built as a ferryman's home and toll house, "cot" being the local word for the small boat used to cross the river. Owned and run by Russell Buchanan and Rita Gillespie, the hotel is a favourite with fishermen angling on the nearby River Eckaig, famous for its sea trout and salmon, and also with all who appreciate good Scottish food, expertly and imaginatively prepared. The Cot House has received many plaudits for its excellent cuisine which is based on the "Natural Cooking of Scotland" theme, featuring seasonally available local produce from the sea, rivers and glens of Argyll. The extensive choice includes meat, fish and vegetarian options, as well as a children's menu. Vegans can also be catered for. The restaurant has a welcoming log fire, as does the bar where you'll find a great range of malt whiskies and drinks to suit all tastes. In good weather, customers can take advantage of the patio and beer garden which overlook the children's play area set in an idyllic rural environment. The Cot House is ideally located for exploring the Cowal Pensinsula and offers guests a good choice of rooms, all tastefully decorated, well-equipped, and en suite. A good indication of the hotel's standing is the fact that it has won the Licensed Trade News Award for the Family Welcome of the Year, and has also been a runner-up in the Independent Hotel Caterer of the Year Award.

Opening Hours: Mon-Sat, 11.00-23.00; Sun, 12.30-23.00

Food: Mon-Sat, 12.00-21.00; Sun 12.30-21.00

Credit Cards: Visa, Delta, Mastercard, Eurocard, Switch

Accommodation: B&B from £20 per person. All rooms en suite.

Facilities: Restaurant; lounge bar; beer garden; patio; children's play area

Entertainment: Live scottish folk music last Sun of month 14.00-17.00

Local Places of Interest/Activities: Holy Loch nearby; Argyll Forest Park nearby; Arboretum, ½ mile; Golf, 2 miles; Younger Botanic Gardens, 3 miles; Cowal Bird Garden, 3 miles

Internet/Website:
e-mail: cothouse@argyll.org
website: www.cothouse.co.uk

Cuilfail Hotel | 133

Kilmelford,
Argyll PA34 4XA
Tel: 01852 200274
Fax: 01852 200264

Directions:
From Oban take the A816 south towards Lochgilphead. Kilmelford village is about 14 miles along this road

In autumn, when the Virginia creeper cloaking its walls has turned a fiery red, the **Cuilfail Hotel** looks especially picturesque and inviting. Part of the hotel was originally an old drovers' inn, although most of the present hotel was built during the Victorian era. The hotel nestles at the foot of rolling hills, close to the shores of Loch Melford. Appropriately, the name Cuilfail in Gaelic means "sheltered corner". The Cuilfail (pronounced Coolfail) has a long tradition of offering highland hospitality to visitors to the Lorne area, a beautiful corner of Argyll. A fairly recent addition to the hotel's attractions is the Tartan Puffer. Open to residents and non-residents alike, this is an indoor barbecue serving prime Scotch beef, lamb, pork and venison, as well as the best local seafood and shellfish, and lots, lots more. Your meal is cooked in front of your very own eyes on the new indoor barbecue and grill.

Naturally, any self-respecting Scottish hostelry stocks a varied range of whiskies to offer its guests. The Cuilfail, however, boasts no fewer than 700 different varieties, including some extremely rare blends. You can sample them either in the cosy hotel bar or in the spacious residents' lounge, perhaps before retiring to one of the Cuilfail's 12 guest bedrooms. These all have en suite facilities, individually controlled central heating, tea/coffee-making facilities and colour TV. There's a choice of double or twin bedrooms, as well as 2 family suites, both with a separate adjoining children's room. Favourable rates are often available for longer stays and weekend breaks.

Opening Hours: Hotel open all day

Food: Available 12.00-14.30; 18.00-21.30

Credit Cards: All major cards except Amex & Diners

Accommodation: 12 bedrooms, (doubles, twins and 2 family suites), all en suite

Facilities: Beer garden; Tartan Puffer indoor barbecue & grill; bar; residents lounge;

Entertainment: 700 different whiskies!

Local Places of Interest/Activities:
Arduaine Gardens (NTS), 5 miles; Scottish Salmon Centre, Kilninver, 8 miles; Carnasserie Castle, 12 miles; prehistoric stone circles, tombs & cairns, around Kilmartin, 14 miles; Caithness Glass, McCaig's Tower, ferries to western islands, Oban Distillery, all at Oban, 14 miles

Internet/Website:
e-mail: david@cuilfail.co.uk
website: www.cuilfail.co.uk

134 Furnace Inn

Furnace,
Argyll PA32 8XN
Tel: 01499 500200

Directions:

Furnace is on the A83, about 21 miles south-west of Cairndow

Furnace is a beautiful little village occupying a lovely position beside Loch Fyne and looking across to the Cowal Peninsula. At the heart of the village is the award-winning **Furnace Inn**, a delightful old hostelry dating back to the early 1800s which is so picturesque it features on postcards as a typical Argyll scene. The interior is crammed with fascinating bric à brac, both in the spacious lounge bar and the separate restaurant. Here, an excellent choice of traditional Scottish fare is on offer - venison, lamb and locally caught fish and seafood. To complement your meal, there are real ales on tap. Mine host, Gordon Pirie, also offers a choice of accommodation. In the inn itself there are 4 standard rooms, and conveniently next door, a self-catering cottage which can accommodate up to 6 persons.

The inn makes a good base for exploring Loch Fyne and the spectacular countryside all around. A popular short excursion from Furnace is to the Crarae Glen Garden, set in a dramatic gorge that slices down to the lake. Laid out in the early 1900s as a "Himalayan ravine", the garden is notable for its rhododendrons, azaleas, and a wide variety of eucalyptus and conifers. A few miles in the other direction, the Auchindrain Folk Museum is an old township of some 20 thatched cottages furnished and decorated as they would have been in the days before the Clearances. And only a little further afield is Inveraray with its famous castle and forbidding old jail.

Opening Hours: Mon-Thu: 17.00-24.00; Fri: 16.00-24.00; Sat: 12.00-24.00; Sun: 12.30-23.00; Summer opens 12.00 every day

Food: Available 12.30-14.30; 18.00-21.00

Credit Cards: Not accepted

Accommodation: 4 standard rooms; also self-catering cottage for 6

Facilities: Beer garden; parking

Entertainment: Pool; quiz nights; occasional live music

Local Places of Interest/Activities: Auchindrain Folk Museum, 3 miles; Crarae Glen Garden, 5 miles; Argyll Wildlife Park, 8 miles; Inveraray Castle, Inveraray Jail, both 11 miles

The Horseshoe Inn
135

Bridgend, Kilmichael
Glassary, Lochgilphead,
Argyll PA31 8QA
Tel: 01546 606369

Directions:

Bridgend is on the A816 about 34 miles south of Oban, just north of Lochgilphead. The Horseshoe Inn is on the A816

Situated in the heart of Mid-Argyll, **The Horseshoe Inn** provides an ideal base for exploring this beautiful part of Scotland. Dating back to the early 1800s, the inn is owned and run by three lively ladies, Lucy, Mary and Chris who, together with their staff, make sure that their customers receive a warm welcome. They called in a professional designer to redecorate the rather drab interior of the inn which has now been transformed into a stylish, beautifully co-ordinated ensemble. The Horseshoe is also well known for the variety and quality of the food served here. Everything is home cooked and freshly prepared from local produce. The varied menu ranges from hearty steaks through bar meals and snacks. Also on offer are vegetarian options, children's meals, daily specials and desserts, and carry-outs - any meal can be a carry-out if the staff can fit it in a takeaway box!

Accommodation at The Horseshoe is in twin or double rooms, all with en suite facilities, colour televisions with remote control, tea/coffee-making equipment and full central heating. From this comfortable base, guests can explore the many archaeological and historic sites within easy reach: the Kilmichael Glassary Inscribed Stone, Carnasserie Castle and Dunadd Hill, the site of an Iron Age fort where the ancient Kings of Dalriada were crowned. A 5-minute drive will bring you to the National Nature reserve of Moine Mhor, and a little further afield are the Mull of Kintyre and the picturesque port of Oban.

Opening Hours: Easter-New Year: Mon-Wed: 12.00-23.00; Thu: 12.00-24.00; Fri-Sat: 12.00-01.00; Sun:11.00-23.00. New Year-Easter: Mon-Wed:16.00-23.00; Thu: 16.00-M'night; Fri-Sat: 12.00-01.00; Sun: 11.00-23.00

Food: Available whilst Inn is open

Credit Cards: All major cards except Amex & Diners

Accommodation: 3 rooms (2 double, 1 twin, all en suite); 1 self-catering flat

Facilities: Children & dogs welcome; parking

Entertainment: Pool table; quiz nights; occasional live music

Local Places of Interest/Activities: Kilmichael Glassary Inscribed Stone, 1 mile; Kilmory Woodland Park, Lochgilphead, 3 miles; Carnasserie Castle, 10 miles

Internet/Website: horseshoeinn@ic24.net.

136 Kilmartin Hotel

Kilmartin, Lochgilphead,
Argyll PA31 8RQ
Tel/Fax: 01546 510250

Directions:

Kilmartin is on the A816
about 30 miles south of Oban

The area around Kilmartin
is the most important prehistoric site on the Scottish
mainland, dotted with
stone circles, cairns and
chambered tombs dating
back some 5000 years. Lo-

cated right in the heart of the village, the **Kilmartin Hotel** is uniquely situated for those wishing to visit and explore the numerous sights of interest in the area. Built in the 19th century, the hotel lies within a conservation area in this peaceful centre of Mid-Argyll. It's owned and run by Pierre and Cecilia Godts, both of them of Belgian origin, who have fallen in love with this beautiful part of the country and hope to entice many of their countrymen to visit. They took over in the spring of 1999 and their priorities are their guests' relaxation and enjoyment within the homely atmosphere of a family run business.

The hotel provides a very comfortable standard of accommodation in 5 guest bedrooms, 3 of which are en suite and all of which are equipped with TV and tea/coffee-making facilities. Pierre and Cecilia also offer an extensive choice of wholesome fayre from their bar meal and restaurant menus, with traditional Scottish and seafood dishes taking pride of place. There's a superb wine list to choose from, or you might prefer one of the real ales on tap which are regularly changed. In addition to the wealth of prehistoric sites close by, Kilmartin is also conveniently located for visits to many other attractions such as Inveraray Castle, the Cruachan Visitors Centre, the famous Mull of Kintyre and day trips to the beautiful islands which lie off the west coast.

Opening Hours: Hotel, all day; Bar: 11.00-01.00, daily

Food: A la carte & bar meals available 12.00-14.00; 18.00-21.00

Credit Cards: All major cards accepted

Accommodation: 5 rooms (3 en suite)

Facilities: Beer garden; restaurant; lounge

Entertainment: Pool table; darts; live Scottish folk music; quiz nights

Local Places of Interest/Activities:
Prehistoric stone circles & cairns nearby; Carnasserie Castle, 2 miles; Dunadd Fort, Kilmichael Glassary Inscribed Stone, 5 miles; Kilmory Woodland Park, 9 miles; Arduaine Garden (NTS), 10 miles. Fishing and shooting packages available.

Internet/Website:
pierre@kilmartinhotel.fsnet.co.uk

The Kilmun House Hotel | 137

Kilmun, nr Dunoon,
Argyll & Bute PA23 8SB
Tel/Fax: 01369 840418

Directions:

From the ferry at Dunoon, turn right on the A815 towards Strachur. After passing the Cot House Service Station, turn right on to the Kilmun road, proceed about 1.5 miles until the Kilmun Pier is on your right. The Kilmun House Hotel is on the left side of the road

Situated on the seashore overlooking the Holy Loch and the Firth of Clyde, Kilmun House Hotel is a small, friendly and fully licensed hotel commanding views of some of the most dramatic and picturesque scenery in the South West Highlands. The hotel stands in its own grounds, complete with lovely gardens and a lily pond. Napiers Restaurant is a stylish conservatory which enjoys an impressive view of the Holy Loch and provides good Scottish fare including vegetarian dishes and a children's menu. There's also a public bar and a cocktail bar. Centrally heated throughout, all the guest bedrooms are attractively furnished and equipped with colour TV and tea/coffee-making facilities, while the en suite rooms have views overlooking the Holy Loch. Devotees of golf can take advantage of special 3, 5 or 7-day golf breaks and play at Cowal Golf Club nearby.

There's plenty in the Kilmun area to keep visitors busy. The Forestry Commission Arboretum with its fascinating display of exotic trees and shrubs is a very worthwhile walk, with outstanding panoramic views across to the Cowal Hills. Near the Arboretum is the ancient Chapel of Kilmun which is the burial place of the Campbells of Argyll and the grave of the Earl Archibald who was killed at Flodden. Kilmun itself owes a great deal to a remarkable but now largely forgotten Scots engineer, David Napier. In the mid-1800s Napier was building steam ships which plied up and down the Clyde and into many Highland lochs. He saw no good reason why, if steam was so successful when used over the seas, it could not do the same over land. So he proceeded to design the 'Steam-driven Carriage'.

Opening Hours: Hotel open all day

Food: Available 12.00-14.30; and 18.00-22.30

Credit Cards: All major cards except Amex & Diners

Accommodation: En suite or standard rooms available

Facilities: Conservatory restaurant; public bar; cocktail bar

Local Places of Interest/Activities: Argyll Forest Park nearby; Arboretum, 1.5 miles; Golf, 2 miles; Younger Botanic Gardens, 5 miles; Cowal Bird Garden, 6 miles

138 Kingarth Hotel

Kingarth,
Isle of Bute PA20 9LU
Tel/Fax: 01700 831662

Directions:
From Rothesay take the A844 south to Kingarth (7 miles)

With its crow-stepped gables and whitewashed walls, the **Kingarth Hotel** looks the very picture of a traditional Scottish country inn, which is exactly what it is. Originally built in 1783 and extended over the years, the hotel is full of character and warmth. The owners, Simon and Maria Tettmar, have been here since 1996 and they have worked hard to maintain and enhance the inn's attractions as a country hotel. One of the most popular of these is the adjacent bowling green, a soothing place in summer for customers to relax with a pint and watch the play. Use of the green is free to residents of the hotel and all the necessary equipment is supplied.

Another attraction at the Kingarth is the quality of the food on offer. The cuisine is traditional Scottish fare with the emphasis on fresh locally caught seafood. All the dishes are based on local produce, freshly prepared to order and attractively presented. Accommodation at the Kingarth comprises 6 guest bedrooms, (4 doubles, 2 twins), all of them en suite and equipped with TV and tea/coffee-making equipment. Some of the rooms are disabled-friendly, please telephone the hotel for more details. The hotel's location means that all the attractions of this small island are within easy reach. One that should not be missed is just 3 miles up the road. Mount Stuart is a fantastical Victorian Gothic extravaganza built for the outrageously wealthy 7th Marquess of Bute in the 1870s. After sampling the opulence of the interior, visitors can relax in the lovely gardens which were established a hundred years earlier than the present house.

Opening Hours: 12.00 onwards everyday

Food: Available all day

Credit Cards: Cash only

Accommodation: 6 rooms (4 doubles, 2 twins, all en suite); some rooms disabled-friendly

Facilities: Beer garden; bowling green; parking

Entertainment: Pool table; bowling green; restaurant theme nights

Local Places of Interest/Activities: Mount Stuart, 3 miles; St Blane's Church, 3 miles; Rothesay Castle, 7 miles; Ettrick Bay beach, 11 miles

Knipoch Hotel **139**

Knipoch, by Oban,
Argyll PA34 4QT
Tel: 01852 316251
Fax: 01852 316249

Directions:
From Oban take the A816 south towards Kilmartin & Lochgilphead. The Knipoch Hotel is well signposted, about 6 miles along this road, halfway along Loch Feochan

Beautifully located on the shore of Loch Feochan, **Knipoch House** is "a family home with a history". Back in 1592, when it was owned by a member of the Campbell clan, it is recorded that Campbell, Thane of Cawdor, was assassinated at the "House of Knipoch in Lorne". In late Victorian times the house was bought by the Craig family and it is they who still live here. They opened Knipoch as a hotel in 1981 and its idyllic location, quality food and accommodation have been delighting visitors every since.

The family takes food very seriously. It produces its own smoked salmon for which it is famous and which is available both at the hotel and by mail order. The elegant restaurant, with its tables overlooking the loch, has received various awards for its cuisine. As the Craigs say, "Combine good food, nice wine and pleasant company, and you have one of the essential experiences of any civilisation". To complement your meal, the hotel's cellar is stocked with more than 300 wines from around the world, including old favourites as well as new discoveries. The Bar too is very well stocked, offering an exciting selection which includes some very old malt whiskies and cognacs. The perfect accompaniment for your beverage is the hotel's own water, supplied from an ancient spring on the side of the hill. Guests staying at the hotel will find beautifully furnished and decorated bedrooms, all offering private facilities with combined bath and shower, direct dial telephone, TV, radio, hair dryer - and a view either of the surrounding countryside or of Loch Feochan.

Opening Hours: Hotel open all day

Food: À la carte & table d'hôte available 12.30-14.00; 19.30-21.00

Credit Cards: All major cards accepted

Accommodation: All rooms with private facilities

Facilities: Extensive lochside grounds; restaurant; bistro; parking

Local Places of Interest/Activities:
Scottish Salmon Centre, 3 miles; Caithness Glass, Oban Distillery, McCaig's Tower, all in Oban, 6 miles; Arduaine Garden (NTS), 11 miles

140 The Lochnell Arms Hotel

North Connel,
Argyll
PA37 1RP
Tel: 01631 710408
Fax: 01631 710239

Directions:

From Oban take the A85 north to Connel, cross the bridge and the hotel is on the left, 200 yards along the road

From the moment you step inside **The Lochnell Arms Hotel** it's clear that the managers, Sharon and Helmut Werner will do their utmost to ensure that your stay is as relaxing and comfortable as possible. Sharon comes from Fife and Helmut comes from Bavaria, but have been captivated by this beautiful corner of Argyll - and so have most of their guests. While relishing a meal in the restaurant or in the café-bar, they can also enjoy the unrivalled views of Loch Etive and the magnificent mountains and hills which surround it. The hotel gardens extend to the shoreline where nothing obstructs your view of the surging Falls of Lora, the point at which the waters of the loch meet the sea.

If you feel energetic, there's a huge variety of activities available locally - anything from water sports to guided wildlife expeditions; from golf to gliding. You can enjoy a cruise to the upper reaches of Loch Etive, inaccessible except by boat, or go on whole or half day sea cruises. Slightly further afield, guided tours will take you to the sombre beauty of Glencoe and Rannoch Moor. Being a family run hotel, the Lochnell Arms welcomes children and if the hotel's spacious gardens and play area are not enough to keep them amused while you enjoy a leisurely meal or after-dinner drink, don't worry! You can take them to the Sea Life Centre, the Rare Breeds Farm Park, the Argyll Wildlife Park or to Inveraray Jail. Whatever your interests, the Werners will be glad to assist or advise you on making the most of the many interesting sights and activities available in the area.

Opening Hours: Hotel open all day

Food: Available 12.30-14.30; 18.00-21.00, daily

Credit Cards: All major cards except Amex & Diners

Accommodation: 8 rooms, all en suite

Facilities: Conservatory restaurant; café-bar; spacious gardens; children's play area;

disabled facilities

Local Places of Interest/Activities: Cruises on Loch Etive depart close by; Dunstaffnage Castle, 3 miles; McCaig's Tower, Caithness Glass, Oban Distillery, all at Oban, 5 miles; Barcaldine Castle, 5 miles; Sea Life Centre, 6 miles; Bonawe Iron Furnace, 12 miles

The Lorne

141

Chalmers Street,
Ardrishaig,
Argyll PA30 8DY
Tel: 01546 603231

Directions:

Ardrishaig is on the A83, about 3 miles south of Lochgilphead

To experience the authentic flavour of a Scottish country pub, you can hardly do better than pay a visit to **The Lorne** in the small village of Ardrishaig, set beside Loch Gilp. Outside, the ground floor wall is painted a rich, royal blue, with the pub name picked out in gold, while two signs promise "A fine collection of malt whiskies" and a "Friendly Atmosphere". The Lorne is a genuine "local", a place where everyone comes to catch up with the gossip and to enjoy a companionable pint or two. The pub was built in 1893 and still has its grand original open fire which adds to the welcoming ambience. Landlady Catrione McDougall makes sure that there's also plenty of entertainment. In addition to the pool table, darts and Sky TV, she also arranges regular quiz nights and karaoke nights as well as live music evenings. No wonder this is such a popular pub and undoubtedly will become more so when Catrione's plans to provide bar snacks and meals come to fruition, hopefully by the winter of 2000.

Opening Hours: Sun-Thu: 11.00-23.00; Fri-Sat: 11.00-24.00

Food: From late 2000, bar snacks will be available

Credit Cards: Cash only

Entertainment: Pool; darts; Sky TV; karaoke; quiz nights; live music

Local Places of Interest/Activities: Kilmory Woodland Park, 3 miles; Dunadd Fort, 7 miles; Kilmichael Glassary Inscribed Stone, 7 miles; Carnasserie Castle, 12 miles

142   The Oyster Inn

Connel,
nr Oban, Argyll
PA37 1PJ
Tel: 01631 710666
Fax: 01631710042

Directions:
From Oban take the
A85 north to Connel
(5 miles)

At Connel the shores of Loch Etive are at their narrowest point and the waters of the 21-mile long loch seethe and rage as they rush over an underlying ledge of rock. **The Oyster Inn** overlooks the Falls of Lora where whirlpools and spectacular white water flows at the ebb and flood tides. The hotel also enjoys magnificent views to the mountains of Movern and Mull and is strategically placed for visiting Argyll's main attractions. It was built originally in the early 19th century to serve ferry passengers but the ferry has since been made redundant by the modern road bridge alongside the splendid cantilever railway bridge of 1903.

At the time of writing, the hotel is being extensively refurbished but by the time you read this everything should be up and running - and extremely spick and span. Sally Davies took over here in the summer of 2000 and already the hotel has seen some substantial improvements. The 7 guest bedrooms are all en suite, very well appointed, and equipped with TV and hospitality tray. The cuisine on offer is traditional Scottish fare, with fresh local seafood a speciality. The regular menu is supplemented by daily chalkboard specials and the hotel boasts an outstanding wine list. This is a lively place, especially at weekends when the hotel hosts ceilidhs and a Sunday quiz, with karaoke evenings and live music at other times. As a place to stay, the hotel is highly recommended.

Opening Hours: Sun-Thurs 11.00-23.00, Fri-Sat 11.00-01.00

Food: 12.00-14.30; 17.30-21.00

Credit Cards: Mastercard, Visa, Switch

Accommodation: 7 rooms, all en suite. (Due for expansion in2001)

Entertainment: Pool; darts; quiz after-noons, Sunday; karaoke; weekend ceilidhs; live music; theme parties

Local Places of Interest/Activities: Dunstaffnage Castle, 3 miles; McCaig's Tower, Caithness Glass, Oban Distillery, all at Oban, 5 miles; Barcaldine Castle, 5 miles; Sea Life Centre, 6 miles; Bonawe Iron Furnace, 12 miles

Internet/Website: sallyd@supanet.com

The Regent Hotel & Dizzy Bar | 143

23 Battery Place,
Rothesay,
Bute PA2 9DU
Tel/Fax: 01700 502006

Directions:

From the ferry terminal in Rothesay, turn left and The Regent Hotel is about half a mile along this road, on the left

Built in 1840, **The Regent Hotel** has a very distinctive frontage with tall ground floor windows, a first floor balcony and a ground floor patio where customers can sit and watch the world go by. There's also a peaceful beer garden to the rear. Inside, the rooms are spacious and attractively furnished and decorated in modern style. The owners of the Regent, Lorraine and Ivor Haverson, provide their customers with an unusually interesting choice of cuisine, offering a menu that ranges from traditional Scottish fare to dishes from the Far East and Mexico. The hotel's convenient location, within walking distance of the town centre, makes it an ideal place to stay on the island. The accommodation comprises 8 rooms, 5 of which are en suite and all of which are equipped with TV, radio and tea/coffee-making facilities. Several of the rooms enjoy sea views across to the mainland.

Opening Hours: Hotel open all day

Food: Available 12.30-14.30; 18.00-21.00

Credit Cards: Access, Visa

Accommodation: 8 rooms, (5 en suite)

Facilities: Restaurant; beer garden; balcony garden

Entertainment: Pool room; live jazz, Wednesday evenings; theme nights

Local Places of Interest/Activities: Rothesay Castle nearby; Mount Stuart, 5 miles; Ettrick Bay beach, 7 miles

144 St Catherine's Old Ferry Inn

St Catherine's,
Cairndow,
Argyll PA25 8AZ
Tel: 01499 302321

Directions:
From Glasgow, take the A82 to Loch Lomond. At Tarbet, turn left on the A83 to Campbeltown (10 miles). Turn left on A815 to Dunoon for 5 miles

Enjoying a lovely lochside location, **St Catherine's Old Ferry Inn** is an attractive long, low building parts of which are believed to date back to 1460 when it was known as the Wayfarer's Inn. The building was extended in 1756 and remains basically unchanged since then. This is a hostelry where you can step back in time, relax and enjoy the superb cuisine on offer - fine venison and lamb from local sources, and excellent seafood, all home cooked attractively presented and served in generous portions. Local people praise the food highly and flock here themselves - always a good sign. Cairndow makes a good base for exploring the Cowal Peninsula and the Argyll coast, and the Old Ferry Inn has 4 guest bedrooms available all year round. Guests also have the use of a separate residents' lounge.

Just behind Cairndow village, Ardkinglas Woodland Gardens boasts the tallest trees in Britain - conifers more than 200ft high, along with hundreds of other attractive trees and shrubs, including many exotic rhododendrons. A few miles to the east is Rest and Be Thankful which takes its name from a plaque placed here by army troops when they repaired the old stone road in 1743. The viewpoint provides superb vistas of Beinn an Lochain (2,992ft) and Ben Ime (3,318ft).

Opening Hours: 11.00-00.00 all year

Food: 12.00-15.00; 17.30-21.00

Credit Cards: All major cards except Amex & Diners

Accommodation: 4 standard rooms

Facilities: Ample parking

Entertainment: Quiz night; folk nights

during the season

Local Places of Interest/Activities: Loch Fyne & Ardkinglas Woodland Garden, both nearby; Argyll Forest Park, 6 miles; Inveraray Castle & Inveraray Jail, 11 miles; Loch Lomond, 13 miles; Argyll Wildlife Park, 14 miles

The Stagecoach Inn 145

Cairndow,
Argyll PA26 8BN
Tel: 01499 600286
Fax: 01499 600220

Directions:

From Glasgow, take the A82 to Loch Lomond. At Tarbet, turn left on the A83 to Cairndow (13 miles)

One of the oldest coaching inns in the Highlands, **The Stagecoach Inn** is delightfully located just off the A83, on the upper reaches of Loch Fyne. Here, Douglas and Catherine Fraser extend a warm welcome in the best traditions of Scottish hospitality and the lucky visitor is presented with a haven of sparkling views, high mountains and magnificent woodlands and rivers. They offer excellent accommodation in 14 bedrooms in a relaxed country atmosphere. All rooms are en suite with central heating, radio and TV, direct dial telephones and tea/coffee-making facilities. Two of the rooms are de luxe with 2-person spa baths and king-size beds. The inn has a residents' lounge, sauna, sunbed and for the more energetic a multi-gym. Afterwards, you can relax in the friendly bar and lounge where you can sample a wide range of malt whiskys and enjoy a chat with the locals.

The stables from the inn's coaching days have been converted into the Stables Restaurant, replete with old world charm. Here you can dine by candlelight and admire the views over the loch. Both table d'hôte and à la carte menus are offered and they include superbly prepared dishes such as sauté haunch of venison in red wine sauce and Loch Fyne salmon steaks. A suitable wine list is available to complement your meal. Children's meals are also catered for and packed lunches are available when desired. 'Pub Grub' is also served in the bar all day. The location of the inn makes it an ideal centre for a touring holiday visiting such places as Loch Lomond, the Trossachs, the Mull of Kintyre, the Cowal Peninsula, the famous Inveraray Castle, ancient seat of the Clan Campbell, and the nearby Inveraray Jail which has been voted Scotland's top new attraction.

Opening Hours: Hotel open all day

Food: Available 12.30-14.30; 18.00-21.00. Bar food available all day

Credit Cards: All major cards accepted

Accommodation: 14 rooms, all en suite, including 2 de luxe bedrooms with 2-person spa baths

Facilities: Sauna; sunbed; multi-gym; parking

Local Places of Interest/Activities: Loch Fyne & Ardkinglas Woodland Garden, both nearby; Argyll Forest Park, 6 miles; Inveraray Castle & Inveraray Jail, 11 miles; Loch Lomond, 13 miles; Argyll Wildlife Park, 14 miles

146 | Tayvallich Inn

Tayvallich,
Argyll PA31 8PL
Tel: 01546 870282
Fax: 01546 870333

Directions:
Tayvallich is about 45
miles south of Oban,
via the A816/B8025

The Knapdale area of
Argyle has been des-
ignated a National
Scenic Area and it's
here, hidden away in the village of Tayvallich, that you'll find the **Tayvallich Inn**, an
outstanding hostelry which is well worth seeking out. Considering it's glorious position on the shore of Loch Sween it's not surprising to find that the inn's speciality is
fresh seafood - Loch Sween Moules Marinières or oysters, for example, locally smoked
salmon with a hint of rum, or pan-fried Sound of Jura Scallops, (just to get your mouth
watering).

Jilly and Andrew Wilson, took over this lochside restaurant in early 1999 and
have made it a popular and well-recommended place to wine and dine. Andrew is the
chef and in addition to the wonderful fish dishes also offers meat, poultry and vegetarian options. Snack lunches are served from 12.30 until 14.00, bar suppers between
18.00 and 20.00, and dinner from 19.00. Booking for the restaurant, especially at
weekends and during the main season, is essential. The Tayvallich Inn is an attractive
building with clean-cut lines and large windows overlooking the loch so it's incredible to learn that it was actually built some 40 years ago as a bus garage, only becoming
an inn some 20 years later.

Opening Hours: Main season: Sun-Thu:
11.00-24.00; Fri-Sat: 11.00-01.00. Off
season: 11.00-15.00; 17.00-23.00, daily

Food: Available 12.30-14.00; 18.00-20.00

Credit Cards: All major cards except Amex
& Diners

Facilities: Restaurant;

Entertainment: Quiz nights; occasional

live music

Local Places of Interest/Activities: Forest
walks nearby; Prehistoric stone circles,
chamber tombs, cairns, around Kilmartin,
12 miles; Kilmory Woodland Park,
Lochgilphead, 15 miles

Internet/Website:
e-mail: tayvallich.inn@virgin.net

6 Perthshire and Kinross

PLACES OF INTEREST:

Aberfeldy 149
Amulree 149
Auchterarder 149
Blair Atholl 149
Crieff 150
Dunkeld 151
Gleneagles 151

Kinloch Rannoch 151
Kinross 151
Meigle 151
Perth 152
Pitlochry 153
Strathtummel 153

PUBS AND INNS:

The Aerodrome, Scone, nr Perth 154
Amulree Hotel & Lonely Inn, Amulree 155
The Bell Tree, Methven 156
The Black Watch Inn, Aberfeldy 157
Coaching Inn, Blackford 158
The Comrie Hotel, Comrie 159
The Crees Inn, Abernethy 160
Cyprus Inn, Bridge of Earn, nr Perth 161

Gwydyr House Hotel, Crieff 162
The Inn, Crook of Devon 163
Kirkstyle Inn, Dunning 164
The Log Cabin, Kirkmichael 165
Marfield Inn, Rattray, nr Blairgowrie 166
The Tower Hotel, Crieff 167
The Two O Eight Hotel, Perth 168
Woodside Inn, Woodside 169

The Hidden Inns of Central and Southern Scotland

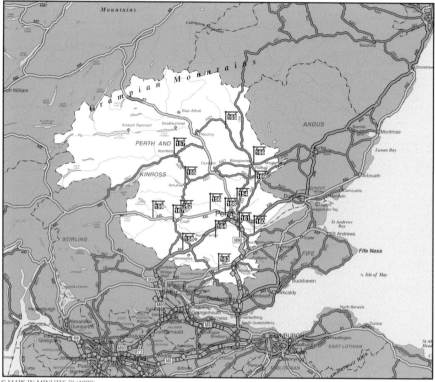

© MAPS IN MINUTES ™ (1999)

154	**The Aerodrome**, Scone, nr Perth	**162**	**Gwydyr House Hotel**, Crieff
155	**Amulree Hotel & Lonely Inn**, Amulree	**163**	**The Inn**, Crook of Devon
156	**The Bell Tree**, Methven	**164**	**Kirkstyle Inn**, Dunning
157	**The Black Watch Inn**, Aberfeldy	**165**	**The Log Cabin**, Kirkmichael
158	**Coaching Inn**, Blackford	**166**	**Marfield Inn**, Rattray, nr Blairgowrie
159	**The Comrie Hotel**, Comrie	**167**	**The Tower Hotel**, Crieff
160	**The Crees Inn**, Abernethy	**168**	**The Two O Eight Hotel**, Perth
161	**Cyprus Inn**, Bridge of Earn, nr Perth	**169**	**Woodside Inn**, Woodside

Please note all cross references refer to page numbers

"Perthshire forms the fairest portion of the northern kingdom - the most varied and the most beautiful." That was Sir Walter Scott's opinion, and few visitors to "Scotland in Miniature" would disagree.

The county of Perthshire and Kinross is an area renowned for the splendour of its noble mountains and romantic lochs. The country's tumultuous past is reflected in historic sites such as Loch Leven Castle, where Mary Stuart made a famous escape, ruined Dunkeld Abbey and Scone Palace, where all 42 of Scotland's kings were crowned. Perth itself is one of the stateliest towns in the realm, and the great open spaces make the county ideal for a wealth of outdoor pursuits, shooting, fishing, skiing and, naturally, golf, with a total of 38 courses to choose from.

For lovers of good food, this region represents a lavishly stocked outdoor larder full of prime ingredients - salmon, trout, beef, game and venison.

PLACES OF INTEREST

ABERFELDY

Now simmer blinks on flowery braes,
And o'er the crystal streamlet plays;
Come let us spend the lightsome days
In the birks of Aberfeldy.

Scotland's much-loved poet Robert Burns composed his ballad *The Birks of Aberfeldy* while standing near the dramatic **Falls of Moness** in September 1787. "Birk" means birch, and the beautiful trees he wrote about can still be seen south of this handsome town.

Fifty years before Rabbie Burns came to Aberfeldy and immortalised the silver birches, General Wade was building the distinctive **Wade's Bridge** across the *Fair Tay, flowing by in stately, placid majesty.* Designed by William Adam, architect father of Robert Adam, the four-arched, humpback bridge was the first to span the River Tay.

Aberfeldy today is a dignified town where you will be greeted in spring by golden banks of daffodils. **Aberfeldy Distillery**, an impressive building of 1898 with a genuine "turn of the century charm", welcomes visitors for guided tours, has a well-stocked shop and a pleasant nature trail through the native woodland which surrounds the distillery. In the centre of the town, **Aberfeldy Water Mill** was built in 1825 and, after restoration in 1987, its four grinding stones, each weighing 1.5 tons, are still producing oatmeal made in the traditional Scottish manner. There's an interesting film showing the place of the miller in Scottish history, and visitors can buy stoneground oatmeal straight from the mill.

AMULREE

From this small village at the foot of **Craig Hulich** (1,650 feet), you can strike off along no fewer than five different roads winding their way through the magnificent Perthshire countryside. To the south lies Glen Almond, to the north Strath Braan and Glen Cochill, while to the west, two minor roads run along opposite banks of Loch Freuchie.

AUCHTERARDER

"A city set on a hill cannot be hid" says the promotional brochure for Auchterarder, and although it's an 800 year old Royal Burgh rather than a city, the town certainly enjoys an elevated position with the stunning scenery of the Grampian Mountains as a backdrop. Auchterarder is known locally as ``The Lang Toon'' because of its lengthy High Street.

BLAIR ATHOLL

The village of Blair Atholl is dominated by the

150 gleaming white walls and towers of **Blair Castle**, the most visited privately-owned home in Scotland. The hereditary seat of the Dukes of Atholl, the castle's oldest part is Cummings Tower, built in 1269. The 2nd Duke transformed the castle into a gracious Georgian mansion; a century or so later the 7th Duke remodelled the building in the flamboyant Scottish Baronial style.

Most of the 32 rooms open to visitors at Blair Castle date from this period - a marvellous sequence of grand apartments containing outstanding collections of furniture, painting, china, lace, tapestries, arms and armour. In the

Blair Castle

vast ballroom, where one whole wall is festooned with antlers, look for the portrait of the 7th Duke. Beneath it lies his walking stick, scored with 749 notches, one for each stag he killed.

Visitors to the castle may well find themselves greeted by a piper of the Atholl Highlanders, the Duke's "private army". This 80-strong force is unique in Europe, the legacy of a visit to Blair Castle in 1844 by Queen Victoria. Enormously impressed by the Guard of kilted Highlanders assembled for her visit, Victoria conferred on them the right to carry the Queen's Colours, a privilege which also allowed them to bear arms. Every year, in May, they hold

their annual parade for the Duke's review and complete the Whitsun weekend with the famous **Atholl Gathering**. These historic Highland Games feature internationally known sportspersons, Highland dancing, traditional caber-tossing and local competitions. In August, the **Blair Castle International Horse Trials**, held in the challenging castle grounds, have become a major event and are followed by Sheep Dog Trials.

In addition to Blair Castle's 32 state rooms, visitors may also wander through the extensive parklands, which include a deer park, a restored 18th century walled garden, a gift shop and restaurant.

CRIEFF

It's hard to imagine that the now-peaceful town of Crieff was once the scene of sackings and burnings. Twice in the 18th century this hillside town was attacked and virtually destroyed by rampaging Highlanders, and there are grim tales of dark deeds linked to nearby Drummond Castle.

Clinging to a hillside above the River Earn, Crieff today is a mellow town, with peaceful flower-filled gardens and parks, and streets winding up the steep hill. Once, drovers brought their cattle down from the Highlands to the great market here, and more than 200 years ago the foundations of a great Scottish tradition were laid when a distillery was established on the banks of the river Turret. Founded in 1775, **Glenturret** is the oldest whisky distillery in Scotland: it still produces award-winning malt whisky which visitors can sample, free, at their Visitor Centre.

Located on the edge of the town, **Stuart Crystal** offers an unusual combination of attractions. Visitors can view the skills involved in the decoration of fine crystal glass, browse in the factory shop, and also watch a free display of trained owls and falcons swooping dramatically in response to the falconer's commands.

A couple of miles south of Crieff, **Drummond Castle Gardens** truthfully claim to be among the finest formal gardens in Europe. First laid out in the early 1600s, the gardens visitors see today were replanted in the 1950s, preserving features such as the ancient yew hedges and the copper beech trees planted by Queen Victoria to commemorate her visit in 1842. In the centre of the magnificent Victorian parterre stands John Mylne's famous multiple sundial, dating from 1630. As a backdrop to these superb gardens, rise the towers and turrets of Drummond Castle, home of the Earls of Perth and not open to the public.

DUNKELD

Set in idyllic surroundings on the east bank of the Tay, **Dunkeld Cathedral** is one of the noblest and most historic buildings in the country. Back in 850, Kenneth MacAlpin moved the religious centre of the country to Dunkeld from Iona and the town also became the seat of the royal court. The present Cathedral was built between the 12th and 15th centuries and although its nave is roofless, the choir remains intact and is still used as the parish church. The "leper's squint" is still in place and the cathedral generously allowed an impressive tomb of the "Wolf of Badenoch" to be installed. Otherwise known as Alexander Stewart, Earl of Buchan, the Wolf was notorious for his lawlessness. His most infamous deed was the sacking of Elgin Cathedral in 1390 as a measured response to the Bishop's criticism of the Earl's marital infidelity.

From this appealing little town with its beautifully-restored 17th century houses, Thomas Telford's lovely seven-arched bridge of 1809 leads to the village of **Birnam** where the **Beatrix Potter Garden** recalls the popular writer who spent many childhood holidays in the area.

Birnam Wood, or its impersonation by Macduff's soldiers, played a crucial part in the downfall of Macbeth, according to Shakespeare. The story of the much-maligned king is presented at **The Macbeth Experience** where visitors can also see the famous Birnam Oak, all that remains of the ancient forest of Birnam Beeches.

GLENEAGLES

In Perthshire, golf is a way of life with almost every town and village seeming to have its own golf links. Some of the best known are the four picturesque courses at Gleneagles, although these are reserved for club members and hotel residents only. Elsewhere, visitors are welcome and are often pleasantly surprised by the modest green fees and the fact that, even in summer, most courses are quiet.

KINLOCH RANNOCH

This little village at the eastern end of Loch Rannoch is popular with anglers and backpackers setting off for the vast expanses of Rannoch Moor, where there are no roads and only a single railway line. West of Kinloch Rannoch, the B846 runs through the increasingly desolate expanses of Rannoch Moor for 15 miles before coming to a dead end at Rannoch Station on the Glasgow to Fort William line. This is the heart of wilderness country, Perthshire's Empty Quarter, and yet another aspect of the county's varied landscapes.

KINROSS

Once the capital of one of Scotland's smallest counties, Kinross-shire, the town grew up beside Loch Leven, now a National Nature Reserve and the most important freshwater lake in Britain for migratory and breeding waterfowl.

Overlooking the loch is **Kinross House**, a fine late-17th century mansion whose enchanting gardens are open to the public during the summer. From the nearby pier, a five-minute ferry trip takes visitors to the island on which stand the ruins of **Loch Leven Castle**. Mary Stuart was imprisoned here for 11 months in 1567-8 but managed to escape with the sole help of an 18 year old lad, William Douglas. He stole the castle keys, arranged a boat and, as they rowed away, threw the keys into the loch. Three centuries later, a bunch of keys was recovered from the loch floor near the castle.

MEIGLE

Tucked away at the foot of the Sidlaw Hills, the tiny village of Meigle has become a place of pilgrimage for anyone interested in Scotland's distant past. In the little churchyard here were found no fewer than 30 of the most remarkable early Christian and Pictish inscribed stones ever discovered in Scotland. They date from the seventh to the tenth centuries and it remains a mystery why so many of them should have been erected at Meigle. The most impressive of them all is a 7-foot high cross, delicately carved with both biblical characters and mythological creatures. According to tradition, this graceful memorial - red sandstone at its base, merging into grey at the top - is the gravestone of Queen Guinevere, but the meaning of the enigmatic symbols has yet to be deciphered. This striking collection is now housed in the **Meigle Museum**.

152

PERTH

For a hundred years, until 1437, the "Fair City of Perth" was Scotland's capital. It still carries an air of distinction. A regular winner of the "Britain in Bloom" competition, it has also received the accolade of "Best Quality of Life in Britain".

Beautifully set beside the River Tay, the compact city centre is framed by two extensive parks, the **North Inch** and **South Inch**. The North Inch was the site of a bloody tournament in 1396 which became known as the Battle of the Clans and later provided the background to Scott's novel *The Fair Maid of Perth*. The historical Fair Maid was Catherine Glover, who lived in a house in Northport, the oldest dwelling in the city. **The Fair Maid's House** was restored in 1893 but can only be viewed from the outside.

Just around the corner from the Fair Maid's House, the city's imposing **Art Gallery & Museum** has displays on Perth's history and local industries. Prominent among these is whisky, since three major producers all had their origins here - Dewar's, Bell's, and Famous Grouse. There's more industrial history at **Lower City Mills** where a massive working waterwheel still grinds out one of Scotland's staple foods, oatmeal. (You can also see quality glass being made at **Caithness Glass** on the outskirts of the city.)

In the heart of the city stands the striking medieval **St John's Kirk**. It was here, in 1559, that John Knox preached a rabble-rousing sermon that provoked an anti-Catholic riot in which four monasteries were razed to the ground, including the historic Abbey at Scone, two miles north of the town. It was a defining moment in the movement for Church reform in Scotland. South of St John's, the splendid **Fergusson Gallery** is a must for art lovers. Housed in the former Perth Waterworks (now a Grade A Listed Building), the Gallery boasts the largest single collection of works by Scotland's foremost "Colourist" painter, J. D. Fergusson.

When **Balhousie Castle** was built in the 1400s, it stood well outside the city but now stands rather uncomfortably on the edge of a residential area. The Castle was formerly the home of the Earls of Kinnoull but is now devoted to the **Black Watch Museum**, celebrating the exploits of the historic regiment founded in 1739.

The area around Perth has a rich agricultural heritage which is explored with the aid of an audio-visual presentation at the **Perth Mart Visitor Centre**, next door to the Auction Market which sells more pedigree beef cattle than anywhere else in Europe. Children will love the Highland animals in the Mart's Animal Farm; they can also marvel at the majestic Clydesdales at the **Fairways Heavy Horse Centre**, just outside Perth.

To the west of Perth, **Huntingtower Castle** (Historic Scotland) was the scene of the Earl of Gowrie's kidnapping of James VI in 1582. The Earl invited the 16-year-old king to his stern-looking 15th century castellated mansion and held him prisoner there for nine months. The conspirators had planned to coerce James into dismissing his favourites. The plot failed and Gowrie was later beheaded. Today, Huntingtower is notable for its richly painted walls and ceilings.

Two miles north of Perth, **Scone Palace** is one of the most historic sites in the country. Between AD 840 and 1296, all 42 of Scotland's kings were "made" (not "crowned") on the Stone of Scone. The Stone, also known as Stone of Destiny, was brought here by the first King of All Scotland, Kenneth McAlpin. Kenneth had acquired the throne by the rather sneaky method of inviting his Pictish enemies to a feast at Scone, waiting until they were helpless with drink, and then massacring the lot of them. An odd feature of the king-making at Scone was that all the nobles in attendance carried some earth from their own lands inside their boots. The mound on which the later Abbey stood was supposedly formed as they emptied their footwear after the ceremony. The Abbey no longer stands. It was one of those destroyed by the Perth mob after John Knox's inflammatory sermon in 1559. Strangely the rioters spared the Bishop's Palace, and this forms the core of the present building. Since 1604 the Palace has been the home of the Murray family, now Earls of Mansfield. It was the 3rd Earl who, in 1802, began enlarging the house in the Gothic style popular at the time, creating what Queen Victoria called "*a fine-looking house of reddish stone*".

Scone's treasures include a priceless collection of Meissen and Sèvres porcelain accumulated by the 2nd Earl during his assignments as Ambassador to Dresden, Vienna and Paris, along with exquisite sets from Chelsea, Derby and Worcester. With such a huge collection, the Earl was able to ensure that distinguished guests never dined twice off the same service. In the Ambassador's Room stands the magnificent bed presented to the Earl by George III, its rich crimson hangings liberally sprinkled with the royal cypher and coats of arms. Nearby hangs Zoffany's enchanting portrait, *Lady Elizabeth Murray with Dido*. Elizabeth was the 1st Earl's daughter, Dido a slave girl he had freed. His unprecedented action helped spark off the Anti-Slavery Movement. Other fine paintings in the Palace include major works by Reynolds and Allan Ramsay. The extensive grounds at Scone include a 100-acre Wild Garden, a historic pinetum nearly 200 years old containing the original British Douglas Fir, a Maze, Adventure Playground, picnic park, gift shop and coffee shop.

PITLOCHRY

This popular resort is set in a particularly beautiful part of the Perthshire Highlands. To the west runs the lovely glen of Strathtummel while to the north the majestic peaks of the Grampians *"pierce the heavens"*.

Over the years Pitlochry has added many other attractions to these natural ones. **The Blair Athol Distillery**, makers of Bell's whisky, was founded in 1798 and is one of Scotland's oldest distilleries. Visitors are welcome and can watch the distilling process as crystal clear water from the Allt Dour, the "burn of the otter", is transformed into amber nectar. Guided tours end with a complimentary dram and there is also a whisky and gift shop, coffee shop and bar.

A sight not to be missed is the **Salmon Ladder** at the Pitlochry Power Station and Dam. In the 1950s the River Tummel was dammed to produce hydroelectric power; in order to permit salmon to pass upstream, the ladder was

constructed. An underwater viewing chamber allows visitors to watch these noble fish flailing their way up the 1,000-foot long tunnel during their annual migration.

153

Nearby stands the world-famous **Pitlochry Festival Theatre** which from May to October presents a full programme of plays, concerts and other entertainments. In the town itself, the summer season brings pipe band concerts, country dancing displays, ceilidhs and many other events.

Nestling in the hills a couple of miles east of Pitlochry, **Edradour Distillery** is the smallest in the country, producing just 12 casks of its prized whisky each week. An old distiller's yardstick states that the smaller the still, the finer the taste, and the Edradour stills are the smallest allowed under Excise regulations - any smaller, the theory goes, and they'd be hidden away on the hillsides! Guided tours begin with the usual complimentary glass and there's a short video recounting Edradour's history since it was founded in 1825.

STRATHTUMMEL

The B8019 running westwards from Pitlochry forms part of the romantic Road to the Isles, and provides magical vistas which are outstanding even in a country where sensational landscapes are almost taken for granted. In 1866 Queen Victoria came to the famous viewpoint in Strathtummel and, like everyone else who has stood here, was enraptured. The astoundingly beautiful view takes in the length of **Loch Tummel** with the conical peak of **Schiehallion** (3,457 feet), the "Fairy Mountain", rising above it. The spot is known as **Queens View**, not because of Victoria, but after Queen Margaret, wife of Robert the Bruce.

154   The Aerodrome

Angus Road,
Scone,
Perth,
Perthshire
PH2 6QU
Tel: 01738 551208

Directions:

Scone is about 3 miles north of Perth, on the A93

Scone Palace is one of the most historic sites in all of Scotland. Between AD 840 and 1296, all 42 of Scotland's kings were "made", (not "crowned"), on the Stone of Scone. An odd feature of the king-making at Scone was that all the nobles in attendance carried some earth from their own lands inside their boots. The mound on which the later Abbey stood was supposedly formed as they emptied their footwear after the ceremony. The Abbey no longer stands. It was one of those destroyed in 1559 by the Perth mob after an inflammatory sermon by John Knox. Strangely, the rioters spared the Bishop's Palace and this forms the core of the present building which is now the hereditary home of the Earls of Mansfield.

A short walk from the Palace is **The Aerodrome**, a friendly and welcoming hostelry owned and run by Brian Gordon, a man with a deep interest in military history. His inn was built in the 1700s as a coaching house and although it has been extended and upgraded over the years it has retained its olde worlde atmosphere. It's a family-friendly pub where children are very welcome and the staff are notably courteous and efficient. The Aerodrome also has a good reputation for the quality of the food on offer - wholesome traditional Scottish food prepared by the pub's own chef.

Opening Hours: Sun-Thu: 11.00-23.00. Fri-Sat: 11.00-24.00

Food: All day every day

Credit Cards: Cash only

Facilities: Beer garden; function room; parking

Entertainment: Pool; large screen TV; karaoke evenings; live music; occasional discos

Local Places of Interest/Activities: Scone Palace nearby; City of Perth, 3 miles; Branklyn Garden (NTS), 3 miles

Amulree Hotel & Lonely Inn | 155

Amulree,
Perthshire
PH8 0EF
Tel: 01350 725218

Directions:

Amulree is on the A822 Crieff to Dunkeld road, about 12 miles north of Crieff

Also known as "The Lonely Inn", **The Amulree Hotel & Coaching Inn** stands close to the geographic centre of both Perthshire and Scotland. A tiny Highland village boasting a shop, a Kirk, the hotel and just half a dozen houses, Amulree is set amidst some of the finest scenery in Scotland yet is only one hour from both Edinburgh and Glasgow. The Amulree Hotel was built in the early 1700s as a Drovers Inn, became a Kings House and evolved as a small coaching inn before being extended to its present size in the 1930s. It stands in 3 acres of lovely grounds, bordered by the River Braan.

The inn is noted for its fine food. Owners Grahame and Kate Stewart's policy of offering home prepared dishes using only the very finest of local produce has contributed greatly to the hotel's growing reputation. Guests can enjoy an excellent 3-course dinner for as little as £10 currently: those with lesser appetites are free to order just one or two courses as required. Hot meals and snacks are available all afternoon to residents and non-residents alike. The hotel has 12 guest bedrooms, 8 of which have private facilities. All rooms are centrally heated and provided with colour TV and tea/coffee-making facilities. It was William Wordsworth who bestowed the name "The Lonely Inn" when he visited the area in 1803. Other notable people to have passed this way include Bonnie Prince Charlie whose demoralised army trudged over Amulree bridge on its way to make a last stand at fateful Culloden; Annie S. Swan, whose novel Sheila is based on Amulree and its people; and show business celebrities such as Greer Garson, Geraldo and Jimmy Logan.

Opening Hours: Sun-Thu: 11.00-23.00; Fri-Sat: 11.00-23.45

Food: Available 12.00-21.00, daily

Credit Cards: All major cards except Diners

Accommodation: 12 rooms, (8 en suite)

Facilities: Beer garden; parking

Entertainment: Occasional traditional live music

Local Places of Interest/Activities: The Hermitage (NTS), 7 miles; Dunkeld Cathedral, 8 miles; Glenturret Distillery, Crieff, 12 miles

Internet/Website:
e-mail: thelonelyinn@aol.com

156 The Bell Tree

54 Main Street,
Methven,
Perthshire PH1 3PT
Tel: 01738 840201

Directions:

From Perth take the A85 towards Crieff. Methven is on this road, about 6 miles west of Perth. The Bell Tree is on the right hand side, midway through the village

The Bell Tree is a striking looking building with its "chess board" pattern of grey granite inlaid with darker blocks. The Bell is very much a family business, with Ken and Margaret Melville aided by their daughter. Ken and Margaret are both from the local area and have a vast knowledge of the surrounding countryside so if you want to know the best places to visit, or where you can golf, fish, go swimming, curling or bowling, just ask! Margaret does most of the cooking, assisted by a chef at weekends, serving bar lunches 7 days a week and evening meals from 6pm to 9.30pm. Her menu offers a good choice of homemade dishes, (soups, steak pie, fish, chicken & duck, for example), with an emphasis on traditional Scottish favourites and all at very sensible prices. Customers can enjoy their meals either in the cosy bar with its soft lighting and comfortable soft fabric wall seating, or in the attractive 20-seater restaurant which is hung with landscape pictures and has a feature wall of exposed stone. Ken is in charge of the bar which in addition to all the usual spirits on optics, has Scottish & Newcastle beers, lager on font, and a good display of various malts on show.

Opening Hours: Mon-Thurs: 11.30-14.30 & 17.00-23.00; Fri-Sun: 11.30-23.45

Food: Home made bar lunches; evening meals 18.00-21.30 daily

Credit Cards: Cash only

Facilities: Lounge bar; restaurant

Local Places of Interest/Activities: Golf, river & loch fishing, all within easy reach; Methven Castle, 1 mile; Caithness Glass, 6 miles; City of Perth, 6 miles; Scone Palace, 12 miles; Crieff Distillery, 12 miles

The Black Watch Inn | **157**

Bank Street,
Aberfeldy,
Perthshire
PH15 2BB
Tel: 01887 820699
Directions:
From the A9, 25 miles north ofPerth, turn left on the A827 to Aberfeldy (9 miles). The Black Watch Inn is in the main street of the town

Occupying a prime position in the main street of this dignified, mostly Victorian, little town, **The Black Watch Inn** takes its name from the peacekeeping force of Highlanders assembled by Gen. Wade in 1769. Some 30 years earlier, the general had constructed the bridge over the River Tay here that bears his name. Designed by William Adam, architect father of Robert Adam, the 4-arched, humpback bridge was the first to span the Tay. At the southern end of the bridge stands the Black Watch Monument, the figure of a thoughtful, kilted soldier erected in 1887.

It was around that time the Black Watch Inn opened for business. A handsome, spacious building, bright and meticulously clean, it has a large lounge and a separate public bar with a long, long bar and plenty of seating. The inn is owned and run by Ian Menzies who has been here since 1987 and has steadily increased the good reputation of this friendly hostelry. Food is available every lunchtime and evening, offering traditional Scottish pub fare at very reasonable prices. The well-stocked bar offers a wide range of all the leading brands including, naturally, a selection of whiskys. Whisky connoisseurs will want to sample the product of the local Aberfeldy Distillery which stands just to the east of the town. An impressive building of 1898, the distillery welcomes visitors for guided tours, has a well-stocked shop and a pleasant Nature Trail through the surrounding native woodland.

Opening Hours: Sun-Thu: 11.00-23.00;Fri-Sat: 11.00-23.45

Food: Available daily, 12.00-14.15; 17.00-20.45

Credit Cards: All major cards except Amex & Diners

Facilities: Beer garden; parking

Entertainment: Pool table; occasional live music & quiz nights

Local Places of Interest/Activities: Black Watch Monument, nearby; Falls of Moness, ½ mile; Aberfeldy Distillery, 1½ miles; Castle Menzies, 2 miles; Loch Tay, 6 miles; Dunkeld Cathedral, 15 miles

158   Coaching Inn

Moray Street, Blackford,
Perthshire PH4 1QF
Tel: 01764 682497
Fax: 01764 682877

Directions:

Blackford village is off the A9
Perth to Stirling road, about
17 miles southwest of Perth

Dating back to the 1830s,
the **Coaching Inn** is a delightful black-and-white
building with witch's hat turrets and a lantern above the front entrance. The inn is a
privately run hotel and conference centre owned by Kipp and Euan who pride themselves on providing a warm welcoming atmosphere. Guests can dine by a coal fire in
the Tavern Bar or enjoy a meal by candlelight in the newly opened Scottish Restaurant. The cuisine in both is wholesome traditional Scottish fare, freshly prepared by
the hotel's chefs. If you are lucky with your fishing they will even cook your catch to
your own recipe. Whisky connoisseurs will surely want to sample the local malt,
Tullibardine, and perhaps some others from the wide range on offer.

Accommodation at the Coaching Inn is of a very high standard. You can sleep in
a turret bedroom in a 4-poster bed and all the rooms are en suite and equipped with
TV, fridge, telephone and tea/coffee-making facilities. Fresh fruit and locally produced
mineral water from Gleneagles Spring are provided as standard.

The Coaching Inn is unique in that it house a Coaching and Development Consultancy. The consultancy's aim for clients over the last 10 years has been to facilitate
personal coaching and organisational development programmes which make a difference. The fully equipped conference and training rooms are designed to encourage
focused learning, positive thinking and the productive exchange of ideas.

Opening Hours: Hotel open all day

Food: All day every day

Credit Cards: All major cards except
Diners

Accommodation: All rooms en suite; 4-
poster room

Facilities: Special golf, fishing or theatre
weekends arranged; Training & Conference
facilities; chauffeur service from railway
station or airport

Entertainment: Pool; large screen TV;
video; live music locally

Local Places of Interest/Activities: Golf,
fishing, falconry, all nearby; Drummond
Castle Gardens, 10 miles; Doune Motor
Museum, 12 miles; Doune Castle, 13 miles;
Blair Drummond Safari Park, 14 miles;
Stirling Castle, Wallace Monument, 16
miles

Internet/Website:
e-mail: coachinginn@hotmail.com

The Comrie Hotel 159

Comrie,
Perthshire PH6 2DY
Tel: 01764 670239
Fax: 01764 670330

Directions:

Comrie is on the A85, about 25 miles west of Perth

The Romans called it Victoria, the Picts knew it as Aberlednock, but the Gaelic-speaking Scots gave Comrie the name it now bears. It comes from comruith, meaning the meeting of streams and the tumbling waters of three rivers, with a backdrop of wooded glens and steep hills, give this picturesque little town its beautiful setting. Many of Comrie's pleasant buildings are 19th century or older. The unusual white church with its castellated steeple dates from 1804 and a turn of the century Charles Rennie Mackintosh building houses a traditional ironmongers in Melville Square.

One of the town's most striking buildings is **The Comrie Hotel** which was purpose built as an upmarket hotel in 1887. Ivy clings to its impressive frontage and inside, the spacious rooms are immaculately furnished and decorated. The hotel is owned and run by Colin and Christine Mackay, attentive hosts who will do all they can to make sure your stay is as pleasant and relaxed as possible. They pay particular attention to the food on offer - traditional quality Scotch fare with salmon and steaks the house specialities. There are 11 guest bedrooms, 2 of them on the ground floor, and all of them en suite and equipped with TV and tea/coffee-making facilities. An additional attraction at this friendly hotel is the peaceful beer garden which is a veritable sun trap.

Opening Hours: Every day: 11.00-14.00, 18.00-23.00

Food: Available Sun-Thu: 12.00-14.00; 18.00-21.00. Fri-Sat: 11.00-14.00; 17.00-23.00

Credit Cards: All major cards except Amex & Diners

Accommodation: 11 rooms, all en suite

Facilities: Beer garden; residents' lounge; parking

Entertainment: Occasional live music; Quiz Nights

Local Places of Interest/Activities: Deil's Cauldron Waterfall, Lord Melville's Monument, both 1.5 miles; Loch Earn, 7 miles; Glenturret Distillery, Crieff, 8 miles; Drummond Castle Gardens, 8 miles

160 The Crees Inn

Main Street,
Abernethy,
Perthshire PH2 9LA
Tel: 01738 850714

Directions:

From Exit 9 of the M90, take the A921 south. About 2 miles along this road, turn left on the A913 to Abernethy (2 miles)

Once the ancient Pictish capital of Scotland, the village of Abernethy is now best known for its 12th century Irish-style Round Tower, one of only two such towers in Scotland. The tower was part of a Saxon church where, according to tradition, Malcolm Canmore swore fealty to William the Conqueror. Another building of interest nearby is Lindores Abbey at Newburgh. Also dating back to the 12th century, only the west tower still stands but from its elevated position there are some stunning views across the River Tay.

Back in Abernethy, the place to seek out for refreshment is undoubtedly **The Crees Inn**, a sturdy building of Scottish stone whose history stretches back to 1781. It is now a listed building. Inside, ongoing renovations have extended the bar area to include a cosy seating area with stone fireplace. Mine host, Brian Johnston, is a genial gentleman who takes great pains to ensure that the food, drink and service at the inn maintains the great traditions of Scottish hospitality. A very varied menu is available, all the dishes based on fresh local produce, lovingly prepared. To complement your meal there's a choice of real ales and malt whiskies along with all the popular beverages, and soft drinks, tea and coffee are always on offer. And if you want to have a private meeting, there's a charming snug available. A restaurant and en-suite bedrooms will be available by Easter 2001.

Opening Hours: Mon-Fri: 11.00-15.00 and 17.00-23.00; Sat: 11.00-00.00; Sun: 12.30-23.00.

Food: Bar meals available every day.

Credit Cards: Access, Delta, Mastercharge & Visa

Facilities: Beer garden; Snug for private meetings; parking

Entertainment: Occasional entertainment

Local Places of Interest/Activities: Round Tower nearby; Pitmedden Forest, 1.5 miles; Lindores Abbey, 4 miles; City of Perth, 10 miles

Cyprus Inn

161

Back Street,
Bridge of Earn,
Perth,
Perthshire
PH2 9AB
Tel: 01738 812313

Directions:

From Exit 9 of the M90 take the A912 to Bridge of Earn (0.5 miles)

Located near the centre of the town, the **Cyprus Inn** opened in 1790 and takes its name from the 18th century ships that were at that time used to transport sherry. The inn retains many original features which the owner, John Bain, would be happy to show you. This is very much a traditional Scottish pub - the public bar always busy with local people. There's also a lounge bar, an excellent place in which to enjoy the wholesome food on offer. An interesting feature in the main bar is a striking mural which captures the attention of many customers. You can play pool here and there are regular karaoke nights and evenings with live entertainment. Outside, there's a pleasant beer garden for those sunny days of summer. This is definitely a hostelry for those who want to experience a really Scottish pub and if you plan to stay in the area, the inn has 4 good quality rooms, all en suite and equipped with TV and tea/coffee-making facilities.

Opening Hours: Sun-Thu: 11.00-23.00; Fri-Sat: 11.00-24.00

Food: Bar snacks served all day

Credit Cards: Access, Delta, Mastercharge & Visa

Accommodation: 4 rooms, all en suite

Facilities: Beer garden; parking

Entertainment: Pool table; karaoke nights; live music

Local Places of Interest/Activities: Ochil Hills to the south & west; Round Tower, Abernethy, 5 miles; City of Perth, 6 miles; Loch Leven Castle & Kinross House Gardens, 14 miles

162 Gwydyr House Hotel

Comrie Road, Crieff,
Perthshire PH7 4BP
Tel/Fax: 01764 653277

Directions:

Crieff is on the A85, 17 miles west of Perth.
Continue along the A85 (signposted to
Crianlarich), and Gwydyr House Hotel can
be found opposite MacRosty Park

Only a five minute walk from the centre of Crieff, **Gwydyr House Hotel**
stands in its own grounds amidst informal gardens and enjoys a wonderfully
peaceful situation overlooking Macrosty
Park on the western edge of the town.
The hotel was built as a private villa in
1875, to the very high standards of that time, and was converted to hotel use in 1973.
Now over 120 years old, it combines present day comfort and amenities with the grace,
architectural style and character of the past. Guests can relax in the lounge bar with a
drink before dining in the elegant restaurant looking out to the mountains. The hotel
faces southwest and commands superb views over the Vale of Strathearn, Glen Artney
and the Grampian mountains, with Ben Vorlich (rising to 3224ft above sea level)
being the prominent feature. A wonderful setting in which to enjoy the hotel chef's
interesting choice of meals -all freshly prepared from the best local produce and complemented by an extensive selection of wines.

The accommodation at Gwydyr House maintains the same high standards. All 8
en suite bedrooms are well-appointed and equipped with colour television, hospitality trays, shaver points, hairdryers and heating. They all offer private bathrooms or
private shower room facilities. The hotel's central location makes it perfect for runs
out to the coasts: Oban and Fort William in the west; St Andrews and the fishing
villages of the Neuk of Fife to the east. A short journey to the north brings you to
Dunkeld and Pitlochry; to the south, Callander, Aberfoyle and the Trossachs are all
within easy reach.

Opening Hours: Bar open from midday
but drinks only with food

Food: Table d'hote available on request

Credit Cards: Visa, Mastercard

Accommodation: 8 rooms, all en suite
Facilities: Gardens

Local Places of Interest/Activities:

Glenturret Distillery, Stuart Crystal, both
nearby; Golf, 2 miles; Falls of Turret, 3
miles; Drummond Castle Gardens, 5 miles;
City of Perth, 17 miles

Internet/Website:
e-mail: george.blackie@iclweb.com
website: www.Smoothhound.co.uk/hotels/
gwydyr.html

The Inn

163

Crook of Devon,
Kinross-shire KY13 0VR
Tel: 01577 840207

Directions:
From Exit 6 of the M90, take the A977 to Crook of Devon (6 miles)

Located in the heart of this much sought after village, **The Inn** at Crook of Devon is an attractive old building dating back to the 1740s. With its long, low whitewashed frontage, dotted with hanging baskets and tubs of flowers, it looks very inviting and the interior is just as appealing. The owner is Marco Palmieri whose hobby is witnessed by the photographs of racing cars and bikes scattered around the walls. As his name suggests, Marco is of Italian descent but his Scots brogue is as authentic as any you will hear in Kinross-shire! Together with his wife, he has made The Inn a popular venue for anyone who appreciates good food and drink. In the 50-seater Stables Restaurant you'll find a good choice of traditional Scottish fare, supplemented by daily specials, and complemented by an extensive selection of wines and ales.

Incidentally, the village takes its rather unusual name from a bend in the River Devon which at this point makes a 180° turn before continuing on its way to join the River Forth near Alloa.

Opening Hours: Every day: 11.30-14.30, 17.00-23.00

Food: Available 12.00-14.00; 17.00-21.30

Credit Cards: Cash only

Facilities: Restaurant; parking

Entertainment: Occasional live music

Local Places of Interest/Activities: Loch Leven, Kinross House Gardens, Loch Leven Castle, all at Kinross, 7 miles; Dollar Glen, Castle Campbell (NTS), 9 miles

164   Kirkstyle Inn

Kirkstyle Square,
Dunning,
Perthshire PH2 0RR
Tel: 01764 684248
Fax: 01764 684695

Directions:

From Perth take the A9 south towards Stirling. After about 8 miles, turn left on the B9141 to Dunning (2 miles). The Kirkstyle Inn is in the centre of the village

This attractive little village was once the capital of the Picts and it was here that Kenneth I, King of the Picts and Scots, died in 860AD. During the Jacobite rebellion, the whole village was destroyed, an outrage which proved to be something of a blessing in disguise since it was rebuilt in handsome Georgian style. The only building to escape the devastation was St Serfs Church, a striking Norman structure whose crow-stepped tower dominates the village. Just to the west of Dunning is a pile of stones surmounted by a cross and inscribed with the words: "Maggie Wall, Burnt here, 1657". The unfortunate lady had been convicted as a witch.

In Dunning itself, just across the road from St Serfs Church, stands the **Kirkstyle Inn**, an imposing Georgian building which has provided food and drink for travellers for more than 200 years. Many alterations have been made over the years, but the inn still remains unpretentious and attractive in appearance - those who come today will see little change in both the Kirkstyle Inn and the village. Inside you will find a warm and welcoming bar, with an open fire, where you can catch up on the local news, via the locals, newspapers and television. There's excellent bar food here, served by friendly, courteous staff. Families are welcome in the comfortable Snug (high chairs provided), or you can enjoy a meal in the Dining Room which offers the best of local produce, cooked to the highest standards.

The immediate countryside provides a whole range of outdoor pursuits - hill walking, tennis, golf, bowls, microlighting, off road driving and more. After all that, the Kirkstyle Inn is the place to go for some well-earned rest.

Opening Hours: Mon-Fri: 11.00-14.30; 17.00-24.00. Sat: 11.00-24.00. Sun: 12.30-23.00

Food: Available every lunchtime & evening

Credit Cards: All major cards accepted

Facilities: Beer garden; parking

Entertainment: Pool table; games room; ceilidhs

Local Places of Interest/Activities: St Serfs Church nearby; Ochil Hills to the south; City of Perth, 10 miles

The Log Cabin 165

Kirkmichael,
Perthshire PH10 7NA
Tel: 01250 881288
Fax: 01250 881206

Directions:

From Exit 11 of the M90, take the A93
north to Blairgowrie. Continue on the
A93 to Bridge of Cally (5 miles) then
turn left on the A924 to Kirkmichael
(7 miles). In the centre of Kirkmichael,
turn left over the River Ardle and continue up tarmac road for 1 mile to the hotel

As the name suggests, **The Log Cabin Hotel** is of solid log construction with a warm and comfortable atmosphere. A massive open fire burner in the main lounge provides a focal point for visitors and the pine floors and ceilings make you feel as if you have arrived at a Scandinavian ski lodge. This unique, family run hotel, built in 1966, stands in secluded woodland which is a haven for wildlife - red squirrels, rabbits, deer, pheasant and buzzards can often be seen from the hotel. From the dining room there are panoramic views of Strathardle and here guests can enjoy a menu which always includes prime Scottish ingredients, freshly prepared and served. The menu also offers a good choice of snacks which can also be enjoyed in the fully licensed Lounge Bar with its open log fire and wide selection of malt whiskies. The hotel has 13 guest bedrooms, all en suite and all on the ground floor, thus providing easy access for the disabled. Some rooms have been specially adapted, so please ask for further details. There's a choice of twin, double and family rooms - some with connecting doors - and each room has tea and coffee-making facilities. A choice of full cooked breakfast is provided for residents, along with cereals, yoghurt, croissants and scones - a hearty repast to set you up for a day exploring this spectacularly scenic part of Perthshire. Within easy range there are facilities for a huge variety of activities - from skiing to swimming and squash, from historic castles such as Scone, Blair, Balmoral and Glamis to distilleries at Pitlochry (one of Scotland's oldest) and Edradour (the smallest in the country) where visitors can enjoy a complimentary dram of the national beverage.

Opening Hours: Hotel open all day

Food: Available 12.00-14.00; 18.30-20.00

Credit Cards: All major cards except Amex & Diners

Accommodation: 13 rooms, all ground floor & en suite, some with disabled facilities

Facilities: Beer garden; restaurant; lounge bar;

Entertainment: Quiz night, Tuesday; karaoke nights; occasional live music

Local Places of Interest/Activities: Tay Forest Park, 3 miles; Skiing at Glenshee, 10 miles; Edradour Distillery, 11 miles; Blair Athol Distillery, Salmon Ladder, Festival Theatre, all at Pitlochry, 12 miles

Internet/Website:
e-mail: mandy@logcabinhotel.co.uk
website:www. logcabinhotel.co.uk

166 Marfield Inn

Hatton Road, Rattray,
Blairgowrie, Perthshire
PH10 7AW
Tel: 01250 872953

Directions:

Rattray is on the A93, 16 miles north of Perth

Rattray and its sister community of Blairgowrie sit on either side of the fast flowing River Ericht, famed for its salmon. This is also the heart of Scotland's fruit growing area. The altitude and soil seem to combine to give perfect growing conditions for the famed raspberries, most of which end up in the Dundee jam factories. The twin towns are at their busiest in the winter when they provide a base for sports enthusiasts skiing at Glenshee just up the road. Anyone interested in Scotland's industrial heritage will want to see Keathbank Mill, located in the centre of Blairgowrie. This massive old jute mill has a steam turbine of 1862 driven by the largest working water wheel in Scotland. The site also boasts the largest model railway set in Britain and workshops where heraldic crests are carved.

Back in Rattray itself, **The Marfield Inn** is everything you would expect of a traditional Scottish pub. Built more than 150 years ago, it stands at the end of a small lane in a peaceful spot with open countryside adjoining. The spacious beer garden has a children's play area, complete with Bouncy Castle, and tucked away nearby are 3 mobile homes which are available to rent. Each of them is fully equipped with all modern facilities and can sleep up to 8 people. The inn is very much at the centre of the community, with all ages welcome and a lively programme of entertainments that includes quiz, karaoke and bingo nights. Landlord William Thomson also provides his customers with a good choice of traditional pub grub, available every day from 11am until 9pm, and offered at very sensible prices.

Opening Hours: Sun-Thu: 11.00-23.00; Fri-Sat: 11.00-24.00

Food: Available 11.00-21.00, daily

Credit Cards: Cash only

Accommodation: 3 mobile homes, each sleeping up to 8 people

Facilities: Beer garden; children's play area; parking

Entertainment: Pool table; quiz, karaoke and bingo nights; occasional live music

Local Places of Interest/Activities: Keathbank Mill, 1.5 miles; Meikleour Beech Hedge, 5 miles; Meigle Museum, 10 miles; Skiing at Glenshee, 10 miles; City of Perth, 16 miles

The Tower Hotel 167

East High Street,
Crieff,
Perthshire PH7 3JA
Tel: 01764 652678
Fax: 01764 652404

Directions:

Crieff is on the A85, 17 miles west of Perth.
The Tower Hotel is located on the main street

Built in 1792 as a church school, **The Tower Hotel** is one of the most striking buildings in this delightful little town. Visitors enter through an impressive entrance hall that leads to an attractively decorated and compact hotel. To the rear is a splendid beer garden that commands stunning views across to the Ochil Hills. The hotel has 8 guest bedrooms, 5 of them en suite, the others with private facilities, and all have full central heating, colour TV, telephone, and tea/coffee-making facilities. The restaurant, which is open to non-residents, provides the diner with an excellent and very varied selection of dishes. The menus change regularly but just as a sample choice you could start your meal with Stilton Cheese & Walnut Pâté, follow this with Fillet of Beef Stroganoff served on a bed of rice, and for dessert, why not try the gorgeous Crème Brulée with fresh raspberries and blackcurrants, a dish fit for a king. There is also a very comprehensive selection of vegetarian and seafood dishes, ranging from Queen Scallops & Smoked Bacon to the oriental tasting Sweet and Sour Vegetables.

Cling to a hillside above the River Earn, Crieff itself is a pleasant town to wander around, perhaps calling in at the Glenturret Whisky Distillery Visitor Centre. Founded in 1775, Glenturret is the oldest whisky distillery in Scotland. It still produces award-winning malt whisky which visitors can sample free at the Visitor Centre. A couple of miles south of Crieff, Drummond Castle Gardens truthfully claims to be one of the finest formal gardens in Europe. First laid out in the early 1600s, the gardens visitors see today were replanted in the 1950s, preserving features such as the ancient yew hedges and the copper beech trees planted by Queen Victoria to commemorate her visit in 1842.

Opening Hours: Sun-Thu: 11.00-23.00; Fri-Sat: 11.00-23.45

Food: Available daily, 12.00-14.30; 17.00-21.00

Credit Cards: All major cards accepted

Accommodation: 8 rooms, (5 en suite)

Facilities: Beer garden; parking

Entertainment: Petanque (French boules); Quiz Nights

Local Places of Interest/Activities: Glenturret Distillery, Stuart Crystal, both nearby; Golf, 2 miles; Falls of Turret, 3 miles; Drummond Castle Gardens, 5 miles; City of Perth, 17 miles

168 Two O Eight Hotel

208 Crieff Road,
Perth,
Perthshire
PH1 2PE
Tel/Fax: 01738 628936
Directions:
From the centre of Perth, take the A85 west towards Crieff. The Two O Eight Hotel is on this road

Beautifully set beside the River Tay, Perth's compact city centre is framed by two extensive parks, the North Inch and South Inch. The North Inch was the site of a bloody tournament in 1396 which became known as the Battle of the Clans and later provided the background to Scott's novel The Fair Maid of Perth. The city boasts a wide range of visitor attractions, amongst them the 15th century Balhousie Castle, home of the Black Watch Museum, and the striking medieval St John's Kirk where in 1559 John Knox preached a rabble-rousing sermon that provoked an anti-Catholic riot in which 4 monasteries were razed to the ground, including the historic Abbey at Scone, a couple of miles north of the town. Scone Palace survived and is one of Scotland's premier stately homes.

Also well worth a visit is **The Two O Eight Hotel** which takes its name from its numbering on the Crieff Road. The hotel was purpose-built in 1975 by the Dorin family and is currently owned and run by Ian Dorin. Immaculately clean and attractively furnished, the rooms are spacious and well laid-out - ideal for family groups. The hotel offers a good choice of traditional bar food, all home cooked, provided at sensible prices and with menus that are regularly changed. There are 8 guest bedrooms, 6 of them en suite, and all equipped with satellite TV and tea/coffee-making facilities. The Two O Eight's location makes it a highly convenient base for exploring this historic city and the spectacular countryside around.

Opening Hours: Sun-Thu: 11.00-23.00; Fri-Sat: 11.00-23.45

Food: Available daily, 12.00-14.00; 18.00-20.00

Credit Cards: All major cards except Amex & Diners

Accommodation: 8 rooms, (6 en suite)

Facilities: Restaurant; parking

Entertainment: Pool table; karaoke, quiz and live music evenings

Local Places of Interest/Activities: Balhousie Castle, St John's Kirk, Art Gallery & Museum, all in Perth; Huntingtower Castle, 2 miles; Scone Palace, 2 miles; Caithness Glass, 2 miles

Internet/Website:
e-mail: 208@easynet.co.uk

Woodside Inn

169

Woodside,
Perthshire
PH13 9NP
Tel: 01828 670254
Fax: 01828 670654

Directions:

Woodside is on the A94, about 11 miles northeast of Perth

During its 150-year history, the excellent **Woodside Inn** has

served as a convalescent home for World War I casualties and as a doctor's surgery before finally finding its proper role as a friendly and relaxing hostelry. Roy and Helen Jacobs bought this attractive white-painted building in 1997 and quickly established a reputation for serving top quality food along with well-kept real ales. There are always 3 or 4 real ales on tap and they change frequently so that during the course of a single year patrons of the inn will have had the opportunity of sampling up to 150 different brews. An interesting feature of the inn's decor is a colourful display of all the beer mats associated with these real ales - smothering the old beams and now spreading across the walls.

Before the Jacobs bought the pub, Roy was chef here and his cooking is the other reason why Woodside Inn is so popular. A glance through the menu explains it all. Haggis & Drambuie Cream amongst the starters, Supreme of Scottish Salmon, Thai Spicy Chicken, and a Mixed Grill "for the hungry only!!!" amongst the main dishes, with a choice of wonderful sweets to follow. It's no surprise to discover that if you plan to eat here over the weekend you would be well-advised to book in advance.

No visit to this corner of Perthshire would be complete without seeing the famous Meikleour Beech Hedge, just a few miles from the Woodside Inn. This extraordinary natural feature has earned itself an entry in the Guinness Book of Records. Planted in 1746, the hedge is now some 750ft long and more than 90ft high.

Opening Hours: Mon-Fri: 12.00-14.00, 17.00-23.00; Sat: 12.00-24.00; Sun: 12.30-23.00

Food: Available Mon-Sat: 12.00-14.00; 17.00-21.00; Sun:12.30-14.30; 16.30-20.30

Credit Cards: All major cards except Amex & Diners

Facilities: Restaurant; parking

Entertainment: Occasional live music & Quiz Nights

Local Places of Interest/Activities: Meikleour Beech Hedge, 4 miles; Meigle Museum, 9 miles; Scone Palace, 12 miles; City of Perth, 13 miles

Internet/Website: e-mail: thewoodsideinn@btinternet.com

The Hidden Inns of Central and Southern Scotland

7 Fife, Dundee and Angus

PLACES OF INTEREST:

Aberdour 173
Anstruther 173
Arbroath 174
Brechin 174
Carnoustie 174
Crail 175
Culross 175
Cupar 175
Dumferline 176
Dundee 176

Falkland 178
Forfar 178
Glamis 178
Glenrothes 179
Kirriemuir 179
Leven 180
Montrose 180
North Queensferry 180
Pittenweem 180
St Andrews 181

PUBS AND INNS:

The Abbey Inn, Newburgh 182

Auchmithie Hotel, Auchmithie, by Arbroath 183

The Balcarres Hotel, Colinsburgh 184

Balcomie Links Hotel, Crail 185

The Bear Tavern, Newburgh 186

The Crusoe Hotel, Lower Largo 187

Lomond Hills Hotel, Freuchie 188

The New Windsor Hotel, Leven 189

The Old Rectory Inn, Dysart, nr Kirkcaldy 190

Path Tavern, Kirkcaldy 191

Red House Hotel, Coupar Angus 192

Salutation Hotel, Inverbervie 193

St Michael's Inn, Leuchars, by St Andrews 194

Thrums Hotel, Kirriemuir 195

The Hidden Inns of Central and Southern Scotland

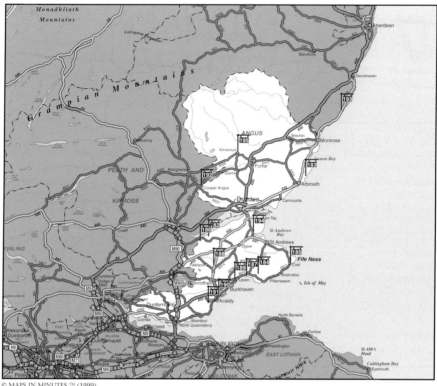

© MAPS IN MINUTES ™ (1999)

182 The Abbey Inn, Newburgh

183 Auchmithie Hotel, Auchmithie, by Arbroath

184 The Balcarres Hotel, Colinsburgh

185 Balcomie Links Hotel, Crail

186 The Bear Tavern, Newburgh

187 The Crusoe Hotel, Lower Largo

188 Lomond Hills Hotel, Freuchie

189 The New Windsor Hotel, Leven

190 The Old Rectory Inn, Dysart, nr Kirkcaldy

191 Path Tavern, Kirkcaldy

192 Red House Hotel, Coupar Angus

193 Salutation Hotel, Inverbervie

194 St Michael's Inn, Leuchars, by St Andrews

195 Thrums Hotel, Kirriemuir

Please note all cross references refer to page numbers

Surrounded on three sides by water (the Tay, the Forth and the North Sea), Fife has retained its identity ever since it was established as a Kingdom by the Picts in the 4th century. Its capital, then as now, is the small market town of Cupar - set in the fertile Howe of Fife, the pastoral heart of the kingdom. Also in the Howe is Falkland, a charming medieval town with a glorious Renaissance Palace.

Over to the east, the handsome and dignified town of St Andrews is surrounded by unspoilt countryside and a coastline edged with extensive sandy beaches. The most picturesque stretch of coast, however, lies to the south in the area known as the East Neuk of Fife. From Leven to Crail, there's a succession of quaint old fishing villages with distinctive pantiled roofs.

Most of Fife's industrial towns are located in the south, but this is where you'll also find the beautifully preserved 16th century village of Culross and historic Dunfermline with its grand old ruined Abbey.

The glorious glens of Angus, carving their way through the southern Grampian mountains, are among the grandest sights in Scotland. Just a few scattered villages are dotted along the quiet minor roads which, for the most part, end at the foot of some unscalable crag. The area includes no fewer than 10 Munros, mountains of 3,000 feet or more, but it is also great walking country where there's a good likelihood of seeing wild deer, golden eagles or ptarmigan.

The Angus coastline offers some fine beaches east of Dundee and there's a fine stretch of cliffs and bays between Arbroath and Montrose. Ruined Arbroath Abbey was the setting in 1320 for the signing of the Scotland's declaration of independence from England, and there's more history to be savoured at Glamis Castle where, according to Shakespeare, Macbeth murdered King Duncan.

In the south, Scotland's fourthh largest city, Dundee, has weathered the loss of its traditional industries and re-emerged as a lively, progressive university city.

PLACES OF INTEREST

ABERDOUR

Aberdour is famous for its silver sands and has even been dubbed the "Fife Riviera". The town also boasts a 14th century **Castle** (HS) with an attractive and spacious 17th century garden where there stands an unusual circular dovecote of the same period. Also in the Castle grounds is **St Fillan's Church**, notable for some fine Norman work.

From the house, scenic walks lead to the old harbour and the village. Also nearby are the ruins of Aberdour Castle, the famous Silversands beach, and the 12th century St Fillan's church, with its ancient Do'cot, as well as Aberdour's award-winning station.

ANSTRUTHER

Fifty years ago, the picturesque port of Anstruther was so busy with fishing boats it was possible to walk from one side of the wide harbour to the other by stepping from boat to boat. Then the North Sea herring shoals, which had brought prosperity to the town for centuries, mysteriously disappeared. The vessels now rocking gently in the harbour are mostly pleasure craft.

The town's long association with the sea is vividly brought to life at the **Scottish Fisheries Museum** beside the harbour. Lovingly restored craft stand beached in the paved courtyard, with a huge anchor alongside. Inside, tableaux, reconstructions, models and paintings give a comprehensive overview of the local fishing industry. On a more poignant note, there's a room devoted to a Memorial to Scottish Fishermen Lost at Sea.

About four miles offshore, on the **Isle of May**, stands a lighthouse built in 1816 by Robert Louis Stevenson's grandfather, and also the ruins of the country's first lighthouse, erected in 1636. The island is now a bird sanctuary with thousands of puffins and eider ducks in permanent residence. Transient birds stopping off

North Carr Lightboat, Anstruther

have boosted the number of different species spotted here to more than 200. There are regular boat trips to the island during the season.

In Anstruther itself, collectors of curiosities will be pleased with Buckie House. Its former owner decorated it outside and inside with buckies, or shells, and as a final touch stipulated that he should be buried in a shell-encrusted coffin.

Arbroath

Arbroath holds a special place of affection in the hearts of Scottish nationalists. Back in 1320, it was at **Arbroath Abbey** that Robert the Bruce signed the Declaration of Arbroath asserting Scotland's independence from England. The Abbey was then one of the wealthiest and grandest churches in the country. Today, the pink sandstone ruins of the Abbey are a melancholy sight but the remnants of its massively proportioned West Front, the Abbot's House and the Gatehouse testify to its former glory. Dr Johnson described the ruins as *"fragments of magnificence"*.

Anyone with the slightest interest in food will immediately link the name of Arbroath with

"smokies". These uniquely tasty delicacies of haddock smoked over oak chips are produced in tiny smokehouses around the picturesque harbour.

Brechin

At Brechin the valley of Strathmore meets the rugged Grampian mountains and the old city is itself set on a hill. Standing at the heart of this small city, **Brechin Cathedral** was founded in the 1100s but time has not been kind to it and most of the structure is the result of extensive restoration in 1900. Pre-dating the Cathedral is the fascinating **Round Tower** of 990 AD, some 80 feet tall. It was built as a refuge for the clergy in times of invasion, which is why its doorway stands six feet above the ground.

Devotees of steam railways will surely want to take a trip on the **Caledonian Railway** which operates a regular summer timetable of passenger trains on the four-mile route from Brechin to Bridge of Dun. The Brechin Railway Society have also restored the station building with its superb glass canopy and opened a small but growing museum in the former telegraph office.

Standing on the banks of the South Esk River, Brechin has long been a centre for visitors wishing to explore this historic corner of Scotland. The city itself is notable for the unusual round tower standing next to the Cathedral. One of only four such towers in Scotland, it dates back to the 10th century when it was built as a refuge from Viking raids. Magical Glamis Castle, childhood home of the Queen Mother, is only 15 miles away, and steam railway enthusiasts can enjoy a trip on the Caledonian Railway Company trains which ply between Brechin's Victorian station and Bridge of Dun during the summer months.

Carnoustie

Carnoustie is internationally famed as host to the British Open Golf Championship and many other major golfing events. Every street in this coastal town seems to lead down to a fairway and a bunker is in the foreground of almost every sea view. Carnoustie's sweeping bay, fringed with fine sandy beaches, has also made it a popular holiday town. There are lovely coastal walks, tennis courts, a bowling green, yachting club, water sports facilities, a leisure centre, as well as two country parks within easy reach.

Two miles west of Carnoustie, **Barry Mill** (National Trust Scotland) was in continuous use from the 18th century to the early 1980s. Its huge waterwheel is now fully functioning once again. The intriguing machinery - fanners, elevators, sieves and sack hoist - are also all still operating. From the Mill there's a delightful walk alongside the lade, or mill-race, to a small apple orchard and picnic area.

CRAIL

The most ancient Royal Burgh in the East Neuk of Fife, Crail also has one of the most photographed harbours in Scotland. Artists, too, love to create paintings of the red-tiled houses cascading down to the shore. Pretty as it is, this picture-postcard village is still a working port, home to Fife's crab and lobster fleet.

About halfway between Crail and St Andrews, at Troywood, is one of Fife's most offbeat visitor attractions: **Scotland's Secret Bunker**. Hidden 100 feet underground and encased in concrete walls 15 feet thick, the bunker was built during the Cold War of the 1950s as a headquarters refuge for government and military officials in the event of a nuclear war. The otherwise austere complex was provided with two cinemas to entertain the expected 300 residents. These now show government information films of the time which advised ludicrously inadequate protective measures for civilians to follow when the four-minute warning of a nuclear bomb attack had been activated.

CULROSS

Culross, pronounced "Cooross", is an outstanding example of a 16th-17th century town, thanks partly to the National Trust for Scotland which has been looking after its picturesque buildings with their crow-stepped gables and red pantiled roofs since 1932. The Trust's Visitor Centre occupies the 16th century **Town House** which has an exhibition and video presentation outlining the burgh's 400 year old history. The house also contains a tiny prison, complete with built-in manacles.

Culross Palace is an impressive ochre-painted mansion built in the late 1500s for a wealthy coal merchant, Sir George Bruce. Inside, there are some remarkable painted ceilings, superb pine panelling and antique furniture and outside, a garden planted with the kinds of herbs and vegetables appropriate for a 16th century garden.

The cobbled alleyway known as **Back Causeway** has a raised centre which was apparently reserved for

the gentry alone. The alley leads to the **Study**, another early 17th century house which takes its name from a room at the top of the tower reached by a turnpike stair. Nearby stands the **Mercat Cross** of 1610 and, a little further up the hill, the ruins of **Culross Abbey**. Only the choir remains intact and now serves as the parish church. Inside, there's a 10th century Celtic cross and a magnificent tomb with alabaster figures portraying Sir George Bruce, his wife, and their eight children. A browse around the graveyard reveals some unusual tombstones with carvings depicting the occupations of the late departed - a gardener with a crossed spade and rake for example.

CUPAR

The capital of Fife, Cupar sits beside the River Eden in the heart of the fertile Howe of Fife for which it serves as the market centre and hosts a regular livestock auction each week. The town is desperately in need of a by-pass to divert the busy A91 which runs through its centre and destroys its medieval character. The 17th century **Mercat Cross** has already been knocked over once by a lorry and the fragments re-assembled.

Two miles south of the town, the **Hill of Tarvit Mansionhouse & Garden** (NTS) is well worth a visit. The house is an Edwardian country mansion designed by Sir Robert Lorimer for a Dundee industrialist, Frederick Bonar Sharp. Sharp was a noted art collector and the house provides a perfect setting for paintings by Raeburn, Ramsay and Dutch artists, as well as superb French, Chippendale and vernacular furniture. In the delightful grounds, there's a restored Edwardian laundry and also **Scotstarvit Tower**, an outstanding example of a late 16th century fortified tower house.

Also within easy reach of Cupar are two family attractions that children in particular will enjoy. The **Scottish Deer Centre** specialises in the rearing of red deer but also raises species of silka, fallow and reindeer. Some of the animals are tame enough to be stroked. The Centre also puts on falconry displays three times a day. Stranger creatures occupy the **Ostrich Kingdom** beside Birnie Loch Nature Reserve. As well as

176

these huge birds, the children's farm is stocked with goats, chickens and pot-bellied pigs.

DUMFERLINE

As the Fife Tourist Board points out, in Dunfermline you can walk through 900 years of history in a day. The capital of Scotland for six centuries until James VI succeeded to the English throne in 1603, the square mile of Dunfermline town centre is rich in history.

A good place to start your walk is, strangely enough, in Glen Bridge car park where you are just yards from **St Margaret's Cave**. In the late 11th century, the pious Margaret, queen to Malcolm III, frequently came to the cave to pray and here she would also wash the feet of the poor.

Just across from the car park, the **Town House** is a gloriously extravagant building, a heady mixture of Scottish Baronial and French Gothic styles. Nearby rises the impressive **Dunfermline Abbey**, originally founded by Queen Margaret and greatly extended by her equally devout son, David I in the early 1100s. Only the nave of the medieval church has survived, its massive Norman columns reminiscent of Durham Cathedral. Robert the Bruce was buried in the Abbey in 1295 but, astonishingly, his resting-place was "lost" and not rediscovered until 1821 when the new parish church was being built. The body was reburied beneath a fine memorial brass thus ensuring that it would not be mislaid again. (His heart, of course, remains at Melrose Abbey.)

Within the Abbey precincts, the 14th century **Abbot House** was formerly the estate office for what was then the richest Benedictine Abbey in Scotland. After being neglected for many years the house has been refurbished and its upper rooms are now dazzlingly colourful with brilliant murals and life-size models illustrating the town's history and people.

Across the road from the Abbey is the entrance to **Pittencroft Park** where a substantial wall, 205 feet long and 60 feet high, is all that remains of the **Royal Palace** in which Charles I was born in 1600. This splendid park, and the Laird's House within it, (now a museum of local history), was a gift to the town from its most famous son, Andrew Carnegie.

Carnegie was born in 1835 in a modest two up-two down cottage in Moodie Street which

is now the **Andrew Carnegie Birthplace Museum**. As a young man Carnegie emigrated to the United States where he rose from bobbin boy, telegraph operator and railroad developer to "Steel King of America". When he sold his businesses inn 1901 for $400 million he became the richest man in the world. He lavished most of his huge fortune on endowing schools, colleges and free public libraries. **The Carnegie Library** at Dunfermline was the first of an eventual 3,000 such buildings. The various Trusts and Foundations established by Carnegie are still operating and dispensing around £100 every minute.

DUNDEE

Approached by either the road or rail bridges over the Tay, Dundee presents a splendid panorama with the city sprawling across the twin hills of Balgay and Law, framed by the often snow-capped Grampians in the distance. The **Tay Rail Bridge**, incidentally, stretches for two miles making it the longest rail bridge in Europe. It replaced the one which collapsed during a storm in December 1879 sending 75 passengers and crew to their deaths. The disaster inspired an out of work actor named William MacGonagall to write *Railway Bridge of the Silvery Tay*. Despite the poem's blithe disregard for metre and its banal sentiments, MacGonagall was lionised in Edinburgh's literary salons and his work still gives enormous pleasure to every new generation of readers.

Any visitor to Dundee will soon hear the term "The Three Js", a reference to the three pillars on which the city's past prosperity was founded - jute, jam, and journalism. In the 19th century Dundee was Britain's leading producer of jute, which was then widely used in the manufacture of coarse sacking, canvas and rope. Dundee's textile heritage is presented in a lively way at **Verdant Works** with the help of vintage working machinery and up-to-the-minute interactive technology.

The association with jam began when a Dundee grocer named Keiller bought a cargo of oranges from a ship taking refuge from a storm. Keiller's wife made marmalade from them and a sweet-tasting success story followed.

The third J, journalism, is still flourishing with D. C. Thomson's ever-popular Beano and Dandy comics delighting children with such characters as Desperate Dan and Dennis the Menace.

Thomson's headquarters stand in Albert Square, across from the city's most imposing Victorian building, the **McManus Art Galleries and Museum** (free). Dundee's 19th century prosperity allowed its citizens to endow the museum with a remarkable collection of Pre-Raphaelite and Scottish paintings. The Museum has a significant display of material from Ancient Egypt and, closer to home, also has the table on which the Duke of Cumberland signed the death warrants of Jacobites captured at the Battle of Culloden.

One of the city's most popular visitor attractions is the **RRS Discovery** which was built at Dundee in 1901 and used by Captain Scott in his expedition to the Antarctic in 1901-1904. The ship lies alongside **Discovery Point**, an award-winning centre where visitors watch an informative film about life on board the Dis-

RRS Discovery

covery (crewmen were permitted one bath every 47 days, for example), before stepping on to the ship with its gleaming brass and scrubbed deck.

A short walk along the waterside brings visitors to another remarkable ship. **HM Frigate Unicorn**, a 46-gun wooden warship, was launched at Chatham in 1824 and is now the oldest British-built ship still afloat. The ship has been restored to her original appearance and provides a fascinating insight into what life was like for its 300 officers and crew just 19 years after the Battle of Trafalgar.

One of the city's unusual attractions is the **Mills Observatory** (free), the only full-time public observatory in Britain. Located in picturesque wooded surroundings on Balgay Hill, it houses a 10-inch refracting telescope and displays illustrating the history of space exploration and astronomy. The best time to visit is during the winter months when the mysteries

of the night sky are explained by the resident astronomer.

Four miles to the east, **Broughty Castle Museum** (free) is an impressive 15th century fort overlooking the Firth of Tay. General Monck "slighted" the castle (made it militarily useless) during the Civil War but it was restored in 1861 as part of Britain's coastal

Jubille Arch, Broughty Ferry

defences. It now houses interesting displays on local history, arms and armour, seashore life and Dundee's whaling history.

EDZELL

Described as the "jewel in the crown of Angus", this pretty village right on the Grampian border is always winning "best-kept village" awards. It's approached through the much-photographed **Dalhousie Arch**, erected in 1887 to the memory of the 13th Earl of Dalhousie and his Countess, who died within a few hours of each other.

Edzell itself is an estate village, created in the 1840s to a regular plan and with trim Victorian houses lining the straight-as-an-arrow main road. About a mile to the west stand the ruins of **Edzell Castle** (HS) an important 15th century tower visited by Mary Stuart and James VI and also used by Cromwell's troops as a garrison. Much of the 16th century castle is ruined, but the beautiful walled garden has survived for more than 350 years and is one of Scotland's unique sights. It was created in 1604 by Sir David Lindsay, Lord Edzell: enclosed by the

178

rosy-coloured sandstone walls of the **Pleasaunce** it still retains its elegant symmetry with sculptured stone panels on the walls and an immaculate box hedge spelling out the family motto: *Dum spiro spero* - "While I breathe I hope."

Northwards from Edzell runs **Glen Esk**, the most easterly and the longest of the Angus Glens. A minor road follows the course of the River North Esk through stunning mountain scenery to The Retreat, a typical glen shooting lodge which houses the **Glenesk Folk Museum**. The museum was founded in 1955 by Mrs Greta Michie and her vast collection of artefacts and records provide an encyclopaedic overview of past life in Glen Esk. There's also a tea room and craft gift shop.

FALKLAND

Set in the Howe (Plain) of Fife, Falkland is a perfect gem, an unspoilt little town which grew up around a superb Renaissance mansion, **Falkland Palace** (NTS). Built between 1501-41, the palace was a favourite seat of the Stuart kings

Falkland Palace

from the time of James V. He extended the building considerably, adding the beautiful Chapel Royal and also a Royal Tennis court in 1539. Both are still in use, and the tennis court is believed to be the oldest in the world.

James was on his deathbed at Falkland when he received news of the birth of his daughter, Mary Stuart. His two sons had died in infancy: now his turbulent kingdom would pass to a woman. He was filled with foreboding: the throne, he said "cam wi' a lass and it will gang wi' a lass". Six days later he was dead and Mary began her ill-fated reign.

Mary, whose experience of castles and palaces was generally pretty melancholy, seems to have spent a happy childhood here, often play-

ing in the splendid gardens which have recently been restored, and frequently returned in later years to ride through the Leven hills.

This enchanting little town was the first in Scotland to be designated a Conservation Area. Concern for protecting Falkland's unique character has even extended to hiding its electricity sub-station in an ordinary house, an idea that could usefully be copied elsewhere.

A stroll around the old town reveals some interesting features such as the "fore-stairs" - outside stairs leading to an upper floor - and "marriage lintels" over front doors inscribed with the initials of the newlywed householders and the year of their marriage.

FORFAR

Forfar, the county town of Angus, stands on what was once the centre of the kingdom of the Picts and the surrounding countryside is scattered with solitary stones carved deep with mysterious shapes. Some of them, along with Neolithic and Celtic examples, are on display at the **Meffan Gallery & Museum** (free) in the High Street which also has an interactive computer archive logging every known Pictish stone in Angus. Other attractions include some inventive simulations of historic street scenes amongst which is a re-creation of a witch hunt. (Forfar was the only town in Angus where witches were executed.)

A more pleasant aspect of the town is the 93-acre park surrounding **Forfar Loch** where rangers organise guided tours and events throughout the year. If you are picnicking here, don't forget to take one of the famous Forfar Bridies, the local equivalent of a Cornish pasty. It was created by Mrs Bridie, a farmer's wife, so that the farmworkers could eat it with work-soiled hands. The crust was simply thrown away.

Two miles northeast of Forfar rise the substantial remains of secluded **Restenneth Priory** (free), mostly 12th century and standing on the site of a Pictish place of worship. It has a striking square tower surmounted by a shapely brooch spire.

GLAMIS

With its Disneyesque towers and turrets, cupolas and bartizans, **Glamis Castle** has an enchanting fairy-tale look about it. The name, (pronounced Glahms), is indissolubly linked with Macbeth's murder of Duncan as presented in Shakespeare's play. In fact, the Bard was playing fast and loose with history since Macbeth actually killed his cousin in a battle near Elgin, some 50 miles away.

All the same, when you step into the 15th century Dunce's Hall, among the oldest and eeriest parts of the castle, it seems an appropriately grim setting for such a dreadful deed. Glamis continued to have close associations with royalty right up to the present day. Mary Stuart stayed in August 1562 and "never merrier", and her son James VI became a close friend of the 9th Lord Glamis whom he elevated to the rank of Earl of Kinghorne.

The Lyon family, now Earls of Strathmore and Kinghorne, have lived at Glamis since 1372. It was to be the childhood home of their most famous descendant, the present Queen Mother, second daughter of the 14th Earl. After her marriage to the Duke of York in 1923, the royal couple spent much of their time at Glamis and it was here that Princess Margaret was born.

The richly furnished Royal Apartments in which the Yorks lived are open to the public and contain notable collections of Dutch and Chinese porcelain, and a dazzling portrait by de Laszlo of the young Duchess of York which hangs in the Queen Mother's Bedroom.

It was the 3rd Earl in the mid-1600s who did most to give Glamis its present appearance, inspired by his love of French chateaux architecture. He transformed the 15th century Great Hall into a sumptuous Drawing Room, still the most splendid apartment in the castle, 60 feet long and 22 feet wide with a fine arched ceiling of delicate plasterwork. A complete west wing was added, and a lovely Chapel whose ceiling and walls are covered with devotional paintings. A generation later, when the Old Pretender, James VIII, was staying at Glamis he came to this Chapel to touch people against the "King's Evil", or scrofula. All those whom the king touched, it was reported, were cured.

The 3rd Earl also laid out the lovely gardens where the formal vistas are enhanced by some fine statuary and a huge baroque sundial with 84 faces. There are delightful walks and a Nature Trail through the extensive landscaped Park, and other attractions include an "Elizabeth of Glamis Exhibition", gift shops and restaurant.

GLENROTHES

About two miles east of the unlovely 20th century architecture of the New Town of Glenrothes, **Balgonie Castle** is a survivor of a more attractive style of building. With its mighty 14th century Keep, the castle is the home of the Laird and Lady of Balgonie and as likely as not it will be one of them who guides you around the partly restored castle. The informative tour provides interesting details about the castle's construction, and its history, which includes a visit by Rob Roy and 200 of his clansmen who were quartered at Balgonie in 1716.

KIRRIEMUIR

This handsome little town is often called the "Gateway to the Glens" and roads lead directly from Kirriemuir to the magnificent scenery of Glen Clova and Glen Prosen. Another, Glen Isla, was frequently visited by Kirrie's most famous son - the creator of the eternally youthful Peter Pan, J. M. Barrie, who was born here in 1860. **Barrie's Birthplace** (NTS) is a modest terraced cottage at 9, Brechin Road where from an early age Barrie dragooned his brothers and sisters into performing his "plays" in the family washhouse. The wash-house is still there, looking much the same as it did more than 130 years ago. Barrie was later to use it as the model for the house that Peter Pan built for Wendy in Never Land.

Barrie's most famous creation is commemorated in the little town square by a winsome **Statue of Peter Pan**. Towards the end of his life, Barrie presented his home town with the rather unorthodox gift of a cricket pavilion with a camera obscura within it. It stands on Kirriemuir Hill and provides some grand views across Strathmore and along the Glens.

Although Barrie was offered burial in Westminster Abbey, he chose to be interred in Kirrie's St Mary's Episcopal Church, just along the road from the house where he was born.

A few hundred yards from the town square, the **Aviation Museum** houses the private collection of Richard Moss who has amassed a wealth of wartime photographs, uniforms, medals, models and other Second World War memorabilia. The museum is open to the public every day in summer: admission is free but donations for local charities are welcome.

180

Just west of Kirriemuir, off the B951, is Lintrathen by Kirriemuir. "In Glen Isla", most westerly of the lovely Glens of Angus, "at the foot of the Knock of Formal", "by the waters of the Loch of Lintrathen", "hard by the waterfall of Reekie Linn" which tumbles 80 feet into a deep pool known as "the Black Dub" - the place names in this region are as entrancing as the magical views.

LEVEN

The area to the east of Leven is known as the East Neuk (nook, or corner) of Fife. Its coastline is dotted with pretty villages and there's a long stretch of excellent sandy beaches around the broad curve of Largo Bay. Leven is the largest of the towns on the bay, popular with holiday-makers enjoying its fine beach, lively Promenade offering all the usual seaside attractions, and two peaceful public parks.

MONTROSE

Montrose stands on a bulbous peninsula with the North Sea washing into its natural harbour on the east, and the two-mile wide **Montrose Lagoon** defines its western boundary. The Lagoon is a wildlife sanctuary of international importance, its mussel and reed beds providing a nature reserve for migrant birds. Seals, thousands of ducks and geese are regular visitors; osprey and kingfishers have also been spotted here. At the **Montrose Basin Wildlife Centre** you can join one of the regular guided walks or view the wildlife through powerful binoculars and on live remote-control television.

The town's natural harbour has been its focal point for generations. Skins, hides and cured salmon were the earliest exports, contraband goods flooded in during the great days of smuggling, and currently the port services the North Sea oil industry. It was from Montrose that the Old Pretender sailed for France after the failure of the 1715 rising.

Montrose Museum (free), built in 1841, is one of the oldest in Scotland. The stately neoclassical building contains comprehensive displays on local life as well as an interesting collection of Napoleonic items, include a cast of the Emperor's death mask. Also within the museum is the **William Lamb Sculpture Studio** commemorating the town's best known artist. Born in 1893, Lamb was famous for making sculpture with subjects such as the Queen and Princess Margaret when they were children. The studio, designed by Lamb himself, has been preserved as it would have been when the artist worked there.

Three miles west of Montrose, the **House of Dun** (NTS) is an imposing Georgian mansion designed by William Adam and built in 1730 for David Erskine, Lord Dun. Outside, the house has an elegant and restrained appearance but inside there's a riot of baroque plasterwork and sumptuous furnishings. One of William IV's daughters lived here and the house contains many royal mementoes. Within the grounds there's an attractive Victorian walled garden, a miniature theatre, a handloom weaving workshop, icehouses and fine parkland with woodland walks.

NORTH QUEENSFERRY

Nestling beneath two soaring bridges, the village of North Queensferry acquired its name from the medieval Queen Margaret who regularly used the ferry on the way to her favourite home at Dunfermline. With the opening of the Forth Road Bridge, the ferry's 800-year-old history came to an abrupt end and North Queensferry reverted to being a peaceful backwater. It's well worth visiting for its grand views of the Firth and two magnificent bridges.

On the edge of the village, **Deep Sea World** boasts the largest underwater tunnel in the world, some 120 yards long. Its transparent upper half allows visitors excellent close-up views of the more than 3,000 fish in the aquarium, among them the largest collection of Sand Tiger Sharks in Europe. A team of experienced divers regularly hand feed the fish and the latest communication technology allows visitors to put questions to the divers. Exhibits include a Touch Tank, where children can touch all kinds of marine species, including small friendly sharks, and an Amazonian Rain Forest display complete with piranhas and a tropical thunderstorm.

PITTENWEEM

Many of the small houses in this coastal village have been restored by the National Trust for Scotland and the quiet streets and lanes leading up from the harbour invite a leisurely exploration. Pittenweem's unusual name is derived from an ancient term for sea caves and, sure enough, here is **St Fillan's Cave**. Once the retreat of the early Christian missionary, the cave has for the most part been respected as a shrine, although at one time fishermen used it to store their nets. The cave was re-dedicated in the 1930s and services are still held in this unconventional setting.

A couple of miles inland, **Kellie Castle & Garden** (NTS) is an outstanding example of Lowland domestic architecture. Dating from the 14th century, the castle was sympathetically restored by the Lorimer family in the late 1800s. The castle contains magnificent plaster ceilings and painted panelling, as well as fine furniture designed by Sir Robert Lorimer.

The Victorian nursery and kitchen are both fascinating and the late-Victorian garden features a collection of organically cultivated old-fashioned roses and herbaceous plants.

St Andrews

A measure of the historic importance of this elegant town is the fact that almost the whole of its town centre enjoys the protection of Listed Building status. The most striking of these buildings is the ruined magnificence of **St Andrews Cathedral**. Masons started to build it in 1160; their descendants finally completed the largest church ever built in Scotland in 1318. Robert the Bruce attended its consecration in that same year. Two and a half centuries later, this beacon of Christian faith was effectively snuffed out when John Knox arrived in St Andrews. On the 5th of June, 1559, Knox delivered a rabble-rousing sermon inciting his Protestant congregation to attack the Catholic church. The mob stripped St Andrew's Cathedral of its treasures (never recovered), and enthusiastically mutilated any stone images of saints and prophets within reach of their axes. The people of St Andrews never found the heart, money or will to restore their desecrated Cathedral.

Standing alongside the ruins of the Cathedral is **St Rule's Tower**, an extraordinary survival from 1130 when, according to legend, it was built to house the sacred relics of St Andrew. No one knows where those relics are nowadays.

Within St Rule's tower, a 174-step corkscrew staircase leads to a platform from which there are grand views across the town and surrounding countryside.

The tower was part of the Augustinian Priory that once stood on this site and the only other building to survive is the massive 14th century gatehouse known as **The Pends**. From here, it's just a short walk to the rocky coastline and the ruins of **St Andrews Castle** surrounded by the sea on three sides, by a moat on the fourth. The castle witnessed some grim scenes during the turbulent years of the Reformation. In 1546 the Protestant reformer George Wishart was burned at the stake in front of the castle while the Bishop of St Andrews, Cardinal Beaton, seated himself on the balcony *"to feed and glut his eyes with the sight of it"*. Less than three months later, Knox's supporters stabbed the Cardinal to death and hung his body from the castle wall. Later, it was dumped into the "bottle dungeon", a 24 feet deep pit gouged out of solid rock which can be seen in the Sea Tower.

Many of the impressive buildings in the city centre are part of St Andrews University, founded in 1410 and the oldest in Scotland. Two of the college quads are open to the public, **St Salvator's** and **St Mary's**, and during the summer vacation guided tours are available.

For golfers around the world St Andrews is a holy place. Back in 1754 the Society of St Andrews Golfers was formed to organise an annual competition on the natural links to the west of the town. Eighty years later it became the Royal & Ancient Golf Club, now the governing body for the rules of golf in most countries. In all, St Andrews has six golf courses; visitors can book a round on any of them at the **Golf Information Centre** or find out more about the game and its history at the British Golf Museum.

St Andrews also boasts one of Scotland's best beaches at **West Sands** where scenes for *Chariots of Fire* were filmed. And the **Botanic Garden**, now a hundred years old, is renowned for its collections of cacti and other exotic plants.

182 The Abbey Inn

Eastport, Cupar Road,
Newburgh, Fife KY14 6EZ
Tel: 01337 840761
Fax: 0870 7059747

Directions:

From Exit 9 of the M90, take the A912 to Aberargie (2 miles). Turn left on the A913 to Abernethy and Newburgh (7 miles)

Built in 1737 to service the stage coach traffic between Perth and St Andrews, The Abbey Inn is a striking 3-storey structure which is now a listed building. It takes its name from nearby Lindores Abbey, founded in the 1100s and today a romantic ruin from which there are grand views across the River Tay. The inn has a wonderfully atmospheric interior - low ceilings, thick walls, narrow corridors, an original ceiling and an interesting feature fireplace in the lounge bar. The owners, George and Sally Buchanan, have been steadily refurbishing and upgrading the inn's decoration and amenities while preserving its character and tradition. The results are completely successful.

The inn offers quality home cooked food every lunchtime and evening, except on Mondays, with menus based on local produce and offered at sensible prices. There are special choices for children and OAPs and real ale lovers will find a regularly changing selection of brews on tap. In good weather, customers can enjoy their refreshments in the attractive beer garden and cobbled courtyard at the rear of the inn. The Abbey Inn also has 3 guest bedrooms, available all year round. The 2 doubles and 1 twin have a 4-star tourist board rating and are all en suite and equipped with television and tea/coffee-making equipment.

Opening Hours: Mon, Wed &Sun 11.00-23.00; Tue, Thu & Sat 11.00-24.00; Fri 11.00-01.00

Food: Available every lunchtime & evening except Mondays

Credit Cards: Access; Mastercard; Visa & Switch

Accommodation: 3 rooms, (2 doubles, 1 twin), all en suite and rated 4-star

Facilities: Beer garden

Entertainment: Occasional live music

Local Places of Interest/Activities: Lindores Abbey, Laing Museum, waterside walks, all nearby; Round Tower, Abernethy, 3 miles; Falkland Palace (NTS), 8 miles;

Internet/Website: www.theabbeyinn-newburgh.co.uk

Auchmithie Hotel 183

Auchmithie by Arbroath,
Angus DD11 5SQ
Tel: 01241 873010 Fax: 01241 879957

Directions:

From Dundee take the A92 to Arbroath. Continue on the A92 for about a mile north of Arbroath then turn right on a minor road to Auchmithie (3 miles)

This picturesque little fishing village can be reached either by road or by a coastal footpath from Arbroath which offers some grand views along the way. There are more superb sea views to be enjoyed from the restaurant at the **Auchmithie Hotel**, a welcoming hostelry which enjoys a splendid Clifton location. The hotel is owned and run by Douglas and Mary Stewart who arrived here in the early summer of 2000 and have speedily established a reputation for serving good, wholesome food and quality ales, as well as providing comfortable accommodation. The hotel was originally built as an ale-house in the 1600s but that building was destroyed by fire. The present inn is very attractively furnished and decorated, with lots of large comfortable settees and huge, glass-fronted fires. Both Robert Burns and Sir Walter Scott stayed here.

The most striking feature however is the staggering view across the North Sea to be enjoyed as you savour your meal in the restaurant. The menu offers an excellent choice of home cooked seafood, steaks and traditional Scottish fare, all freshly prepared and attractively presented. The hotel's accommodation comprises 1 twin and 4 double bedrooms, all with en suite facilities, TV and hospitality tray. Alternatively, if you prefer self-catering, there's also a self-contained flat with a large family bathroom, kitchen, sitting room and 3 double bedrooms, one of which is en suite. Ideal as a base for exploring this corner of Angus, especially if you love golf since there are 25 or more championship golf courses within a 30-minute drive, including the famous courses at Carnoustie and St Andrews.

Opening Hours: 12.00-24.00 every day

Food: 12.00-14,30, 18.00-20.30

Credit Cards: Access, Mastercard, Visa

Accommodation: 5 rooms (4 doubles, 1 twin), all en suite; 1 self-contained flat with 3 double bedrooms

Facilities: Restaurant with sea view; lounge bar; public bar; parking

Entertainment: Pool table; quiz night; live music

Local Places of Interest/Activities: Coastal footpath, nearby; 25+ championship golf courses within 30 minutes travel; Arbroath Abbey, 3 miles; Brechin Cathedral, Round Tower, Caledonian Railway, all at Brechin, 14 miles; House of Dun (NTS), 17 miles

Internet/Website: e-mail: auchmithiehotel@rbroath.fsbusiness.co.uk

184 The Balcarres Hotel

59 Main Street,
Colinsburgh,
Fife KY9 1LS
Tel: 01333 340600

Directions:
Colinsburgh is on the B942, about 12 miles south of St Andrews

The Balcarres Hotel is one of those friendly places where, if you don't see your favourite dish listed on the menu, just say what you would like and if the kitchen has the ingredients available, they will cook it for you. This kind of flexibility is typical of Ian and Anne Cooper's welcoming hostelry, a delightful old 18th century coaching inn still complete with its arched entrance leading to the former stables at the rear. (The neighbouring building, incidentally, is a former Army barracks, its dungeon and morgue both intact although happily neither is in use). Ian and Anne arrived at the Balcarres Hotel in September 1996 as managers, became its owners in May 1999 and, while they are constantly improving the inn's amenities, are careful to preserve its unique charm and character.

The food here enjoys a very good reputation, with appetising bar snacks available throughout the day until around 21.00. There's also a very good selection of beverages, including a heady "Scrumpy Jack". Children are welcome inside until 20.00, there's a lovely beer garden to the rear, and every other Saturday customers are entertained with live music, or entertain each other with a lively karaoke. If you are planning to stay in this delightful part of Fife, the inn has 3 guest bedrooms, sharing 2 bathrooms, all attractively furnished and decorated and equipped with TV and a hospitality tray.

Opening Hours: Mon-Wed:12.00-23.00; Thu: 12.00-24.00; Fri: 12.00-01.00; Sat: 11.00-01.00; Sun: 12.30-24.00

Food: Bar snacks and meals available 12.00-20.00

Credit Cards: Cash only

Accommodation: 3 rooms, 2 bathrooms

Facilities: Beer garden; residents' lounge; parking

Entertainment: Pool table; live music or karaoke every other Saturday

Local Places of Interest/Activities: Kellie Castle (NTS), 3 miles; Scottish Fisheries Museum, Anstruther, 6 miles; Scotland's Secret Bunker, 9 miles

Balcomie Links Hotel | 185

Balcomie Road, Crail,
Fife KY10 3TN
Tel: 01333 450237 Fax: 01333 450546

Directions:
From Kirkcaldy take the A917 towards St Andrews. Crail is about 11 miles along this road. In the town centre, the A917 turns sharp left - keep straight on and the Balcomie Links Hotel is on the left.

The most ancient Royal Burgh in the East Neuk of Fife, Crail also has one of the most photographed harbours in Scotland. Artists, too, love to make paintings of the red-tiled houses with their crow stepped gables and whitewashed walls cascading down to the shore. Pretty as it is, this picture postcard village is still a working port, home to Fife's crab and lobster fleet. It's also home to the **Balcomie Links Hotel**, a small friendly family-run establishment under the personal supervision of its resident owners, Mike and Debbie Kadir.

In the comfortable lounge, bar lunches and suppers for all the family are served daily, while the restaurant offers a full Chef's menu backed by an excellent wine list. The small cosy public bar stocks a wide range of fine ales, beers and spirits, while the adjoining games room is enjoyed by both locals and visitors alike. Every weekend there is live entertainment in the lounge provided by a wide variety of acts. Purpose built as a hotel in the 1920s, the hotel has 15 bedrooms all of which are en suite with double glazing and central heating, and some command a wonderful view over the Firth of Forth. There's plenty to keep the holiday visitors occupied, with a links course less than a mile from the hotel and St Andrews, the 'Home of Golf', just 9 miles away. The Scottish Fisheries Museum overlooks the harbour at Anstruther; Elie, with its fine crescent sandy beach is a favourite with sea sport enthusiasts, and the most southerly of the East Neuk villages, Largo, was the birth place of Alexander Selkirk, the real life castaway who was the model for Daniel Defoe's Robinson Crusoe.

Opening Hours: Mon-Fri, 11.00-24.00; Sat-Sun 11.00-01.00

Food: Available every lunchtime & evening

Credit Cards: All major cards accepted excpet Amex

Accommodation: 15 rooms, all en suite

Facilities: Special golf packages

Entertainment: Live music at weekends

Local Places of Interest/Activities: Golf, 1 mile; Scotland's Secret Bunker, Troywood, 4 miles; Fisheries Museum, Anstruther, 4 miles; Kellie Castle & Garden, 6 miles; St Andrews, 9 miles

186 The Bear Tavern

47 High Street, Newburgh,
Fife KY14 6AH
Tel/Fax: 01337 840365

Directions:

From Exit 9 of the M90, take the A912 to Aberargie (2 miles). Turn left on the A913 to Abernethy and Newburgh (7 miles)

Occupying a prime position in the very heart of the village, **The Bear Tavern** is well placed to act as a community pub, which it does. Newburgh's junior soccer team have chosen the pub as their base and the tavern has a thriving darts team. Occasional live music evenings add to the vitality of the inn. Ronnie Alexander bought the pub in the summer of 2000 and since then has been energetically updating and improving The Bear's amenities while retaining the more attractive features of the early-19th century building. By the time you read this, a 36-seater restaurant should be up and running, serving quality food freshly prepared from local produce. Meals will be available every lunchtime and evening.

Newburgh village itself stands on the south shore of the Firth of Tay and enjoys grand views across the water. Just to the east of the village stands the 14th century tower of Lindores Abbey - a romantic ruin which is all that remains of a Benedictine foundation of around 1150. Also of interest in the village is the Laing Museum which houses a collection of antiques and geological specimens gathered in the area by the banker and historian Dr Alexander Laing who donated the collection to the village in 1892.

Opening Hours: Mon-Thu: 11.00-23.00; Fri: 11.00-01.00; Sat: 11.00-24.00; Sun: 12.30-23.00

Food: From late 2000, restaurant serving lunchtime & evening meals

Credit Cards: Access, Visa

Entertainment: Occasional live music

Local Places of Interest/Activities: Lindores Abbey, Laing Museum, waterside walks, all nearby; Round Tower, Abernethy, 3 miles; Falkland Palace (NTS), 8 miles

The Crusoe Hotel

Lower Largo, Fife KY8 6BT
Tel: 01333 320759
Fax: 01333 320865

Directions:

Follow the M90 over the Forth Road Bridge heading north. Turn off at Junction 2A onto the A92 to Kirkcaldy. From Kirkcaldy follow the A915 to Leven and on to Lundin Links. In Lundin Links turn right down to Lower Largo (0.5 miles)

Lower Largo is famed as the birthplace of Alexander Selkirk, the real life castaway whose adventures inspired Daniel Defoe's Robinson Crusoe. Hence the name of **The Crusoe Hotel** which occupies an ideal position beside the harbour from which Selkirk sailed on his fateful journey. This spacious hotel offers a good choice of eating options. In the Castaway Restaurant the A La Carte menu provides a wide selection of dishes largely using local produce complimented by a reasonably priced wine list.The Largo Lounge provides a historical and informal setting with it's old timber clad seafaring walls and "Man Friday" footprint highlighted in the floor. Another option is the Crusoe Bar which is open every day to residents and non-residents. The olde worlde ambience, beamed ceiling, fireplace and views of the harbour make this the ideal place to relax. Bar food is served daily in the lounge and bar.

The hotel also offers top quality accommodation. There are 2 single and 13 double or twin luxury en suite bedrooms, most of which have spectacular sea views. Alternatively, spoil yourself in one of our suites each with its own sitting room, bedroom and balcony with outstanding views across the Firth of Forth to the Bass Rock. All the rooms have colour TV, tea/coffee making facilities, hairdryer, trouser press and direct dial telephone. Lower Largo is surrounded by the finest golf courses in Scotland and is perfectly positioned for a golfing break. Other local activities include sailing, riding, windsurfing, coastal walks, bird watching and pleasure cruises to the Isle of May

Opening Hours: Mon-Sat: 11.00-24.00; Sun: 12.30-24.00

Food: Restaurant serving modern Scottish food; Bar food

Credit Cards: All major cards except Diners

Accommodation: 15 rooms, all en suite, most with sea views, 2 suites

Facilities: Restaurant; bistro; bar

Local Places of Interest/Activities: The Selkirk Experience, nearby; sandy beaches, nearby; Kellie Castle, 9 miles; Scottish Fisheries Museum, 12 miles; St Andrews, Old Course

Internet/Website:
e-mail: relax@crusoehotel.co.uk
website: www.crusoehotel.co.uk

188   Lomond Hills Hotel

Freuchie, Fife KY15
Tel: 01337 857329,
857498 or 858180
Tel/Fax: 01337 857329

Directions:

Freuchie village is on the A92, about 2 miles north of Glenrothes. The Lomond Hills Hotel is located in the centre of the village

Providing 3-star comfort at 2-star prices, the **Lomond Hills Hotel** also provides its guests with a comprehensive variety of amenities. The outstanding Cobblers Restaurant offers a small selection of Scottish specialities together with some popular French flambé dishes to create an appetising à la carte menu. There's a large choice of wines, sherries and liqueurs to complement your meal and the intimate, candlelit atmosphere, coupled with courteous service, makes dining here a memorable experience. Guests can also enjoy a relaxing drink in the attractive Lounge with its theme of copper and Blue Delft. Other facilities include a sauna, gym, a swimming pool and a jacuzzi. Outside, there's a small children's play area and a small pleasant garden. The Lomond Function suite is completely self-contained, with bar and cloakroom facilities, and caters for conferences, receptions and other functions for between 20 and 200 people. The hotel has 25 bedrooms, all of them en suite and equipped with direct dial telephone, colour television, radio, hair dryer, trouser press and tea and coffee-making facilities. The two honeymoon suites feature lace-trimmed 4-poster beds and combine romance with all modern amenities. Freuchie itself is a picturesque village where, in olden times, courtiers out of favour at nearby Falkland Palace were banished. Even today, the derisory saying "Awa tae Freuchie and eat mice" is used in some parts of Scotland. Today, the village's location in the heart of Fife make it an ideal base for golf (there are some 30 golf courses within easy reach), fishing, sailing, gliding and pony trekking.

Opening Hours: Hotel is open all day

Food: 12.00-14.15; 18.00-22.00

Credit Cards: All major cards accepted

Accommodation: 25 bedrooms, including 2 honeymoon suites, all en suite

Facilities: Swimming pool; sauna; gym; children's pool; jacuzzi; garden; outside children's play area; roof terrace; function suite; piano lounge

Local Places of Interest/Activities: Falkland Palace (NTS), 2.5 miles; Balbirnie Country Park, golf, 3 miles; Balgonie Castle, 5 miles; Lindores Abbey, 10 miles

Internet/Website: e-mail: sales@theindependents.co.uk website: www.lomond.activebooking.com

The New Windsor Hotel   189

42/44 High Street, Leven,
Fife KY8 4NA
Tel/Fax: 01333 429575

Directions:
Leven is on the A915/A955 about 7 miles
northwest of Kirkcaldy

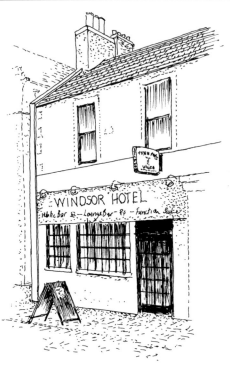

Located in the pedestrianised heart of
this busy little resort, **The New Windsor Hotel** looks quite small from the
outside but the interior is surprisingly
spacious, comprising a lounge bar,
public bar, separate restaurant and a
function suite. Mine host James
Walker, a local man, takes great pride
and pleasure in continually extending
and upgrading the amenities here and
his hundred year old inn is attractively
furnished and decorated throughout.
He also offers a wholesome choice of
food during the morning and at
lunchtime, with specials for OAPs, a
menu for children and good package
deals for group bookings. The dishes are traditional Scottish fare, all home cooked and
with "nothing out of a tin". To complement your meal, there's an excellent selection
of draught beers and wines. The hotel has 6 guest bedrooms, which share 2 bathrooms. All are comfortably furnished and equipped with cable TV and tea/coffee-mak-
ing facilities.

Leven is the largest of the towns on the bay, popular with holidaymakers enjoying
its fine beach, its lively Promenade offering all the usual seaside attractions, and its
two peaceful public parks. The area to the east of the town is known as the East Neuk
(nook, or corner) of Fife. Its coastline is dotted with pretty villages and there's a long
stretch of excellent sandy beaches around the broad curve of Largo Bay.

Opening Hours: 11.00-24.00 every day

Food: Available 9.30-14.30; evening meals
for residents

Credit Cards: Cash only

Accommodation: 6 rooms, 2 bathrooms

Facilities: Function suite

Entertainment: Occasional live music

Local Places of Interest/Activities: Golf,
sandy beach, nearby; Balgonie Castle, 7
miles; Kellie Castle (NTS), 11 miles;
Scottish Fisheries Museum, 15 miles

190   The Old Rectory Inn

West Quality Street,
Dysart,
Kirkcaldy KY1 2TE
Tel: 01592 651211
Fax: 01592 655221

Directions:

From the centre of Kirk-
caldy take the A955 to-
wards Buckhaven. Just be-
fore the sign for Dysart
turn left and The Old Rectory Inn is on the left

A handsome Georgian
building with ivy-clad
walls, the building known today as **The Old Rectory Inn** was built by a prominent
Dysart merchant, James Reddie, in 1771. The new dwelling was known as Rectory
House even though no minister was to reside in it until almost 90 years later when it
was sold to the Earl of Rosslyn. He decided to use it as a residence for a succession of
ministers and it remained part of the Rosslyn estate until 1950 by which time the
family's fortunes had deteriorated to the point that a recent Earl was working as a
police constable in London. The house has fared better, retaining its Georgian charm
with features such as the Roman Doric doorpiece, moulded eaves cornice and pan-
elled chimneys. In the east wall, visitors can see an old circular opening which is now
sealed. It was used as a means of passing small objects such as food and drink to
persons waiting outside. This avoided opening the door and running the risk of harm
or theft!

The Rectory became a restaurant in 1966 and is now owned and run by David and
Gareth who offer their customers an excellent choice of both traditional Scottish and
Continental cuisine. There are 3 different menus: one for lunch, one for supper and
an à la carte for dinner. All three menus offer dishes based on top quality local fresh
produce. The restaurant has three separate dining areas, all of them immaculately
maintained and elegantly designed.

Opening Hours: Tue-Sat: 12.00-15.00,
19.00-23.00; Sun: 12.30-16.00

Food: Traditional Scottish & Continental
cuisine available every lunchtime &
evening

Credit Cards: Access, Amex, Mastercharge,
Visa & Switch

Local Places of Interest/Activities: In
Dysart - National Trust Pan Ha' and
Harbour; Balgonie Castle, 4 miles;
Balbirnie Country Park, 6 miles; Falkland
Palace, 13 miles

Path Tavern 191

Mid Street,
Kirkcaldy
KY1 2PC
Tel: 01592 263671

Directions:

Kirkcaldy is off the A92, about 15 miles E of Dunfermline. In the town, follow the High Street northwards along the sea front and the Path Tavern is at the very end on the left

September 26th, 2000 was a rather special day for everyone at the **Path Tavern** for it was on that very day, back in 1750, that the original hostelry received its licence. The building has changed during the two and a half centuries since it first opened its doors but the inn is still dispensing friendly and welcoming hospitality. The Path Tavern is very much a family business, run by John Hutchinson, his sister and his mum, a cheerful trio who have made the inn a popular venue for both locals and visitors alike. Part of the appeal is undoubtedly the food on offer - really tasty and appetising dishes which change daily and are listed on the chalk board. Meals can be enjoyed in the attractive "half moon"-shaped lounge or in the cosy bar. The inn will also have a special appeal for lovers of malt whisky since it stocks a huge selection of different varieties of Scotland's favourite beverage. Another popular amenity at the Path Tavern is its enormous function room which enjoys lovely views across the Firth of Forth. The inn stands at the northern end of Kirkcaldy's famous 4-mile long esplanade which was constructed in 1922-23, partly to alleviate the terrible unemployment of the time.

Opening Hours: Mon-Sat: 11.00-24.00. Sun: 12.30-24.00

Food: Mon-Sat: bar lunches

Credit Cards: Cash only

Facilities: Large function room with sea views

Entertainment: Weekly Comedy Club; regular live music

Local Places of Interest/Activities: Kirkcaldy Museum & Art Gallery, Ravenscraig Castle, both close by; Balgonie Castle, 8 miles; Falkland Palace, 13 miles

Internet/Website:
e-mail: johnpath@freeuk.com

192   Red House Hotel

Coupar Angus,
Tayside
PH13 9AL
Tel: 01828 628500
Fax: 01828 628574

Directions:

From the A90 Perth to Dundee road, about 4 miles west of Dundee, turn left on the A923 to Coupar Angus (11 miles)

Set beside the River Isla, the little town of Coupar Angus has one of best-preserved medieval street patterns in Scotland and when the Abbey here was flourishing its incomes were equal to Holyrood and exceeded those of the Border abbeys of Melrose and Kelso. Today, it's a busy little place and well worth visiting to enjoy the excellent food, fine wines and ales on offer at the **Red House Hotel**. As the name indicates, it is built of a lovely local red sandstone which positively glows when the sun is shining.

Over the years, the pub has been greatly extended and modernised, and the interior is now very spacious and attractively decorated with lots of solid pine and thick tartan carpets. There's a delightful conservatory restaurant serving a very varied menu, with something for every palate and at remarkable value for money prices. The inn's owner, Alan Bannerman, has also created an excellent wine list to complement the appetising cuisine. Alan has been here for more than 20 years and has spent generously on upgrading and improving the hotel's amenities. Children are very welcome and so too are coach parties by arrangement.

Opening Hours: 11.00-23.00

Food: Available 12.00-21.00, daily

Credit Cards: All major cards except Diners

Facilities: Conservatory restaurant; lounge bar; public bar; ample parking

Entertainment: Snooker, squash, sauna, gymnasium

Local Places of Interest/Activities: Meikleour Beech Hedge, 4 miles; Sculptured stone Museum, Meigle, 6 miles; Scone Palace, 11 miles; City of Perth, 13 miles; Dunkeld Cathedral, 14 miles; City of Dundee, 15 miles

Internet/Website:
email:stay@red-house-hotel.co.uk

Salutation Hotel

193

Inverbervie,
Aberdeenshire
DD10 0RG
Tel: 01561 361455
Fax: 01561 361397

Directions:

From Montrose take the A92 coastal road towards Stonehaven and Aberdeen. Inverbervie is on this road, about 13 miles north of Montrose

The pretty little village of Inverbervie stands close to the sea at Bervie Bay and at the heart of the village stands the **Salutation Inn**. Mine host, Gordon Meldrum, has owned and run this friendly traditional tavern for more than 21 years so there's little about the village and the surrounding area that he isn't familiar with! His white-painted inn was built more than a century ago and has a very welcoming and relaxing atmosphere. Everything is spick and span, with tables well-spaced around the bar. Here, customers can enjoy the wholesome food on offer - tasty traditional Scottish fare based on fresh local produce and locally caught fish. During the summer, there are tables to the front of the inn where you can sup your pint and watch the village life passing by. A pool table and game machines are available in the bar and Gordon arranges karaoke evenings and occasional live entertainment.

Amongst the many visitor attractions within easy reach is Dunnottar Castle, a few miles up the coast. Reckoned to be one of the finest of Scotland's ruined castles, it featured as the backdrop to Franco Zeffirelli's film version of Hamlet. Even closer is the village of Arbuthnot, home of the celebrated local author Lewis Grassic Gibbon whose many novels were set in this area, known as the Mearns. And lovers of fine whisky will want to travel a little further inland to Fettercairn and its distillery which is one of the oldest in Scotland and provides free tours and a complimentary dram.

Opening Hours: Mon-Thu: 11.00-00.00; Fri-Sat: 11.00-01.00; Sun: 12.30-00.00

Food: Mon-Thu: 12.00-14.30; Fri-Sat: 12.00-14.30, 17.00-21.00; Sun: 12.30-20.00

Credit Cards: Access, Mastercard, Visa & Switch

Facilities: Seating at front in summer

Entertainment: Pool; game machines; karaoke nights; occasional live music

Local Places of Interest/Activities: Grassic Gibbon Centre, Arbuthnot, 3 miles; St Cyrus beach, 8 miles; Dunnottar Castle, 9 miles; Fettercairn Distillery, 13 miles; Fasque House, 15 miles; House of Dun (NTS), 17 miles

194 St Michael's Inn

Leuchars,
by St Andrews,
Fife KY16 0DU
Tel: 01334 839220
Fax: 01334 838299

Directions:

From the south, follow signs to Cupar, continue on the A91 through Dairsie. At the next roundabout, take the left exit (A92). Pass through Balmullo and continue for 1.5 miles and you will arrive at St Michaels Inn

More than 200 years old, **St Michaels Inn** was formerly a coaching inn. It has been greatly extended over the years but there's a reminder of those days in the inn's Public Bar which was originally the stables for the coach horses. This friendly bar is a good place to catch up on the local gossip or to enjoy a game of pool. There's also a Lounge Bar, complete with low ceilings, relaxing chairs and traditional flame fires, which offers a wide selection of Scottish beers, malt whiskies and good wines. Since St Michaels was acquired by the McKinney family in 1992, the inn has gained an excellent reputation for good quality and value for money food. The McKinneys try to use as much fresh local produce and the menus are wide and varied with trout, salmon and venison always available. Special diets can be catered for with prior warning and it's always advisable to reserve your table in the 24-seater restaurant.

For special events, there's also a large, self-contained function suite which can accommodate up to 100 guests for a sit down meal. With its adjacent patio and landscaped gardens, St Michaels makes an ideal venue for weddings, anniversaries, birthdays, retirals or more private occasion. A small marquee can be erected on the patio to create extra space. The inn can provide a menu to suit your party and your pocket, and entertainment can also be arranged. If you are planning to stay in the area, the inn has 8 guest bedrooms, all with private facilities, self control central heating, colour television and a tray of complimentary tea and coffee. Leuchars is a convenient base for exploring the Kingdom of Fife, with the Mecca for golfers, St Andrews, only 6 miles away and approximately 60 golf courses within an hour's drive from the inn!

Opening Hours: Open all day

Food: 12.00-21.30

Credit Cards: Access, Mastercharge, Visa and Switch accepted

Accommodation: 8 rooms, all en suite

Facilities: Beer garden; function room; ample parking

Entertainment: Pool; gaming machines

Local Places of Interest/Activities: St Andrews Cathedral, St Andrews Castle, Botanic Garden, Golf Information Centre, all at St Andrews, 6 miles; Tents Muir woods, 3 miles; Tentsmuir Sands, 5 miles

Internet/Website:
e-mail: grahame@st-michaels-inn.co.uk
website: www.st-michaels-inn.co.uk

Thrums Hotel

195

Bank Street,
Kirriemuir,
Angus DD8 4BE
Tel/Fax: 01575 572758

Directions:

From the A90, 15 miles
north of Dundee, turn left
on the A925 to Kirriemuir
(6 miles). The Thrums Ho-
tel is located in the centre
of the town

Although Kirriemuir first appears in written records in 1201, it was as the birthplace of Sir J.M. Barrie, the novelist, dramatist and creator of 'Peter Pan', that the little town became known around the world. A statue of the elfin child stands in the market square, a short walk from **Thrums Hotel**, an attractive family run inn which has recently been refurbished to a high standard. A listed building, the hotel dates back to the 18th century and is now owned and run by Dave Clarke, a local celebrity who takes pride in the hotel's long established reputation for good service, quality accommodation and excellent home made cuisine. The hotel's chefs create a variety of appetising dishes, many of them based on the best of local produce, including fresh Scottish salmon, marvellous local game and excellent seafood fresh from the East Coast. Meals are served either in the lovely dining room or in the popular lounge bar.

The hotel has 11 guest bedrooms - a combination of singles, twin and family size. Eight of them are en suite and all are equipped with colour TV and tea/coffee-making facilities. Thrums Hotel provides a perfect base for exploring the famed Glens of Angus, two of which, Glen Clova and Glen Prosen, meet near Kirriemuir. Barrie's own favourite was Glen Isla and the celebrated waterfall of Reekie Linn. The name means "smoking fall" and it was so called because the 60ft drop into a deep ravine produces a haze of water mist. In the town itself, 9, Brechin Road is a popular visitor attraction. It was in this small terraced cottage that Barrie was born in 1860 and as a child dragooned his brothers and sisters into performing his "plays" in the family wash house which is still in place.

Opening Hours: Hotel open all day

Food: Available daily, 12.00-14.00; 17.00-22.30

Credit Cards: All major cards except Amex & Diners

Accommodation: 11 rooms (singles, twin and family), 8 of them en suite

Facilities: Dining room; lounge

Entertainment: Pool; game machines; juke box

Local Places of Interest/Activities: Barrie's Birthplace (NTS), nearby; golf, 1 mile; Camera Obscura, 1 mile; Glamis Castle, 5 miles; Reekie Linn Falls, 12 miles

The Hidden Inns of Central and Southern Scotland

ALPHABETIC LIST OF INNS

A

The Abbey Inn	Newburgh, Fife	182
Aberdour Hotel	Dumfries, Dumfries & Galloway	38
The Aerodrome	Scone, nr Perth, Perthshire	154
Allandale House	Brodick, Isle of Arran	63
Amulree Hotel & Lonely Inn	Amulree, Perthshire	155
The Annfield House Hotel	Irvine, Ayrshire	64
Ardbrecknish House	South Lochaweside, nr Dalmally, Argyll	126
Ardfillayne Country House Hotel	West Bay, nr Dunoon, Argyll	127
Auchmithie Hotel	Auchmithie, by Arbroath, Angus	183
The Auld Cross Keys	Denholm, Roxburghshire	12
The Auld Hoose Restaurant	Dunoon, Argyll	128

B

The Balcarres Hotel	Colinsburgh, Fife	184
Balcomie Links Hotel	Crail, Fife	185
The Bank	Prestwick, Ayrshire	65
The Bear Tavern	Newburgh, Fife	186
The Beech Tree Inn	Dumgoyne, Stirlingshire	92
The Bell Tree	Methven, Perthshire	156
Bird in the Hand Hotel	Johnstonebridge, Renfrewshire	93
Black Bull Hotel	Moffat, Dumfries & Galloway	39
The Black Bull Hotel	Duns, Berwickshire	13
The Black Watch Inn	Aberfeldy, Perthshire	157
The Boat	Rothesay, Bute	129
The Boswell Arms	Auchinleck, Ayrshire	66
The Bridgend Hotel	East Linton, East Lothian	94
The Burgh	Musselburgh, East Lothian	95

C

Cairnbaan Hotel	Cairnbaan, by Lochgilphead, Argyll	130
The Cardwell Inn	Gourock, Renfrewshire	96
The Carrutherstown Hotel	Carrutherstown, Dumfries & Galloway	40
The Castle Hotel	Coldstream, Berwickshire	14
Catacol Bay Hotel	Catacol, Isle of Arran	67
Churches Hotel	Eyemouth, Berwickshire	15
Clachan Bar	Largs, Ayrshire	68
Coaching Inn	Blackford, Perthshire	158
Colintraive Hotel	Colintraive, Argyll	131
The Commercial Inn	Coldstream, Berwickshire	16
The Comrie Hotel	Comrie, Perthshire	159
The Cot House Hotel	Sandbank, nr Dunoon, Argyll	132
The Courtyard	Eaglesfield, by Lockerbie, Dumfries & Galloway	41
The Coylton Arms	Low Coylton, Ayrshire	69
Craigdarroch Arms Hotel	Moniaive, Dumfries & Galloway	42
The Craw Inn	Auchencrow, nr Reston, Berwickshire	17
The Crees Inn	Abernethy, Perthshire	160
Cressfield Country House Hotel	Ecclefechan, Dumfries & Galloway	43
The Crooked Arm	Bridge of Allan, Stirlingshire	97

198   *ALPHABETIC LIST OF INNS*

The Cross Keys Hotel	Canonbie, Dumfries & Galloway	44
The Crown Hotel	Coldstream, Berwickshire	18
The Crown Hotel	Tarbolton, Ayrshire	70
The Crusoe Hotel	Lower Largo, Fife	187
Cuilfail Hotel	Kilmelford, Argyll	133
Cyprus Inn	Bridge of Earn, nr Perth, Perthshire	161

D

Devon Park Inn	Devonside, by Tillicoultry, Clackmannanshire	98
Dinwoodie Lodge Hotel	Johnstonebridge, by Lockerbie, Dumfries & Galloway	45
Dryburgh Arms Hotel	Newtown St Boswells, Borders	19

F

The Farmers Inn	Clarencefield, Dumfries & Galloway	46
The Fox & Hounds	Denholm, Roxburghshire	20
Furnace Inn	Furnace, Argyll	134

G

The George Hotel	Stranraer, Dumfries & Galloway	47
The George Hotel	Thornhill, Dumfries & Galloway	48
Goblin Ha' Hotel	Gifford, East Lothian	99
Golfer's Rest	North Berwick, East Lothian	100
Gwydyr House Hotel	Crieff, Perthshire	162

H

The Harbour Bar	Troon, Ayrshire	71
The Horseshoe Inn	Bridgend, nr Lochgilphead, Argyll	135

I

The Inn	Crook of Devon, Kinross-shire	163

J

Jameshaven Inn	Auldhouse, East Kilbride, Strathclyde	101

K

Kilmartin Hotel	Kilmartin, nr Lochgilphead, Argyll	136
The Kilmun House Hotel	Kilmun, nr Dunoon, Argyll	137
Kingarth Hotel	Kingarth, Isle of Bute, Bute	138
Kirkstyle Inn	Dunning, Perthshire	164
Knipoch Hotel	Knipoch, by Oban, Argyll	139

L

The Liddesdale Hotel	Newcastleton, Roxburghshire	21
Linton Hotel	West Linton, Peebleshire	22
The Lochann Inn	Lochans, Dumfries & Galloway	49
The Lochnell Arms Hotel	North Connel, Argyll	140
The Lochside House Hotel	New Cumnock, Ayrshire	72

ALPHABETIC LIST OF INNS | 199

The Log Cabin	Kirkmichael, Perthshire	165
Lomond Hills Hotel	Freuchie, Fife	188
The Lorne Taverna	Dollar, Clackmannanshire	102
The Lorne	Ardrishaig, Argyll	141
Lugton Inn Motel	Dalkeith, Midlothian	103

M

Marfield Inn	Rattray, nr Blairgowrie, Perthshire	166
Masonic Arms	Longcroft, by Bonnybridge, Stirlingshire	104

N

The New Windsor Hotel	Leven, Fife	189
Nithsdale Hotel	Sanquhar, Dumfries & Galloway	50

O

Oak Tree Inn	Balmaha, by Loch Lomond, Central	105
The Old Rectory Inn	Dysart, nr Kirkcaldy, Fife	190
The Oyster Inn	Connel, nr Oban, Argyll	142

P

Path Tavern	Kirkcaldy, Fife	191
The Pheasant Inn	Jedburgh, Roxburghshire	23
The Plough Hotel	Leitholm, Berwickshire	24
The Plough Tavern	Haddington, East Lothian	106

R

Red House Hotel	Coupar Angus, Tayside	192
The Regent Hotel	Rothesay, Bute	143
Roslin Glen Hotel	Roslin, Midlothian	107
The Royal Hotel	Jedburgh, Roxburghshire	25
The Royal Hotel	Bonnybridge, Stirlingshire	108

S

Salutation Hotel	Inverbervie, Aberdeenshire	193
Scoretulloch House	Darvel, Ayrshire	73
The Ship Inn	Melrose, Roxburghshire	26
The Ship Inn	Irvine, Ayrshire	74
St Catherine's Old Ferry Inn	St Catherine's, nr Cairndow, Argyll	144
St Michael's Inn	Leuchars, by St Andrews, Fife	194
The Stagecoach Inn	Cairndow, Argyll	145
The Stair Inn	Stair, nr Mauchline, Ayrshire	75
The Station House Hotel	Annan, Dumfries & Galloway	51

T

Tantallon Inn	North Berwick, East Lothian	109
Tayvallich Inn	Tayvallich, Argyll	146

200   *A*LPHABETIC *L*IST OF *I*NNS

The Thistle Inn	Crossmichael, Dumfries & Galloway	52
Thrums Hotel	Kirriemuir, Angus	195
The Tower Hotel	Crieff, Perthshire	167
Traquair Arms Hotel	Innerleithen, Peeblesshire	27
The Two O Eight Hotel	Perth, Perthshire	168
Tyneside Tavern	Haddington, East Lothian	110

W

The Waterfront	Portpatrick, Wigtownshire	53
Waterside Bistro & Restaurant	Haddington, East Lothian	111
Wee Bush Inn	Carnwath, Lanarkshire	112
West Barns Inn	West Barns, nr Dunbar, East Lothian	113
The Wheatsheaf Inn	Symington, Ayrshire	76
Woodside Inn	Woodside, Perthshire	169

ACCOMMODATION

THE BORDERS

The Black Bull Hotel	Duns, Berwickshire	13
The Castle Hotel	Coldstream, Berwickshire	14
Churches Hotel	Eyemouth, Berwickshire	15
The Craw Inn	Auchencrow, nr Reston, Berwickshire	17
The Crown Hotel	Coldstream, Berwickshire	18
Dryburgh Arms Hotel	Newtown St Boswells, Borders	19
The Fox & Hounds	Denholm, Roxburghshire	20
The Liddesdale Hotel	Newcastleton, Roxburghshire	21
Linton Hotel	West Linton, Peebleshire	22
The Plough Hotel	Leitholm, Berwickshire	24
The Royal Hotel	Jedburgh, Roxburghshire	25
Traquair Arms Hotel	Innerleithen, Peeblesshire	27

DUMFRIES AND GALLOWAY

Aberdour Hotel	Dumfries, Dumfries & Galloway	38
Black Bull Hotel	Moffat, Dumfries & Galloway	39
The Carrutherstown Hotel	Carrutherstown, Dumfries & Galloway	40
The Courtyard	Eaglesfield, by Lockerbie, Dumfries & Galloway	41
Craigdarroch Arms Hotel	Moniaive, Dumfries & Galloway	42
Cressfield Country House Hotel	Ecclefechan, Dumfries & Galloway	43
The Cross Keys Hotel	Canonbie, Dumfries & Galloway	44
Dinwoodie Lodge Hotel	Johnstonebridge, by Lockerbie, Dumfries & Galloway	45
The Farmers Inn	Clarencefield, Dumfries & Galloway	46
The George Hotel	Stranraer, Dumfries & Galloway	47
The George Hotel	Thornhill, Dumfries & Galloway	48
The Lochann Inn	Lochans, Dumfries & Galloway	49
Nithsdale Hotel	Sanquhar, Dumfries & Galloway	50
The Station House Hotel	Annan, Dumfries & Galloway	51
The Waterfront	Portpatrick, Wigtownshire	53

AYRSHIRE AND THE ISLE OF ARRAN

Allandale House	Brodick, Isle of Arran	63
The Annfield House Hotel	Irvine, Ayrshire	64
Catacol Bay Hotel	Catacol, Isle of Arran	67
The Coylton Arms	Low Coylton, Ayrshire	69
The Crown Hotel	Tarbolton, Ayrshire	70
The Lochside House Hotel	New Cumnock, Ayrshire	72
The Stair Inn	Stair, nr Mauchline, Ayrshire	75

CENTRAL SCOTLAND

Bird in the Hand Hotel	Johnstonebridge, Renfrewshire	93
The Bridgend Hotel	East Linton, East Lothian	94
Goblin Ha' Hotel	Gifford, East Lothian	99
Jameshaven Inn	Auldhouse, East Kilbride, Strathclyde	101
The Lorne Taverna	Dollar, Clackmannanshire	102
Lugton Inn Motel	Dalkeith, Midlothian	103

Oak Tree Inn	Balmaha, by Loch Lomond, Central	105
The Plough Tavern	Haddington, East Lothian	106
Roslin Glen Hotel	Roslin, Midlothian	107
The Royal Hotel	Bonnybridge, Stirlingshire	108
Tantallon Inn	North Berwick, East Lothian	109
Waterside Bistro & Restaurant	Haddington, East Lothian	111

ARGYLL AND BUTE

Ardbrecknish House	South Lochaweside, nr Dalmally, Argyll	126
Ardfillayne Country House Hotel	West Bay, nr Dunoon, Argyll	127
Cairnbaan Hotel	Cairnbaan, by Lochgilphead, Argyll	130
Colintraive Hotel	Colintraive, Argyll	131
The Cot House Hotel	Sandbank, nr Dunoon, Argyll	132
Cuilfail Hotel	Kilmelford, Argyll	133
Furnace Inn	Furnace, Argyll	134
The Horseshoe Inn	Bridgend, nr Lochgilphead, Argyll	135
Kilmartin Hotel	Kilmartin, nr Lochgilphead, Argyll	136
The Kilmun House Hotel	Kilmun, nr Dunoon, Argyll	137
Kingarth Hotel	Kingarth, Isle of Bute, Bute	138
Knipoch Hotel	Knipoch, by Oban, Argyll	139
The Lochnell Arms Hotel	North Connel, Argyll	140
The Oyster Inn	Connel, nr Oban, Argyll	142
The Regent Hotel	Rothesay, Bute	143
St Catherine's Old Ferry Inn	St Catherine's, nr Cairndow, Argyll	144
The Stagecoach Inn	Cairndow, Argyll	145

PERTHSHIRE AND KINROSS

Amulree Hotel & Lonely Inn	Amulree, Perthshire	155
Coaching Inn	Blackford, Perthshire	158
The Comrie Hotel	Comrie, Perthshire	159
Cyprus Inn	Bridge of Earn, nr Perth, Perthshire	161
Gwydyr House Hotel	Crieff, Perthshire	162
The Log Cabin	Kirkmichael, Perthshire	165
Marfield Inn	Rattray, nr Blairgowrie, Perthshire	166
The Tower Hotel	Crieff, Perthshire	167
The Two O Eight Hotel	Perth, Perthshire	168

FIFE, DUNDEE AND ANGUS

The Abbey Inn	Newburgh, Fife	182
Auchmithie Hotel	Auchmithie, by Arbroath, Angus	183
The Balcarres Hotel	Colinsburgh, Fife	184
Balcomie Links Hotel	Crail, Fife	185
The Crusoe Hotel	Lower Largo, Fife	187
Lomond Hills Hotel	Freuchie, Fife	188
The New Windsor Hotel	Leven, Fife	189
St Michael's Inn	Leuchars, by St Andrews, Fife	194
Thrums Hotel	Kirriemuir, Angus	195

ALL DAY OPENING

THE BORDERS

The Black Bull Hotel	Duns, Berwickshire	13
The Castle Hotel	Coldstream, Berwickshire	14
Churches Hotel	Eyemouth, Berwickshire	15
The Commercial Inn	Coldstream, Berwickshire	16
The Craw Inn	Auchencrow, nr Reston, Berwickshire	17
The Crown Hotel	Coldstream, Berwickshire	18
Dryburgh Arms Hotel	Newtown St Boswells, Borders	19
The Liddesdale Hotel	Newcastleton, Roxburghshire	21
Linton Hotel	West Linton, Peebleshire	22
The Pheasant Inn	Jedburgh, Roxburghshire	23
The Plough Hotel	Leitholm, Berwickshire	24
The Royal Hotel	Jedburgh, Roxburghshire	25
The Ship Inn	Melrose, Roxburghshire	26
Traquair Arms Hotel	Innerleithen, Peeblesshire	27

DUMFRIES AND GALLOWAY

Aberdour Hotel	Dumfries, Dumfries & Galloway	38
Black Bull Hotel	Moffat, Dumfries & Galloway	39
Craigdarroch Arms Hotel	Moniaive, Dumfries & Galloway	42
Cressfield Country House Hotel	Ecclefechan, Dumfries & Galloway	43
The Cross Keys Hotel	Canonbie, Dumfries & Galloway	44
Dinwoodie Lodge Hotel	Johnstonebridge, by Lockerbie, Dumfries & Galloway	45
The Farmers Inn	Clarencefield, Dumfries & Galloway	46
The George Hotel	Stranraer, Dumfries & Galloway	47
The George Hotel	Thornhill, Dumfries & Galloway	48
The Lochann Inn	Lochans, Dumfries & Galloway	49
Nithsdale Hotel	Sanquhar, Dumfries & Galloway	50
The Thistle Inn	Crossmichael, Dumfries & Galloway	52
The Waterfront	Portpatrick, Wigtownshire	53

AYRSHIRE AND THE ISLE OF ARRAN

Allandale House	Brodick, Isle of Arran	63
The Annfield House Hotel	Irvine, Ayrshire	64
The Bank	Prestwick, Ayrshire	65
Catacol Bay Hotel	Catacol, Isle of Arran	67
Clachan Bar	Largs, Ayrshire	68
The Coylton Arms	Low Coylton, Ayrshire	69
The Crown Hotel	Tarbolton, Ayrshire	70
The Harbour Bar	Troon, Ayrshire	71
The Lochside House Hotel	New Cumnock, Ayrshire	72
The Stair Inn	Stair, nr Mauchline, Ayrshire	75
The Wheatsheaf Inn	Symington, Ayrshire	76

CENTRAL SCOTLAND

The Beech Tree Inn	Dumgoyne, Stirlingshire	92
Bird in the Hand Hotel	Johnstonebridge, Renfrewshire	93
The Burgh	Musselburgh, East Lothian	95
The Cardwell Inn	Gourock, Renfrewshire	96
The Crooked Arm	Bridge of Allan, Stirlingshire	97
Devon Park Inn	Devonside, by Tillicoultry, Clackmannanshire	98
Golfer's Rest	North Berwick, East Lothian	100
Jameshaven Inn	Auldhouse, East Kilbride, Strathclyde	101
The Lorne Taverna	Dollar, Clackmannanshire	102
Lugton Inn Motel	Dalkeith, Midlothian	103
Masonic Arms	Longcroft, by Bonnybridge, Stirlingshire	104
Oak Tree Inn	Balmaha, by Loch Lomond, Central	105
The Plough Tavern	Haddington, East Lothian	106
Roslin Glen Hotel	Roslin, Midlothian	107
The Royal Hotel	Bonnybridge, Stirlingshire	108

ARGYLL AND BUTE

Ardfillayne Country House Hotel	West Bay, nr Dunoon, Argyll	127
The Boat	Rothesay, Bute	129
Cairnbaan Hotel	Cairnbaan, by Lochgilphead, Argyll	130
Colintraive Hotel	Colintraive, Argyll	131
The Cot House Hotel	Sandbank, nr Dunoon, Argyll	132
Cuilfail Hotel	Kilmelford, Argyll	133
Kilmartin Hotel	Kilmartin, nr Lochgilphead, Argyll	136
The Kilmun House Hotel	Kilmun, nr Dunoon, Argyll	137
Kingarth Hotel	Kingarth, Isle of Bute, Bute	138
Knipoch Hotel	Knipoch, by Oban, Argyll	139
The Lochnell Arms Hotel	North Connel, Argyll	140
The Lorne	Ardrishaig, Argyll	141
The Oyster Inn	Connel, nr Oban, Argyll	142
The Regent Hotel	Rothesay, Bute	143
St Catherine's Old Ferry Inn	St Catherine's, nr Cairndow, Argyll	144
The Stagecoach Inn	Cairndow, Argyll	145
Tayvallich Inn	Tayvallich, Argyll	146

PERTHSHIRE AND KINROSS

The Aerodrome	Scone, nr Perth, Perthshire	154
Amulree Hotel & Lonely Inn	Amulree, Perthshire	155
The Black Watch Inn	Aberfeldy, Perthshire	157
Coaching Inn	Blackford, Perthshire	158
Cyprus Inn	Bridge of Earn, nr Perth, Perthshire	161
The Log Cabin	Kirkmichael, Perthshire	165
Marfield Inn	Rattray, nr Blairgowrie, Perthshire	166
The Tower Hotel	Crieff, Perthshire	167
The Two O Eight Hotel	Perth, Perthshire	168

ALL DAY OPENING

FIFE, DUNDEE AND ANGUS

The Abbey Inn	Newburgh, Fife	182
Auchmithie Hotel	Auchmithie, by Arbroath, Angus	183
The Balcarres Hotel	Colinsburgh, Fife	184
Balcomie Links Hotel	Crail, Fife	185
The Crusoe Hotel	Lower Largo, Fife	187
Lomond Hills Hotel	Freuchie, Fife	188
The New Windsor Hotel	Leven, Fife	189
Path Tavern	Kirkcaldy, Fife	191
Red House Hotel	Coupar Angus, Tayside	192
Salutation Hotel	Inverbervie, Aberdeenshire	193
St Michael's Inn	Leuchars, by St Andrews, Fife	194
Thrums Hotel	Kirriemuir, Angus	195

CHILDRENS FACILITIES

THE BORDERS

Dryburgh Arms Hotel	Newtown St Boswells, Borders	19
The Fox & Hounds	Denholm, Roxburghshire	20
The Plough Hotel	Leitholm, Berwickshire	24
The Royal Hotel	Jedburgh, Roxburghshire	25
The Ship Inn	Melrose, Roxburghshire	26

DUMFRIES AND GALLOWAY

Black Bull Hotel	Moffat, Dumfries & Galloway	39
Dinwoodie Lodge Hotel	Johnstonebridge, by Lockerbie, Dumfries & Galloway	45
The Thistle Inn	Crossmichael, Dumfries & Galloway	52

AYRSHIRE AND THE ISLE OF ARRAN

Catacol Bay Hotel	Catacol, Isle of Arran	67
The Harbour Bar	Troon, Ayrshire	71
Scoretulloch House	Darvel, Ayrshire	73

CENTRAL SCOTLAND

The Beech Tree Inn	Dumgoyne, Stirlingshire	92
Bird in the Hand Hotel	Johnstonebridge, Renfrewshire	93
The Burgh	Musselburgh, East Lothian	95
Goblin Ha' Hotel	Gifford, East Lothian	99

ARGYLL AND BUTE

Ardbrecknish House	South Lochaweside, nr Dalmally, Argyll	126
The Cot House Hotel	Sandbank, nr Dunoon, Argyll	132
The Horseshoe Inn	Bridgend, nr Lochgilphead, Argyll	135
The Lochnell Arms Hotel	North Connel, Argyll	140

PERTHSHIRE AND KINROSS

The Aerodrome	Scone, nr Perth, Perthshire	154
Marfield Inn	Rattray, nr Blairgowrie, Perthshire	166

FIFE, DUNDEE AND ANGUS

Lomond Hills Hotel	Freuchie, Fife	188
Red House Hotel	Coupar Angus, Tayside	192

CREDIT CARDS ACCEPTED 207

THE BORDERS

The Auld Cross Keys	Denholm, Roxburghshire	12
The Black Bull Hotel	Duns, Berwickshire	13
The Castle Hotel	Coldstream, Berwickshire	14
Churches Hotel	Eyemouth, Berwickshire	15
The Craw Inn	Auchencrow, nr Reston, Berwickshire	17
The Crown Hotel	Coldstream, Berwickshire	18
The Fox & Hounds	Denholm, Roxburghshire	20
The Liddesdale Hotel	Newcastleton, Roxburghshire	21
Linton Hotel	West Linton, Peebleshire	22
The Pheasant Inn	Jedburgh, Roxburghshire	23
The Royal Hotel	Jedburgh, Roxburghshire	25
The Ship Inn	Melrose, Roxburghshire	26
Traquair Arms Hotel	Innerleithen, Peeblesshire	27

DUMFRIES AND GALLOWAY

Aberdour Hotel	Dumfries, Dumfries & Galloway	38
Black Bull Hotel	Moffat, Dumfries & Galloway	39
The Carrutherstown Hotel	Carrutherstown, Dumfries & Galloway	40
The Courtyard	Eaglesfield, by Lockerbie, Dumfries & Galloway	41
Craigdarroch Arms Hotel	Moniaive, Dumfries & Galloway	42
The Cross Keys Hotel	Canonbie, Dumfries & Galloway	44
Dinwoodie Lodge Hotel	Johnstonebridge, by Lockerbie, Dumfries & Galloway	45
The Farmers Inn	Clarencefield, Dumfries & Galloway	46
The George Hotel	Stranraer, Dumfries & Galloway	47
The George Hotel	Thornhill, Dumfries & Galloway	48
Nithsdale Hotel	Sanquhar, Dumfries & Galloway	50
The Waterfront	Portpatrick, Wigtownshire	53

AYRSHIRE AND THE ISLE OF ARRAN

The Annfield House Hotel	Irvine, Ayrshire	64
The Bank	Prestwick, Ayrshire	65
Catacol Bay Hotel	Catacol, Isle of Arran	67
The Lochside House Hotel	New Cumnock, Ayrshire	72
Scoretulloch House	Darvel, Ayrshire	73
The Ship Inn	Irvine, Ayrshire	74
The Stair Inn	Stair, nr Mauchline, Ayrshire	75
The Wheatsheaf Inn	Symington, Ayrshire	76

CENTRAL SCOTLAND

The Beech Tree Inn	Dumgoyne, Stirlingshire	92
Bird in the Hand Hotel	Johnstonebridge, Renfrewshire	93
The Bridgend Hotel	East Linton, East Lothian	94
The Cardwell Inn	Gourock, Renfrewshire	96
The Crooked Arm	Bridge of Allan, Stirlingshire	97
Goblin Ha' Hotel	Gifford, East Lothian	99
Jameshaven Inn	Auldhouse, East Kilbride, Strathclyde	101

208

CREDIT CARDS ACCEPTED

The Lorne Taverna	Dollar, Clackmannanshire	102
Lugton Inn Motel	Dalkeith, Midlothian	103
Masonic Arms	Longcroft, by Bonnybridge, Stirlingshire	104
Oak Tree Inn	Balmaha, by Loch Lomond, Central	105
The Plough Tavern	Haddington, East Lothian	106
Roslin Glen Hotel	Roslin, Midlothian	107
The Royal Hotel	Bonnybridge, Stirlingshire	108
Tantallon Inn	North Berwick, East Lothian	109
Tyneside Tavern	Haddington, East Lothian	110
Waterside Bistro & Restaurant	Haddington, East Lothian	111
Wee Bush Inn	Carnwath, Lanarkshire	112
West Barns Inn	West Barns, nr Dunbar, East Lothian	113

ARGYLL AND BUTE

Ardbrecknish House	South Lochaweside, nr Dalmally, Argyll	126
Ardfillayne Country House Hotel	West Bay, nr Dunoon, Argyll	127
The Auld Hoose Restaurant	Dunoon, Argyll	128
The Boat	Rothesay, Bute	129
Cairnbaan Hotel	Cairnbaan, by Lochgilphead, Argyll	130
Colintraive Hotel	Colintraive, Argyll	131
The Cot House Hotel	Sandbank, nr Dunoon, Argyll	132
Cuilfail Hotel	Kilmelford, Argyll	133
The Horseshoe Inn	Bridgend, nr Lochgilphead, Argyll	135
Kilmartin Hotel	Kilmartin, nr Lochgilphead, Argyll	136
The Kilmun House Hotel	Kilmun, nr Dunoon, Argyll	137
Knipoch Hotel	Knipoch, by Oban, Argyll	139
The Lochnell Arms Hotel	North Connel, Argyll	140
The Oyster Inn	Connel, nr Oban, Argyll	142
The Regent Hotel	Rothesay, Bute	143
St Catherine's Old Ferry Inn	St Catherine's, nr Cairndow, Argyll	144
The Stagecoach Inn	Cairndow, Argyll	145
Tayvallich Inn	Tayvallich, Argyll	146

PERTHSHIRE AND KINROSS

Amulree Hotel & Lonely Inn	Amulree, Perthshire	155
The Black Watch Inn	Aberfeldy, Perthshire	157
Coaching Inn	Blackford, Perthshire	158
The Comrie Hotel	Comrie, Perthshire	159
The Crees Inn	Abernethy, Perthshire	160
Cyprus Inn	Bridge of Earn, nr Perth, Perthshire	161
Gwydyr House Hotel	Crieff, Perthshire	162
Kirkstyle Inn	Dunning, Perthshire	164
The Log Cabin	Kirkmichael, Perthshire	165
The Tower Hotel	Crieff, Perthshire	167
The Two O Eight Hotel	Perth, Perthshire	168
Woodside Inn	Woodside, Perthshire	169

CREDIT CARDS ACCEPTED 209

FIFE, DUNDEE AND ANGUS

The Abbey Inn	Newburgh, Fife	182
Auchmithie Hotel	Auchmithie, by Arbroath, Angus	183
Balcomie Links Hotel	Crail, Fife	185
The Bear Tavern	Newburgh, Fife	186
The Crusoe Hotel	Lower Largo, Fife	187
Lomond Hills Hotel	Freuchie, Fife	188
The Old Rectory Inn	Dysart, nr Kirkcaldy, Fife	190
Red House Hotel	Coupar Angus, Tayside	192
Salutation Hotel	Inverbervie, Aberdeenshire	193
St Michael's Inn	Leuchars, by St Andrews, Fife	194
Thrums Hotel	Kirriemuir, Angus	195

210 GARDEN, PATIO OR TERRACE

THE BORDERS

The Black Bull Hotel	Duns, Berwickshire	13
The Castle Hotel	Coldstream, Berwickshire	14
Churches Hotel	Eyemouth, Berwickshire	15
The Craw Inn	Auchencrow, nr Reston, Berwickshire	17
Dryburgh Arms Hotel	Newtown St Boswells, Borders	19
The Fox & Hounds	Denholm, Roxburghshire	20
The Plough Hotel	Leitholm, Berwickshire	24
The Ship Inn	Melrose, Roxburghshire	26

DUMFRIES AND GALLOWAY

The Carrutherstown Hotel	Carrutherstown, Dumfries & Galloway	40
Dinwoodie Lodge Hotel	Johnstonebridge, by Lockerbie, Dumfries & Galloway	45
The Lochann Inn	Lochans, Dumfries & Galloway	49
The Station House Hotel	Annan, Dumfries & Galloway	51
The Waterfront	Portpatrick, Wigtownshire	53

AYRSHIRE AND THE ISLE OF ARRAN

The Annfield House Hotel	Irvine, Ayrshire	64
Catacol Bay Hotel	Catacol, Isle of Arran	67
The Coylton Arms	Low Coylton, Ayrshire	69
The Crown Hotel	Tarbolton, Ayrshire	70
Scoretulloch House	Darvel, Ayrshire	73
The Ship Inn	Irvine, Ayrshire	74
The Stair Inn	Stair, nr Mauchline, Ayrshire	75
The Wheatsheaf Inn	Symington, Ayrshire	76

CENTRAL SCOTLAND

The Beech Tree Inn	Dumgoyne, Stirlingshire	92
Bird in the Hand Hotel	Johnstonebridge, Renfrewshire	93
The Burgh	Musselburgh, East Lothian	95
Goblin Ha' Hotel	Gifford, East Lothian	99
Oak Tree Inn	Balmaha, by Loch Lomond, Central	105
The Plough Tavern	Haddington, East Lothian	106
Tyneside Tavern	Haddington, East Lothian	110
Waterside Bistro & Restaurant	Haddington, East Lothian	111
West Barns Inn	West Barns, nr Dunbar, East Lothian	113

ARGYLL AND BUTE

Ardbrecknish House	South Lochaweside, nr Dalmally, Argyll	126
Cairnbaan Hotel	Cairnbaan, by Lochgilphead, Argyll	130
The Cot House Hotel	Sandbank, nr Dunoon, Argyll	132
Cuilfail Hotel	Kilmelford, Argyll	133
Furnace Inn	Furnace, Argyll	134
Kilmartin Hotel	Kilmartin, nr Lochgilphead, Argyll	136
Kingarth Hotel	Kingarth, Isle of Bute, Bute	138

GARDEN, PATIO OR TERRACE | 211

Knipoch Hotel	Knipoch, by Oban, Argyll	139
The Lochnell Arms Hotel	North Connel, Argyll	140
The Regent Hotel	Rothesay, Bute	143

PERTHSHIRE AND KINROSS

The Aerodrome	Scone, nr Perth, Perthshire	154
Amulree Hotel & Lonely Inn	Amulree, Perthshire	155
The Black Watch Inn	Aberfeldy, Perthshire	157
The Comrie Hotel	Comrie, Perthshire	159
The Crees Inn	Abernethy, Perthshire	160
Cyprus Inn	Bridge of Earn, nr Perth, Perthshire	161
Kirkstyle Inn	Dunning, Perthshire	164
The Log Cabin	Kirkmichael, Perthshire	165
Marfield Inn	Rattray, nr Blairgowrie, Perthshire	166
The Tower Hotel	Crieff, Perthshire	167

FIFE, DUNDEE AND ANGUS

The Abbey Inn	Newburgh, Fife	182
The Balcarres Hotel	Colinsburgh, Fife	184
Lomond Hills Hotel	Freuchie, Fife	188
Salutation Hotel	Inverbervie, Aberdeenshire	193
St Michael's Inn	Leuchars, by St Andrews, Fife	194

212

LIVE ENTERTAINMENT

THE BORDERS

The Auld Cross Keys	Denholm, Roxburghshire	12
The Black Bull Hotel	Duns, Berwickshire	13
The Castle Hotel	Coldstream, Berwickshire	14
The Craw Inn	Auchencrow, nr Reston, Berwickshire	17
Dryburgh Arms Hotel	Newtown St Boswells, Borders	19
The Fox & Hounds	Denholm, Roxburghshire	20
Linton Hotel	West Linton, Peebleshire	22
The Pheasant Inn	Jedburgh, Roxburghshire	23
The Plough Hotel	Leitholm, Berwickshire	24
The Royal Hotel	Jedburgh, Roxburghshire	25

DUMFRIES AND GALLOWAY

The Carrutherstown Hotel	Carrutherstown, Dumfries & Galloway	40
Cressfield Country House Hotel	Ecclefechan, Dumfries & Galloway	43
Dinwoodie Lodge Hotel	Johnstonebridge, by Lockerbie, Dumfries & Galloway	45
The George Hotel	Stranraer, Dumfries & Galloway	47
The George Hotel	Thornhill, Dumfries & Galloway	48
Nithsdale Hotel	Sanquhar, Dumfries & Galloway	50
The Station House Hotel	Annan, Dumfries & Galloway	51
The Thistle Inn	Crossmichael, Dumfries & Galloway	52

AYRSHIRE AND THE ISLE OF ARRAN

The Boswell Arms	Auchinleck, Ayrshire	66
Catacol Bay Hotel	Catacol, Isle of Arran	67
Clachan Bar	Largs, Ayrshire	68
The Crown Hotel	Tarbolton, Ayrshire	70
The Harbour Bar	Troon, Ayrshire	71
The Lochside House Hotel	New Cumnock, Ayrshire	72

CENTRAL SCOTLAND

The Bridgend Hotel	East Linton, East Lothian	94
The Burgh	Musselburgh, East Lothian	95
Goblin Ha' Hotel	Gifford, East Lothian	99
Golfer's Rest	North Berwick, East Lothian	100
Jameshaven Inn	Auldhouse, East Kilbride, Strathclyde	101
Lugton Inn Motel	Dalkeith, Midlothian	103
Oak Tree Inn	Balmaha, by Loch Lomond, Central	105
West Barns Inn	West Barns, nr Dunbar, East Lothian	113

ARGYLL AND BUTE

Ardbrecknish House	South Lochaweside, nr Dalmally, Argyll	126
The Boat	Rothesay, Bute	129
The Cot House Hotel	Sandbank, nr Dunoon, Argyll	132
Furnace Inn	Furnace, Argyll	134
The Horseshoe Inn	Bridgend, nr Lochgilphead, Argyll	135

LIVE ENTERTAINMENT

Kilmartin Hotel	Kilmartin, nr Lochgilphead, Argyll	136
The Lorne	Ardrishaig, Argyll	141
The Oyster Inn	Connel, nr Oban, Argyll	142
The Regent Hotel	Rothesay, Bute	143
St Catherine's Old Ferry Inn	St Catherine's, nr Cairndow, Argyll	144
Tayvallich Inn	Tayvallich, Argyll	146

PERTHSHIRE AND KINROSS

The Aerodrome	Scone, nr Perth, Perthshire	154
Amulree Hotel & Lonely Inn	Amulree, Perthshire	155
The Black Watch Inn	Aberfeldy, Perthshire	157
Coaching Inn	Blackford, Perthshire	158
The Comrie Hotel	Comrie, Perthshire	159
Cyprus Inn	Bridge of Earn, nr Perth, Perthshire	161
The Inn	Crook of Devon, Kinross-shire	163
Kirkstyle Inn	Dunning, Perthshire	164
The Log Cabin	Kirkmichael, Perthshire	165
Marfield Inn	Rattray, nr Blairgowrie, Perthshire	166
The Two O Eight Hotel	Perth, Perthshire	168
Woodside Inn	Woodside, Perthshire	169

FIFE, DUNDEE AND ANGUS

The Abbey Inn	Newburgh, Fife	182
Auchmithie Hotel	Auchmithie, by Arbroath, Angus	183
The Balcarres Hotel	Colinsburgh, Fife	184
Balcomie Links Hotel	Crail, Fife	185
The Bear Tavern	Newburgh, Fife	186
The New Windsor Hotel	Leven, Fife	189
Path Tavern	Kirkcaldy, Fife	191
Salutation Hotel	Inverbervie, Aberdeenshire	193

214   *RESTAURANT/DINING AREA*

THE BORDERS

The Black Bull Hotel	Duns, Berwickshire	13
Churches Hotel	Eyemouth, Berwickshire	15
The Craw Inn	Auchencrow, nr Reston, Berwickshire	17
Linton Hotel	West Linton, Peebleshire	22
The Plough Hotel	Leitholm, Berwickshire	24
Traquair Arms Hotel	Innerleithen, Peeblesshire	27

DUMFRIES AND GALLOWAY

Black Bull Hotel	Moffat, Dumfries & Galloway	39
The Courtyard	Eaglesfield, by Lockerbie, Dumfries & Galloway	41
Craigdarroch Arms Hotel	Moniaive, Dumfries & Galloway	42
Cressfield Country House Hotel	Ecclefechan, Dumfries & Galloway	43
The Cross Keys Hotel	Canonbie, Dumfries & Galloway	44
Dinwoodie Lodge Hotel	Johnstonebridge, by Lockerbie, Dumfries & Galloway	45
The George Hotel	Thornhill, Dumfries & Galloway	48
The Station House Hotel	Annan, Dumfries & Galloway	51
The Thistle Inn	Crossmichael, Dumfries & Galloway	52
The Waterfront	Portpatrick, Wigtownshire	53

AYRSHIRE AND THE ISLE OF ARRAN

Allandale House	Brodick, Isle of Arran	63
The Annfield House Hotel	Irvine, Ayrshire	64
The Coylton Arms	Low Coylton, Ayrshire	69
The Lochside House Hotel	New Cumnock, Ayrshire	72
Scoretulloch House	Darvel, Ayrshire	73
The Ship Inn	Irvine, Ayrshire	74
The Stair Inn	Stair, nr Mauchline, Ayrshire	75

CENTRAL SCOTLAND

The Beech Tree Inn	Dumgoyne, Stirlingshire	92
The Burgh	Musselburgh, East Lothian	95
Goblin Ha' Hotel	Gifford, East Lothian	99
Jameshaven Inn	Auldhouse, East Kilbride, Strathclyde	101
Oak Tree Inn	Balmaha, by Loch Lomond, Central	105
The Plough Tavern	Haddington, East Lothian	106
Roslin Glen Hotel	Roslin, Midlothian	107
The Royal Hotel	Bonnybridge, Stirlingshire	108
Tantallon Inn	North Berwick, East Lothian	109
Waterside Bistro & Restaurant	Haddington, East Lothian	111

ARGYLL AND BUTE

Ardbrecknish House	South Lochaweside, nr Dalmally, Argyll	126
Ardfillayne Country House Hotel	West Bay, nr Dunoon, Argyll	127
The Auld Hoose Restaurant	Dunoon, Argyll	128

RESTAURANT/DINING AREA 215

Cairnbaan Hotel	Cairnbaan, by Lochgilphead, Argyll	130
Colintraive Hotel	Colintraive, Argyll	131
The Cot House Hotel	Sandbank, nr Dunoon, Argyll	132
Cuilfail Hotel	Kilmelford, Argyll	133
Furnace Inn	Furnace, Argyll	134
Kilmartin Hotel	Kilmartin, nr Lochgilphead, Argyll	136
The Kilmun House Hotel	Kilmun, nr Dunoon, Argyll	137
Knipoch Hotel	Knipoch, by Oban, Argyll	139
The Lochnell Arms Hotel	North Connel, Argyll	140
The Regent Hotel	Rothesay, Bute	143
The Stagecoach Inn	Cairndow, Argyll	145
Tayvallich Inn	Tayvallich, Argyll	146

PERTHSHIRE AND KINROSS

Amulree Hotel & Lonely Inn	Amulree, Perthshire	155
The Bell Tree	Methven, Perthshire	156
Coaching Inn	Blackford, Perthshire	158
The Comrie Hotel	Comrie, Perthshire	159
The Crees Inn	Abernethy, Perthshire	160
Gwydyr House Hotel	Crieff, Perthshire	162
The Inn	Crook of Devon, Kinross-shire	163
Kirkstyle Inn	Dunning, Perthshire	164
The Log Cabin	Kirkmichael, Perthshire	165
The Tower Hotel	Crieff, Perthshire	167
The Two O Eight Hotel	Perth, Perthshire	168
Woodside Inn	Woodside, Perthshire	169

FIFE, DUNDEE AND ANGUS

Auchmithie Hotel	Auchmithie, by Arbroath, Angus	183
Balcomie Links Hotel	Crail, Fife	185
The Bear Tavern	Newburgh, Fife	186
The Crusoe Hotel	Lower Largo, Fife	187
Lomond Hills Hotel	Freuchie, Fife	188
The New Windsor Hotel	Leven, Fife	189
The Old Rectory Inn	Dysart, nr Kirkcaldy, Fife	190
Red House Hotel	Coupar Angus, Tayside	192
St Michael's Inn	Leuchars, by St Andrews, Fife	194
Thrums Hotel	Kirriemuir, Angus	195

The Hidden Inns of Central and Southern Scotland

A

Aberdour 173
Aberfeldy 149
Alloway 57
Amulree 149
Ancrum 3
Anstruther 173
Arbroath 174
Arniston 80
Auchterarder 149
Ayr 58
Ayton 3

B

Ballantrae 58
Balquhidder 80
Biggar 80
Blair Atholl 149
Blantyre 80
Bowhill 4
Brechin 174
Brodick 58

C

Caerlaverock 31
Cairndow 118
Callander 81
Campbeltown 118
Carnoustie 174
Carsaig 119
Castle Douglas 31
Coldstream 5
Colvend 32
Craignure 119
Crail 175
Crieff 150
Crossmichael 32
Culross 175
Cupar 175

D

Dalbeattie 32
Dalkeith 81
Dalmellington 59
Dervaig 119
Dirleton 81
Dumbarton 81
Dumferline 176
Dumfries 32
Dunbar 82
Dundee 176
Dunkeld 151
Dunoon 120
Duns 5

E

East Linton 82
Ecclefechan 34
Edinburgh 82

F

Fairlie 59
Falkirk 84
Falkland 178
Fionnphort 121
Forfar 178

G

Galashiels 6
Galston 59
Glamis 178
Glasgow 85
Glenbarr 121
Gleneagles 151
Glenluce 34
Glenrothes 179
Gretna Green 34

H

Haddington 86
Hamilton 86
Hawick 6

I

Innerleithen 7
Inveraray 121
Irvine 59

J

Jedburgh 7

K

Kelso 8
Killin 87
Kilmarnock 59
Kilmartin 122
Kilmun 122
Kinloch Rannoch 151
Kinross 151
Kirkcudbright 34
Kirkoswald 60
Kirriemuir 179

L

Lamlash 60
Lanark 87
Largs 60
Lauder 9
Lerags 122
Leven 180

Linlithgow 88
Lochgoilhead 122
Lockerbie 35

M

Mauchline 60
Maybole 61
Meigle 151
Melrose 9
Moffat 35
Montrose 180

N

New Abbey 35
New Galloway 36
Newton Stewart 36
North Berwick 88
North Queensferry 180

O

Oban 123

P

Paisley 89
Patna 62
Peebles 10
Perth 152
Pitlochry 153
Pittenweem 180
Port Appin 124
Port Logan Bay 37

R

Rest and Be Thankful 124
Roslin 89
Rothesay 124

S

Saltcoats 62
Selkirk 11
South Queensferry 89
St Abb's 10
St Andrews 181
Stirling 90
Stoneykirk 37
Stranraer 37
Strathtummel 153

T

Tarbert 125
Tarbolton 62
Tobermory 125
Troon 62
Tyndrum 91

W

Wanlockhead 37
Whithorn 37

Hidden Inns Reader Reaction

The *Hidden Inns* research team would like to receive reader's comments on any visitor attractions or places reviewed in the book and also recommendations for suitable entries to be included in the next edition. This will help ensure that the *Hidden Inns* series continues to provide its readers with useful information on the more interesting, unusual or unique features of each attraction or place ensuring that their stay in the local area is an enjoyable and stimulating experience.

To provide your comments or recommendations would you please complete the forms below and overleaf as indicated and send to:The Research Department, Travel Publishing Ltd, 7a Apollo House, Calleva Park, Aldermaston, Reading, RG7 8TN.

Your Name:

Your Address:

Your Telephone Number:

Please tick as appropriate: Comments ☐ Recommendation ☐

Name of *"Hidden Inn"*:

Address:

Telephone Number:

Name of Contact:

Hidden Inns Reader Reaction

Comment or Reason for Recommendation:

....

....

....

....

....

....

....

....

....

....

....

....

Hidden Inns Reader Reaction

The *Hidden Inns* research team would like to receive reader's comments on any visitor attractions or places reviewed in the book and also recommendations for suitable entries to be included in the next edition. This will help ensure that the *Hidden Inns* series continues to provide its readers with useful information on the more interesting, unusual or unique features of each attraction or place ensuring that their stay in the local area is an enjoyable and stimulating experience.

To provide your comments or recommendations would you please complete the forms below and overleaf as indicated and send to:The Research Department, Travel Publishing Ltd, 7a Apollo House, Calleva Park, Aldermaston, Reading, RG7 8TN.

Your Name:

Your Address:

Your Telephone Number:

Please tick as appropriate: Comments ☐   Recommendation ☐

Name of *"Hidden Inn"*:

Address:

Telephone Number:

Name of Contact:

Hidden Inns Reader Reaction

Comment or Reason for Recommendation:

....

....

....

....

....

....

....

....

....

....

....

....

HIDDEN INNS ORDER FORM

To order any of our publications just fill in the payment details below and complete the order form *overleaf*. For orders of less than 4 copies please add £1 per book for postage and packing. Orders over 4 copies are P & P free.

Please Complete Either:

I enclose a cheque for £ .... made payable to Travel Publishing Ltd

Or:

Card No: ☐☐☐☐ ☐☐☐☐ ☐☐☐☐ ☐☐☐☐

Expiry Date: ☐☐ ☐☐

Signature: ....

NAME: ....

ADDRESS: ....

....

....

POSTCODE: ....

TEL NO: ....

Please either send or telephone your order to:

Travel Publishing Ltd   Tel : 0118 981 7777
7a Apollo House   Fax: 0118 982 0077
Calleva Park
Aldermaston
Berks, RG7 8TN

	Price	Quantity	Value
Hidden Places Regional Titles			
Cambridgeshire & Lincolnshire	£7.99	....	....
Channel Islands	£6.99	....	....
Cheshire	£7.99	....	....
Chilterns	£7.99	....	....
Cornwall	£8.99	....	....
Derbyshire	£7.99	....	....
Devon	£8.99	....	....
Dorset, Hants & Isle of Wight	£7.99	....	....
East Anglia	£8.99	....	....
Essex	£7.99	....	....
Gloucestershire & Wiltshire	£7.99	....	....
Heart of England	£7.99	....	....
Hereford, Worcs & Shropshire	£7.99	....	....
Highlands & Islands	£7.99	....	....
Kent	£7.99	....	....
Lake District & Cumbria	£7.99	....	....
Lancashire	£7.99	....	....
Northeast Yorkshire	£6.99	....	....
Northumberland & Durham	£6.99	....	....
North Wales	£7.99	....	....
Nottinghamshire	£6.99	....	....
Potteries	£6.99	....	....
Somerset	£7.99	....	....
South Wales	£7.99	....	....
Suffolk	£7.99	....	....
Surrey	£6.99	....	....
Sussex	£7.99	....	....
Thames Valley	£7.99	....	....
Warwickshire & West Midlands	£6.99	....	....
Yorkshire	£7.99	....	....
Hidden Places National Titles			
England	£9.99	....	....
Ireland	£9.99	....	....
Scotland	£9.99	....	....
Wales	£11.99	....	....
Hidden Inns Titles			
West Country	£5.99	....	....
South East	£5.99	....	....
South	£5.99	....	....
Central and Southern Scotland	£5.99	....	....
Wales	£5.99	....	....

*For orders of less than 4 copies please add £1 per book for postage &
packing. Orders over 4 copies P & P free.*